Classical Encryption: Classical Ciphers

Contents

Chapter 1

Classical cipher

In cryptography, a **classical cipher** is a type of cipher that was used historically but now has fallen, for the most part, into disuse. The term includes the simple systems used since Greek and Roman times; the elaborate Renaissance ciphers, World War II cryptography such as the Enigma machine and beyond.

In contrast, modern strong cryptography relies on new algorithms and computers developed since the 1970s.

1.1 Types of Classical ciphers

Classical ciphers are often divided into *transposition ciphers* and *substitution ciphers*.

1.1.1 Substitution ciphers

In a substitution cipher, letters (or groups of letters) are systematically replaced throughout the message for other letters (or groups of letters).

A well-known example of a substitution cipher is the Caesar cipher. To encrypt a message with the Caesar cipher, each letter of message is replaced by the letter three positions later in the alphabet. Hence, A is replaced by D, B by E, C by F, etc. Finally, X, Y and Z are replaced by A, B and C respectively. So, for example, "WIKIPEDIA" encrypts as "ZLNLSHGLD". Caesar rotated the alphabet by three letters, but any number works.

Another method of substitution cipher is based on a keyword. All spaces and repeated letters are removed from a word or phrase, which the encoder then uses as the start of the cipher alphabet. The end of the cipher alphabet is the rest of the alphabet in order without repeating the letters in the keyword. For example, if the keyword is CIPHER, the cipher alphabet would look like this:

The previous examples were all examples of monoalphabetic substitution ciphers, where just one cipher alphabet is used. It is also possible to have a polyalphabetic substitution

cipher, where multiple cipher alphabets are used. The encoder would just make up two or more cipher alphabets using whatever techniques he or she chooses, and then encode their message, alternating what cipher alphabet is used with every letter or word. This makes the message much harder to decode because the codebreaker would have to figure out both cipher alphabets.

Another example of a polyalphabetic substitution cipher that is much more difficult to decode is the Vigenère square, an innovative encoding method. With the square, there are 26 different cipher alphabets that are used to encrypt text. Each cipher alphabet is just another rightword Caesar shift of the original alphabet. This is what a Vigenère square looks like:

```
A B C D E F G H I J K L M N O P Q R S T U V W X Y
Z B C D E F G H I J K L M N O P Q R S T U V W X Y
Z A C D E F G H I J K L M N O P Q R S T U V W X Y
Z A B D E F G H I J K L M N O P Q R S T U V W X Y
Z A B C E F G H I J K L M N O P Q R S T U V W X Y
Z A B C D F G H I J K L M N O P Q R S T U V W X Y
Z A B C D E G H I J K L M N O P Q R S T U V W X Y
Z A B C D E F H I J K L M N O P Q R S T U V W X Y
Z A B C D E F G I J K L M N O P Q R S T U V W X Y
Z A B C D E F G H J K L M N O P Q R S T U V W X Y
Z A B C D E F G H I K L M N O P Q R S T U V W X Y
Z A B C D E F G H I J L M N O P Q R S T U V W X Y
Z A B C D E F G H I J K M N O P Q R S T U V W X Y
Z A B C D E F G H I J K L N O P Q R S T U V W X Y Z
A B C D E F G H I J K L M O P Q R S T U V W X Y Z
A B C D E F G H I J K L M N P Q R S T U V W X Y Z
A B C D E F G H I J K L M N O Q R S T U V W X Y Z
A B C D E F G H I J K L M N O P R S T U V W X Y Z
A B C D E F G H I J K L M N O P Q S T U V W X Y Z
A B C D E F G H I J K L M N O P Q R T U V W X Y Z
A B C D E F G H I J K L M N O P Q R S U V W X Y Z
A B C D E F G H I J K L M N O P Q R S T V W X Y Z
A B C D E F G H I J K L M N O P Q R S T U W X Y Z
A B C D E F G H I J K L M N O P Q R S T U V X Y Z A
B C D E F G H I J K L M N O P Q R S T U V W Y Z A
B C D E F G H I J K L M N O P Q R S T U V W X Z A
```

B C D E F G H I J K L M N O P Q R S T U V W X Y

To use the Vigenère square to encrypt a message, you first choose whatever keyword you want to use and then repeat it until it is the same length as the message you wish to encode. Let's say we use LEMON as the keyword. Each letter of the repeated keyword will tell you what cipher (what row) you'll use for each letter of the message to be coded. The cipher alphabet on the second row uses B for A and C for B etc. That would be cipher alphabet 'B'. Each cipher alphabet is named by the first letter in it. For example, if you have a keyword of LEMON and the message you want to encode is ATTACKATDAWN, this is what you would do:

Some substitution ciphers involve using numbers instead of letters. An example of this is the Great Cipher, where numbers were used to represent syllables. There is also another number substitution cipher that involves having four different number pair options for a letter based on a keyword.

Instead of numbers, symbols can also be used to replace letters or syllables. One example of this is Zodiac alphabet, where signs of the zodiac were used to represent different letters, for example, the symbols for the sun stood for A, Jupiter stood for B, and Saturn stood for C. Dots, lines, or dashes could also be used, one example of this being Morse Code, which isn't really a cipher, but uses dots and dashes as letters nonetheless. The pigpen cipher uses a grid system or lines and dots to establish symbols for letters. There are various other methods that involve substituting letters of the alphabet with symbols or dots and dashes.

1.1.2 Transposition ciphers

In a transposition cipher, the letters themselves are kept unchanged, but their order within the message is scrambled according to some well-defined scheme. Many transposition ciphers are done according to a geometric design. A simple (and once again easy to crack) encryption would be to write every word backwards. For example, "Hello my name is Alice." would now be "olleH ym eman si ecilA." A scytale is a machine that aids in the transposition of methods.

In a columnar cipher, the original message is arranged in a rectangle, from left to right and top to bottom. Next, a key is chosen and used to assign a number to each column in the rectangle to determine the order of rearrangement. The number corresponding to the letters in the key is determined by their place in the alphabet, i.e. A is 1, B is 2, C is 3, etc. For example, if the key word is CAT and the message is THE SKY IS BLUE, this is how you would arrange your message:

C A T 3 1 20 T H E S K Y I S B L U E

Next, you take the letters in numerical order and that is how you would transpose the message. You take the column under A first, then the column under C, then the column under T, as a result your message "The sky is blue" has become: HKSUTSILEYBE

In the Chinese cipher's method of transposing, the letters of the message are written from right to left, down and up columns to scramble the letters. Then, starting in the first row, the letters are taken in order to get the new ciphertext. For example, if the message needed to be enciphered was THE DOG RAN FAR, the Chinese cipher would look like this:

R R G T A A O H F N D E

The cipher text then reads: RRGT AAOH FNDE

Many transposition ciphers are similar to these two examples, usually involving rearranging the letters into rows or columns and then taking them in a systematic way to transpose the letters. Other examples include the Vertical Parallel and the Double Transposition Cipher.

More complex algorithms can be formed by mixing substitution and transposition in a product cipher; modern block ciphers such as DES iterate through several stages of substitution and transposition.

1.2 Cryptanalysis of classical ciphers

Classical ciphers are commonly quite easy to break. Many of the classical ciphers can be broken even if the attacker only knows sufficient ciphertext and hence they are susceptible to a ciphertext-only attack. Some classical ciphers (e.g. the Caesar cipher) have a small key space. These ciphers can be broken with a brute force attack, that is by simply trying out all keys. Substitution ciphers can have a large key space, but are often susceptible to a frequency analysis, because for example frequent letters in the plaintext language correspond to frequent letters in the ciphertexts. Polyalphabetic ciphers such as the Vigenère cipher prevent a simple frequency analysis by using multiple substitutions. However, more advanced techniques such as the Kasiski examination can still be used to break these ciphers.

On the other hand, modern ciphers are designed to withstand much stronger attacks than ciphertext-only attacks. A good modern cipher must be secure against a wide range of potential attacks including known-plaintext attacks and chosen-plaintext attacks as well as chosen-ciphertext attacks. For these ciphers an attacker should not be able to find the key even if he knows any amount of plaintext and corresponding ciphertext and even if he could select plaintext or ciphertext himself. Classical ciphers do not satisfy these much stronger criteria and hence are no longer of interest for serious applications.

1.3 See also

- History of cryptography

1.4 References

- Hand Ciphers Pencil-and-paper ciphers on Ciphermachines & Cryptology

- Trinity College Department of Computer Science: Historical Cryptography Information about many different types of encryption algorithms including substitution and transposition ciphers

- Singh, Simon. The Code Book: The Science of Secrecy from Ancient Egypt to Quantum Cryptography. New York: Anchor, 2000.

- D'Agapeyeff, Alexander. Codes and Ciphers. Oxford UP, 1939.

- Laffin, John. Codes and Ciphers: Secret Writing through the Ages. Abelard-Schuman, 1964.

- Wrixon, Fred B. Codes, Ciphers, and Secret Languages. New York: Bonanza Books, 1989.

Chapter 2

A-1 (code)

A-1 was the designation for a code used by the United States Navy during World War I that replaced the Secret Code of 1887, SIGCODE and another system designed for radio communication. The cryptographic system was developed by Lt. W.W. Smith in the Office of Naval Operations by randomly associating key words with 5 letter patterns.[1]

2.1 References

[1] Newton, David E. (1997). *Encyclopedia of Cryptography*. Santa Barbara California: Instructional Horizons, Inc. p. 1.

Chapter 3

Acme Commodity and Phrase Code

Acme Commodity and Phrase Code was a book published in 1923 by the Acme Code Company which contained a standard book of codes and condensed terms used to shorten telegrams and save money. The book was extremely popular amongst businesses in the 1930s.[1]

3.1 References

[1] Newton, David E. (1997). *Encyclopedia of Cryptography*. Santa Barbara California: Instructional Horizons, Inc. p. 4.

Chapter 4

ADFGVX cipher

In cryptography, the **ADFGVX** cipher was a field cipher used by the German Army on the Western Front during World War I. ADFGVX was in fact an extension of an earlier cipher called **ADFGX**.

Invented by Lieutenant[1] Fritz Nebel (1891–1977)[2] and introduced in March 1918, the cipher was a fractionating transposition cipher which combined a modified Polybius square with a single columnar transposition.

4.1 Nomenclature

The cipher is named after the six possible letters used in the ciphertext: A, D, F, G, V and X. These letters were chosen deliberately because they sound very different from each other when transmitted via Morse code. The intention was to reduce the possibility of operator error.

Nebel designed the cipher to provide an army on the move with encryption more convenient than trench codes but still secure. In fact, the Germans believed the ADFGVX cipher was unbreakable.[3]

4.2 Operation of ADFGX

Suppose we need to send the plaintext message, "Attack at once". First, a secret mixed alphabet is filled into a 5 × 5 Polybius square, like so:

i and j have been combined, to make the alphabet fit into a 5 × 5 grid.

Using this square, the message is converted to fractionated form:

a t t a c k a t o n c e AF AD AD AF GF DX AF AD DF FX GF XF

Next, the fractionated message is subject to a columnar transposition. We write out the message in rows under a transposition key (here, "CARGO"):

C A R G O _____ A F A D A D A F G F D X A F A
D D F F X G F X F

Next, we sort the letters alphabetically in the transposition key (changing CARGO to ACGOR), rearranging the columns beneath the letters along with the letters themselves:

A C G O R _____ F A D A A A D G F F X D F A A
D D F X F F G F X

Then it is read off in columns, in keyword order, yielding the ciphertext:

FAXDF ADDDG DGFFF AFAX AFAFX

In practice, the transposition keys were about two dozen characters long. Long messages sent in the ADFGX cipher were broken into sets of messages of different and irregular lengths, thus making it invulnerable to multiple anagramming.[3] Both the transposition keys and fractionation keys were changed daily.

4.3 ADFGVX

In June 1918, an additional letter, V, was added to the cipher. This expanded the grid to 6 × 6, allowing 36 characters to be used. This allowed the full alphabet (instead of combining I and J), plus the digits from 0 to 9. This mainly had the effect of considerably shortening messages which contained a large number of figures.

The cipher is based on the 6 letters ADFGVX. A table containing a random and secret alphabet is created with these letters as column headings and row identifiers. This results in the following table:

The text 'attack at 1200am' will translate to this:

Then, a new table is created with a key as a heading. Let's use 'PRIVACY' as a key. Usually much longer keys or even phrases were used.

The columns are sorted alphabetically based on the keyword

and the table changes to this:

Then, appending the columns to each other results in the following cipher text:

DGDD DAGD DGAF ADDF DADV DVFA ADVX

Having the keyword, the columns can be reconstructed and placed in the correct order. When using the original table containing the secret alphabet, the text can be deciphered.

4.4 Cryptanalysis

ADFGVX was cryptanalysed by French Army Lieutenant Georges Painvin and the cipher was broken in early June 1918.[4] The work was exceptionally difficult by the standards of classical cryptography, and Painvin became physically ill during it. His method of solution relied on finding messages with stereotyped beginnings, which would fractionate the same, then form similar patterns in the positions in the ciphertext that had corresponded to column headings in the transposition table. (Considerable statistical analysis was required after this step had been reached — all done by hand.) This meant it was only effective during times of very high traffic — but, fortunately for the cryptanalysts, that was also when the most important messages were sent.

However, that was not the only trick Painvin used to crack the ADFGX cipher.[3] He used repeating sections of ciphertext to derive information about the likely length of the key being used. Where the key was an even number of letters in length he knew, due to the way the message was enciphered, that each column consisted entirely of either letter coordinates taken from the top of the Polybius Square, or from the left of the Square, but not a mixture of the two. He also knew that after substitution, but before transposition, the columns would alternately consist entirely of "top" and "side" letters. One of the characteristics of frequency analysis of letters is that while the distributions of individual letters may vary widely from the norm, the law of averages dictates that groups of letters vary less. With the ADFGX cipher, each "side" letter or "top" letter is associated with five plaintext letters. In the example above, the "side" letter "D" is associated with the plaintext letters "d h o z k", while the "top" letter "D" is associated with the plaintext letters "t h f j r". Since these two groups of five letters have different cumulative frequency distributions, then a frequency analysis of the "D" letter in columns consisting of "side" letters will have a distinctively different result from those of the "D" letter in columns consisting of "top" letters. This trick allowed Painvin to tentatively identify which columns consisted of "side" letters and which columns consisted of "top" letters. He could then pair them up and perform a frequency analysis on the pairings to see if they were noise, or real pairings that corresponded to plaintext letters. Once he

had the proper pairings, he could then use frequency analysis to figure out the actual plaintext letters. The result was still transposed, but at that point all he had to do was unscramble a simple transposition. Once he determined the transposition scheme for one message, he would then be able to crack any other message enciphered with the same transposition key.[3]

Painvin broke the ADFGX cipher in April 1918, a few weeks after the Germans launched their Spring Offensive. As a direct result, the French army discovered where Ludendorff intended to attack. The French concentrated their forces at that point and it has been claimed that this stopped the Spring Offensive.

Note, however the claim that Painvin's breaking of the ADFGX cipher stopped the German Spring Offensive of 1918, while frequently made,[5] is disputed by some. In his 2002 review of Sophie de Lastours' book on this subject, *La France gagne la guerre des codes secrets 1914-1918*, in the Journal of Intelligence History, (*Journal of Intelligence History*: volume 2, Number 2, Winter 2002) Hilmar-Detlef Brückner states:

> Regrettably, Sophie de Lastours subscribes to the traditional French view that the solving of a German ADFGVX-telegram by Painvin at the beginning of June 1918 was decisive for the Allied victory in the First World War because it gave timely warning of a forthcoming German offensive meant to reach Paris and to inflict a critical defeat on the Allies. However, it has been known for many years, that the German *Gneisenau* attack of 11 June was staged to induce the French High Command to rush in reserves from the area up north, where the Germans intended to attack later on.
>
> To achieve this, its aim had to be grossly exaggerated. This the German High Command did by spreading rumors that the attack was heading for Paris and beyond; disinformation proved effective then - and apparently still does. But the German offensive was not successful because the French had a sufficient number of reserves at hand to stop the assault and did not need to bring in additional reinforcements.
>
> Moreover, it is usually overlooked that the basic version of the ADFGVX cipher had been particularly created for the German spring offensive in 1918, meant to deal the Allies a devastating blow. It was hoped that the cipher ADFGX would protect German communications against Allied cryptographers during the assault and this is what it indeed did.
>
> Telegrams in ADFGX appeared for the first

time on 5 March, the German attack started on 21 March. When Painvin presented his first solution of the code on 5 April, the German offensive had already petered out.

The ADFGX and ADFGVX ciphers are now regarded as insecure.

4.5 Notes

[1] Friedrich L. Bauer: *Decrypted Secrets, Methods and Maxims of Cryptology.* Springer, Berlin 2007 (4. Aufl.), S. 173, ISBN 3-540-24502-2.

[2] Friedrich L. Bauer: *Decrypted Secrets, Methods and Maxims of Cryptology.* Springer, Berlin 2007 (4. Aufl.), S. 53, ISBN 3-540-24502-2.

[3] "Codes and Codebreaking in World War I".

[4] Newton, David E. (1997). *Encyclopedia of Cryptography.* Santa Barbara California: Instructional Horizons, Inc. p. 6.

[5] "Painvin's manna had saved the French" writes David Kahn in *The Codebreakers - The Story of Secret Writing*, 1967, ISBN 978-0-684-83130-5, Ch. 9. Kahn also details the role that Painvin's decryption of German messages played in the French response to Operation Gneisenau.

4.6 References

• Friedman, William F. Military Cryptanalysis, Part IV: Transposition and Fractionating Systems. Laguna Hills, CA: Aegean Park Press, 1992.

• General Solution of the ADFGVX Cipher System, J. Rives Childs, Aegean Park Press, ISBN 0-89412-284-3

4.7 External links

• A JavaScript implementation of the ADFGVX cipher

• Another JavaScript implementation

• A C implementation of the ADFGVX cipher

Chapter 5

Affine cipher

The **affine cipher** is a type of monoalphabetic substitution cipher, wherein each letter in an alphabet is mapped to its numeric equivalent, encrypted using a simple mathematical function, and converted back to a letter. The formula used means that each letter encrypts to one other letter, and back again, meaning the cipher is essentially a standard substitution cipher with a rule governing which letter goes to which. As such, it has the weaknesses of all substitution ciphers. Each letter is enciphered with the function $(ax + b)$ mod 26, where b is the magnitude of the shift.

5.1 Description

In the affine cipher the letters of an alphabet of size m are first mapped to the integers in the range $0 \ldots m - 1$. It then uses modular arithmetic to transform the integer that each plaintext letter corresponds to into another integer that correspond to a ciphertext letter. The encryption function for a single letter is

$$E(x) = (ax + b) \bmod m,$$

where modulus m is the size of the alphabet and a and b are the key of the cipher. The value a must be chosen such that a and m are coprime. The decryption function is

$$D(x) = a^{-1}(x - b) \bmod m,$$

where a^{-1} is the modular multiplicative inverse of a modulo m. I.e., it satisfies the equation

$$1 = aa^{-1} \bmod m.$$

The multiplicative inverse of a only exists if a and m are coprime. Hence without the restriction on a decryption might not be possible. It can be shown as follows that decryption function is the inverse of the encryption function,

$$
\begin{aligned}
D(E(x)) &= a^{-1}(E(x) - b) \bmod m \\
&= a^{-1}(((ax + b) \bmod m) - b) \bmod m \\
&= a^{-1}(ax + b - b) \bmod m \\
&= a^{-1}ax \bmod m \\
&= x \bmod m.
\end{aligned}
$$

5.2 Weaknesses

Since the affine cipher is still a monoalphabetic substitution cipher, it inherits the weaknesses of that class of ciphers. The Affine cipher is a Caesar cipher when $a = 1$ since the encrypting function simply reduces to a linear shift.

Considering the specific case of encrypting messages in English (i.e. $m = 26$), there are a total of 286 non-trivial affine ciphers, not counting the 26 trivial Caesar ciphers. This number comes from the fact there are 12 numbers that are coprime with 26 that are less than 26 (these are the possible values of a). Each value of a can have 26 different addition shifts (the b value); therefore, there are 12×26 or 312 possible keys. This lack of variety renders the system as highly insecure when considered in light of Kerckhoffs' Principle.

The cipher's primary weakness comes from the fact that if the cryptanalyst can discover (by means of frequency analysis, brute force, guessing or otherwise) the plaintext of two ciphertext characters then the key can be obtained by solving a simultaneous equation. Since we know a and m are relatively prime this can be used to rapidly discard many "false" keys in an automated system.

The same type of transformation used in affine ciphers is used in linear congruential generators, a type of pseudorandom number generator. This generator is not a cryptographically secure pseudorandom number generator for the same reason that the affine cipher is not secure.

5.3 Examples

In these two examples, one encrypting and one decrypting, the alphabet is going to be the letters A through Z, and will have the corresponding values found in the following table.

5.3.1 Encrypting

In this encrypting example,[1] the plaintext to be encrypted is "AFFINE CIPHER" using the table mentioned above for the numeric values of each letter, taking a to be 5, b to be 8, and m to be 26 since there are 26 characters in the alphabet being used. Only the value of a has a restriction since it has to be coprime with 26. The possible values that a could be are 1, 3, 5, 7, 9, 11, 15, 17, 19, 21, 23, and 25. The value for b can be arbitrary as long as a does not equal 1 since this is the shift of the cipher. Thus, the encryption function for this example will be $y = E(x) = (5x + 8) \bmod 26$. The first step in encrypting the message is to write the numeric values of each letter.

Now, take each value of x, and solve the first part of the equation, $(5x + 8)$. After finding the value of $(5x + 8)$ for each character, take the remainder when dividing the result of $(5x + 8)$ by 26. The following table shows the first four steps of the encrypting process.

The final step in encrypting the message is to look up each numeric value in the table for the corresponding letters. In this example, the encrypted text would be IHHWVC-SWFRCP. The table below shows the completed table for encrypting a message in the Affine cipher.

5.3.2 Decrypting

In this decryption example, the ciphertext that will be decrypted is the ciphertext from the encryption example. The corresponding decryption function is $D(y) = 21(y - 8) \bmod 26$, where a^{-1} is calculated to be 21, b is 8, and m is 26. To begin, write the numeric equivalents to each letter in the ciphertext, as shown in the table below.

Now, the next step is to compute $21(y - 8)$, and then take the remainder when that result is divided by 26. The following table shows the results of both computations.

The final step in decrypting the ciphertext is to use the table to convert numeric values back into letters. The plaintext in this decryption is AFFINECIPHER. Below is the table with the final step completed.

5.3.3 Entire alphabet encoded

To make encrypting and decrypting quicker, the entire alphabet can be encrypted to create a one to one map between the letters of the cleartext and the ciphertext. In this example, the one to one map would be the following:

5.3.4 Programming examples

Using the Python programming language, the following code can be used to create an encrypted alphabet using the Roman letters A through Z.

```
#Prints a transposition table for an affine cipher. #a must be coprime to m=26. def affine(a, b): for i in range(26): print(chr(i+65) + ": " + chr(((a*i+b)%26)+65)) #An example call affine(5, 8)
```

Or in Java:

```
public void Affine(int a, int b){ for (int num = 0; num < 26; num++) System.out.println(((char)('A'+num)) + ":" + ((char)('A'+(a*num + b)% 26)) ); } Affine(5,8)
```

Or in Pascal:

```
Procedure Affine(a,b : Integer); begin for num := 0 to 25 do WriteLn(Chr(num+65) , ': ' , Chr(((a*num + b) mod 26) + 65); end; begin Affine(5,8) end.
```

In PHP:

```
function affineCipher($a, $b) { for($i = 0; $i < 26; $i++) { echo chr($i + 65) . ' ' . chr(65 + ($a * $i + $b) % 26) . '<br>'; } } affineCipher(5, 8);
```

5.4 See also

- Affine functions

- Atbash code

- Caesar cipher

- ROT13

- Topics in cryptography

- Perl interface to "Affine cipher"

5.5 References

[1] Kozdron, Michael. "Affine Ciphers" (PDF). Retrieved 22 April 2014.

Chapter 6

Alberti cipher

The **Alberti Cipher** was one of the first polyalphabetic ciphers.

Created in the 15th century (1466/67), it was the peak of cryptography at that time. Its inventor was Leon Battista Alberti, an illegitimate son of an Italian nobleman.

He was also interested in painting and writing, though he is probably best known for his architecture. He created the cipher after a conversation on the art of print with Leonardo Dati in the gardens of the Vatican.

6.1 Description

The Alberti Cipher Disk described by Leon Battista Alberti in his treatise *De Cifris* embodies the first example of polyalphabetic substitution with mixed alphabets and variable period. This device, called *Formula*, is made up of two concentric disks, attached by a common pin, which can rotate one with respect to the other.

The larger one is called *Stabilis* [stationary or fixed], the smaller one is called *Mobilis* [movable]. The circumference of each disk is divided into 24 equal cells.

The outer ring contains one uppercase alphabet for plaintext and the inner ring has a lowercase mixed alphabet for ciphertext. The outer ring also includes the numbers 1 to 4 for the superencipherment of a codebook containing 336 phrases with assigned numerical values.

This is a very effective method of concealing the code-numbers, since their equivalents cannot be distinguished from the other garbled letters. The sliding of the alphabets is controlled by key letters included in the body of the cryptogram.

For an unequivocal study of this cipher two chapters of *De Cifris* are herewith reproduced in English.

Chapter XIV. I will first describe the movable index. Suppose that we agreed to use the letter k as an index letter in the movable disk. At the moment of writing I will position the two disks of the formula as I wish, for example juxtaposing the index letter to capital B, with all other small letters corresponding to the capital letters above them. When writing to you, I will first write a capital B that corresponds to the index k in the formula. This means that if you want to read my message you must use the identical formula you have with you, turning the movable disk until the letter B corresponds to the index k. Thus all small letters in the ciphertext will receive the meaning and sound of those above them in the stationary disk. When I have written three or four words I will change the position of the index in our formula, turning the disk until, say, the index k is under capital R. Then I will write a capital R in my message and from this point onward the small k will no longer mean B but R, and the letters that follow in the text, will receive new meanings from the capital letters above them in the stationary disk. When you read the message you have received, you will be advised by the capital letter, which you know is only used as a signal, that from this moment the position of the movable disk and of the index has been changed. Hence, you will also place the index under that capital letter, and in this way you will be able to read and understand the text very easily. The four letters in the movable disk facing the four numbered cells of the outer ring will not have, so to speak, any meaning by themselves and may be in-

serted as nulls within the text. However, if used in groups or repeated, they will be of great advantage, as I will explain later on.

Chapter XV. We can also choose the index letter among the capital letters and agree between us which of them will be the index. Let us suppose we chose the letter B as an index. The first letter to appear in the message will be a small one at will, say q. Hence, turning the movable disk in the formula you will place this letter under the capital B that serves as an index. It follows that q will take the sound and meaning of B. For the other letters we will continue writing in the manner described earlier for the movable index. When it is necessary to change the set up of the disks in the formula, then I will insert one, and no more, of the numeral letters into the message, that is to say one of the letters of the small disk facing the numbers which corresponds to, let's say, 3 or 4, etc. Turning the movable disk I will juxtapose this letter to the agreed upon index B and, successively, as required by the logic of writing, I will continue giving the value of the capitals to the small letters. To further confuse the scrutinizers you can also agree with your correspondent that the capital letters intermingled in the message have the function of nulls and must be disregarded, or you may resort to similar conventions, which are not worth recalling. Thus changing the position of the index by rotating the movable disk, one will be able to express the phonetic and semantic value of each capital letter by means of twenty-four different alphabetic characters, whereas each small letter can correspond to any capital letter or to any of the four numbers in the alphabet of the stationary disk. Now I come to the convenient use of the numbers, which is admirable.

6.2 Cryptanalysis

Compared to previous ciphers of the time the Alberti Cipher was impossible to break without knowledge of the method. This was because the frequency distribution of the letters was masked and frequency analysis - the only known technique for attacking ciphers at that time - was no help.

6.3 See also

- Alberti cipher disk

6.4 External links

- Example of a Cipher Disc, and a Description of the difference between the Alberti Cipher and the Vigenère Cipher

6.5 References

- Alberti, Leon Battista, *A Treatise on Ciphers*, trans. A. Zaccagnini. Foreword by David Kahn, Galimberti, Torino 1997.

- Buonafalce, Augusto, "An Exercise in Solving the Alberti Disk". *The Cryptogram* LIV, 5, ACA, Plano 1999.

Chapter 7

The Alphabet Cipher

Lewis Carroll published *The Alphabet-Cipher* in 1868, possibly in a children's magazine. It describes what is known as a Vigenère cipher, a well-known scheme in cryptography. While Carroll calls this cipher "unbreakable", Kasiski had published a volume describing how to break such ciphers from five years earlier, and Charles Babbage had secretly found ways to break polyalphabetic ciphers during the Crimean War.

The piece begins with a tabula recta.

7.1 *The Alphabet-Cipher*, Lewis Carroll, 1868

ABCDEFGHIJKLMNOPQRSTUVWXYZ A abcdefghijklmnopqrstuvwxyz A B bcdefghijklmnopqrstuvwxyza B C cdefghijklmnopqrstuvwxyzab C D defghijklmnopqrstuvwxyzabc D E efghijklmnopqrstuvwxyzabcd E F fghijklmnopqrstuvwxyzabcde F G ghijklmnopqrstuvwxyzabcdef G H hijklmnopqrstuvwxyzabcdefg H I ijklmnopqrstuvwxyzabcdefgh I J jklmnopqrstuvwxyzabcdefghi J K klmnopqrstuvwxyzabcdefghij K L lmnopqrstuvwxyzabcdefghijk L M mnopqrstuvwxyzabcdefghijkl M N nopqrstuvwxyzabcdefghijklm N O opqrstuvwxyzabcdefghijklmn O P pqrstuvwxyzabcdefghijklmno P Q qrstuvwxyzabcdefghijklmnop Q R rstuvwxyzabcdefghijklmnopq R S stuvwxyzabcdefghijklmnopqr S T tuvwxyzabcdefghijklmnopqrs T U uvwxyzabcdefghijklmnopqrst U V vwxyzabcdefghijklmnopqrstu V W wxyzabcdefghijklmnopqrstuv W X xyzabcdefghijklmnopqrstuvw X Y yzabcdefghijklmnopqrstuvwx Y Z zabcdefghijklmnopqrstuvwxy Z ABCDEFGHIJKLMNOPQRSTUVWXYZ

7.1.1 Explanation

Each column of this table forms a dictionary of symbols representing the alphabet: thus, in the A column, the symbol is the same as the letter represented; in the B column, A is represented by B, B by C, and so on.

To use the table, some word or sentence should be agreed on by two correspondents. This may be called the 'key-word', or 'key-sentence', and should be carried in the memory only.

In sending a message, write the key-word over it, letter for letter, repeating it as often as may be necessary: the letters of the key-word will indicate which column is to be used in translating each letter of the message, the symbols for which should be written underneath: then copy out the symbols only, and destroy the first paper. It will now be impossible for anyone, ignorant of the key-word, to decipher the message, even with the help of the table.

For example, let the key-word be vigilance, and the message 'meet me on Tuesday evening at seven', the first paper will read as follows—

vigilancevigilancevigilancevi meetme
ontuesdayeveningatsevenhmkbxebpxp
myllyrxiiqtoltfgzzv

The second will contain only 'h m k b x e b p x p m y l l y r x i i q t o l t f g z z v'.

The receiver of the message can, by the same process, retranslate it into English.

If this table is lost, it can easily be written out from memory, by observing that the first symbol in each column is the same as the letter naming the column, and that they are continued downwards in alphabetical order. It would only be necessary to write out the particular columns required by the key-word, but such a paper would afford an adversary the means for discovering the key-word.

Chapter 8

Alphabetum Kaldeorum

The Alphabetum Kaldeorum

The **Alphabetum Kaldeorum** is one of the best known ciphers of the Middle Ages. Its name refers to the Chaldees, whose inhabitants during the medieval era were reputed to have mysterious and magical knowledge.

It can be found in a complete version, together with other non-Latin alphabets, in a manuscript from the year 1428, now in the library at the University of Munich (Cod. 4º 810, fol. 41v). However, its origins lie clearly in an earlier time, as some examples of its practical use demonstrate.

The Alphabetum Kaldeorum was meant primarily for the encipherment of diplomatic correspondence; its alphabet implies that predominantly Latin texts were coded: u and v are equated; w was to be written as double v; j is missing. For frequently arising letters the Alphabetum Kaldeorum provides several different versions, which were used at random so that a decipherment attempt using the classical frequency analysis method should fail. "Nulla", cipher-letters with no plaintext assignment which were to be ignored, were also often added to the enciphered texts to further render frequency-analysis useless.

A possible author of the Alphabetum Kaldeorum is Duke Rudolf IV of Austria (1339–1365), who attributed an Indian origin to them; the letters of the Alphabetum Kaldeorum are probably not, however, at all related to any writing common in India, and are actually independent creations.

Even Rudolf's gravestone in the Stephansdom in Vienna

The decipherment of the epitaph *accompanying the cenotaph, or symbolic tomb, of Duke Rudolph IV in the* Stephansdom *in Vienna.*

carries an inscription enciphered using the Alphabetum Kaldeorum, which gives the names and titles of the duke.

8.1 External links

Media related to Alphabetum Kaldeorum at Wikimedia Commons

Chapter 9

Arnold Cipher

ONE OF THE TREASON LETTERS IN CYPHER

A coded communication. Handwriting by Peggy Shippen Arnold is interspersed with coded communication in Arnold's hand.

The **Arnold Cipher** was a book cipher used by John André and Benedict Arnold during the negotiations that led to Arnold's failed attempt to surrender West Point to the British in 1780.

9.1 Background

In May 1779, Continental Army Major General Benedict Arnold initiated what became a series of communications with British Army Major John André, the adjutant and spy chief to Lieutenant General Sir Henry Clinton, the commander-in-chief of British forces in North America. In these communications, which were at first mediated by Joseph Stansbury, a Philadelphia merchant, Arnold offered his services to the British. André responded to this offer with a letter dated May 10, 1779, in which he described the types of services Arnold might provide, and described a code which they should use to obscure their communications.[1]

The book used as a key to the cipher was either *Commentaries on the Laws of England* by William Blackstone or *Nathan Bailey's Dictionary*. The cipher consisted of a series of three numbers separated by periods. These

numbers represented a page number of the agreed book, a line number on that page, and a word number in that line. Arnold added missing letters or suffixes where he could not find a match in one of the books.[2] For example, 120.9.7 would refer to the 120th page, the 9th line on that page, and the seventh word in that line, which, in the following example is decoded as "general".

The actual communications was often disguised by embedding it in a letter written by Arnold's wife Peggy, where the cipher would be written in invisible ink, but might also be disguised as what appeared to be routine business communications.

9.2 Coded example

This code was generated by Arnold for a message to André dated July 12, 1780:[3]

120.9.7, W------- 105.9.5's on the .22.9.14.---- / of 163.8.19 F----- 172.8.7s to 56.9.8 |30.000| 172.8.70 to 11.94. in / 62.8.20. If 179.8.25, 84.8.9'd, 177.9.28. N---- is 111.9.27.'d on / 23.8.10. the 111.9.13, 180.9.19 if his 180.8.21 an .179.8.25., 255.8.17. for / that, 180.9.19, 44.8.9—a—is the 234.8.14 of 189.8.17. I --- / 44.8.9, 145.8.17, 294.9.12, in 266.8.17 as well as, 103.8.11, 184.9.15.---- /80.4.20. ---- I149.8.7, 10.8.22'd the 57.9.71 at 288.9.9, 198.9.26, as, a / 100.4.18 in 189.8.19—I can 221.8.6 the 173.8.19, 102.8.26, 236.8.21's--- / and 289.8.17 will be in 175.9.7, 87.8.7--- the 166.8.11, of the .191.9.16 / are .129.19.21 'of --- 266.9.14 of the .286.8.20, and 291.8.27 to be an --—163.9.4 / 115.8.16 -'a .114.8.25ing --- 263.9.14. are 207.8.17ed, 125.8.15, 103.8.60--- / from this 294.8.50, 104.9.26—If 84.8.9ed— 294.9.12, 129.8.7. only / to 193.8.3 and the 64.9.5, 290.9.20, 245.8.3 be at an, 99.8.14 . / the .204.8.2, 253.8.7s are 159.8.10 the 187.8.11 of a 94.9.9ing / 164.8.24, 279.8.16, but of a .238.8.25, 93.9.28.

9.3 Decoded example

Here is how Jonathan Odell, André's assistant, decoded the message:[4]

General W[ashington]--- expects on the arrival of the F[rench]--- Troops to collect / 30,000 Troops to act in conjunction; if not disappointed, N[ew]. York is fixed / on as the first Object, if his numbers are not sufficient for that Object, / Can-a- is the second; of which I can inform you in time, as well as of / every other design. I have accepted the command at W[est]. P[oint]. As a Post in which / I can render the most essential Services, and which will be in my disposal. / The mass of the People are heartily tired of the War, and wish to be on / their former footing - They are promised great events from this / year's exertion—If - disappointed - you have only to persevere / and the contest will soon be at an end. The present Struggles are / like the pangs of a dying man, violent but of a short duration---

9.4 References

[1] André to Stansbury, May 10, 1779

[2] Secret Methods and Techniques

[3] Arnold to André, July 12, 1780 (Code)

[4] Arnold to André, July 12, 1780 (Decoded)

- "Secret Methods and Techniques". Clements Library, University of Michigan. Retrieved 2010-03-12.

- "July 12, 1780 -- Benedict Arnold to John André (Code)". Clements Library, University of Michigan. Retrieved 2010-03-12.

- "July 12, 1780 -- Benedict Arnold to John André (Decoded)". Clements Library, University of Michigan. Retrieved 2010-03-12.

- "André to Stansbury, May 10, 1779". Clements Library, University of Michigan. Retrieved 2010-03-12.

Chapter 10

Āryabhaṭa numeration

"Sanskrit numerals" redirects here. For the basic numerals of Sanskrit, see Sanskrit grammar § Numerals.

The **Āryabhaṭa numeration** is a system of numerals based on Sanskrit phonemes. It was introduced in the early 6th century in India by Āryabhaṭa, in the first chapter titled *Gītika Padam* of his *Aryabhatiya*. It attributes a numerical value to each syllable of the form consonant+vowel possible in Sanskrit phonology, from *ka* = 1 up to *hau* = 10^{18}.

10.1 History

The basis of this number system is mentioned in the second stanza of the first chapter of Aryabhatiya.

The Varga (Group/Class) letters Ka to Ma are to be placed in the varga (square) places (1st, 100th, 10000th ...etc. places) and Avarga letters like Ya, Ra, La .. have to be placed in Avarga places (10th, 1000th,...etc. places).

The Varga letters 'Ka' to 'Ma' have value from 1, 2, 3 .. up to 25 and Avarga letters 'Ya' to 'Ha' have value 30, 40, 50.. up to 100. In the Varga and Avarga letters, beyond the ninth vowel (place), new symbols can be used.

The values for vowels are as follows : i= 100 ; u = 10000, ru = 1000000 and so on.

Aryabhata used this number system for representing both small and large numbers in his mathematical and astronomical calculations. This system can even be used to represent fractions and mixed fractions. For example, nga is 1/5, nja is 1/10 and Jhardam (jha=9; its half) = 4½

10.2 Example

The traditional Indian digit order is reversed compared to the modern way. By consequence, Āryabhaṭa began with the ones before the tens; then the hundreds and the thousands; then the myriad and the lakh (= 10^5) and so on. (*cf.* *Indian numbering system)*

10.3 Numeral table

In citing the values of Āryabhaṭa numbers, the short vowels अ, इ, उ, ऋ, ऌ, ए, and ओ are invariably used. However, the Āryabhaṭa system did not distinguish between long and short vowels. This table only cites the full slate of क-derived (1×10^x) values, but these are valid throughout the list of numeric syllables.[1]

10.4 See also

- Aksharapalli
- Bhutasamkhya system
- Katapayadi system
- IAST

10.5 References

[1] Ifrah, Georges (2000). *The Universal History of Numbers. From Prehistory to the Invention of the Computer*. New York: John Wiley & Sons. pp. 447–450. ISBN 0-471-39340-1.

- Kurt Elfering: *Die Mathematik des Aryabhata I. Text, Übersetzung aus dem Sanskrit und Kommentar*. Wilhelm Fink Verlag, München, 1975, ISBN 3-7705-1326-6

- Georges Ifrah: *The Universal History of Numbers. From Prehistory to the Invention of the Computer*. John Wiley & Sons, New York, 2000, ISBN 0-471-39340-1.

- B. L. van der Waerden: *Erwachende Wissenschaft. Ägyptische, babylonische und griechische Mathematik.* Birkhäuser-Verlag, Basel Stuttgart, 1966, ISBN 3-7643-0399-9

- Fleet, J. F. (January 1911). "Aryabhata's System of Expressing Numbers". *Journal of the Royal Asiatic Society of Great Britain and Ireland*: 109–126. ISSN 0035-869X. JSTOR 25189823.

- Fleet, J. F. (1911). "Aryabhata's System of Expressing Numbers". *The Journal of the Royal Asiatic Society of Great Britain and Ireland*. Royal Asiatic Society of Great Britain and Ireland. **43**: 109–126. doi:10.1017/S0035869X00040995. JSTOR 25189823.

Chapter 11

Atbash

Atbash (Hebrew: אתבש; also transliterated **Atbaš**) is a simple substitution cipher originally used for the Hebrew alphabet, but can be done to any known alphabet.

It is considered 'complex', But, it has a possible key, and it is a simple mono-alphabetic substitution cipher. However, this may not have been an issue at the time when the cipher was first devised.

11.1 History

The name derives from the first, last, second, and second to last Hebrew letters (Aleph-Tav-Beth-Shin).

The Atbash cipher for the modern Hebrew alphabet would be:

11.1.1 In the Bible

Several Biblical verses are described by commentators as being examples of Atbash:

- Jeremiah 25:26 - "The king of *Sheshach* shall drink after them" - Sheshach meaning Babylon in Atbash (ששך=בבל)

- Jeremiah 51:1 - "Behold, I will raise up against Babylon, and against the inhabitants of *Lev-kamai*, a destroying wind." - Lev-kamai meaning Chaldeans (לבקמי=כשדים)

- Jeremiah 51:41 - "How has *Sheshach* been captured! and the praise of the whole earth taken! How has Babylon become a curse among the nations!" - Sheshach meaning Babylon (ששך=בבל)

11.2 Use

It works by substituting the first letter of an alphabet for the last letter, the second letter for the second to last and so on, effectively reversing the alphabet. An Atbash cipher for the Latin alphabet would be as follows:

An easier, simpler and faster way of doing this is:

11.2.1 Examples

A few English words also 'Atbash' into other English words: "irk"="rip", "low"="old", "hob"="sly", "hold"="slow", "holy"="slob", "horn"="slim", "glow"="told", "grog"="tilt" and "zoo"="all". Some other English words Atbash into their own reverses, *e.g.*, "wizard" = "draziw."

11.3 Relationship to the affine cipher

The Atbash cipher can be seen as a special case of the affine cipher.

Under the standard affine convention, an alphabet of m letters is mapped to the numbers 0, 1, ..., $m-1$. (The Hebrew alphabet has $m = 22$, and the standard Latin alphabet has $m = 26$). The Atbash cipher may then be enciphered and deciphered using the encryption function for an affine cipher, by setting $a = b = (m-1)$:

$$E(x) = D(x) = ((m-1)x + (m-1)) \bmod m$$

This may be simplified to:

$$E(x) = (m-1)(x+1) \bmod m$$
$$= -(x+1) \bmod m$$

If, instead, the m letters of the alphabet are mapped to 1, 2, .., m, then the encryption and decryption function for the Atbash cipher becomes:

$$E(x) = (-x \bmod m) + 1$$

11.4 See also

- Temurah (Kabbalah)

- Gematria

- Hebrew language

- ROT13

11.5 References

- Paul Y. Hoskisson. "Jeremiah's Game". *Insights*. Retrieved 30 March 2013.

Chapter 12

Autokey cipher

```
  A B C D E F G H I J K L M N O P Q R S T U V W X Y Z
A A B C D E F G H I J K L M N O P Q R S T U V W X Y Z
B B C D E F G H I J K L M N O P Q R S T U V W X Y Z A
C C D E F G H I J K L M N O P Q R S T U V W X Y Z A B
D D E F G H I J K L M N O P Q R S T U V W X Y Z A B C
E E F G H I J K L M N O P Q R S T U V W X Y Z A B C D
F F G H I J K L M N O P Q R S T U V W X Y Z A B C D E
G G H I J K L M N O P Q R S T U V W X Y Z A B C D E F
H H I J K L M N O P Q R S T U V W X Y Z A B C D E F G
I I J K L M N O P Q R S T U V W X Y Z A B C D E F G H
J J K L M N O P Q R S T U V W X Y Z A B C D E F G H I
K K L M N O P Q R S T U V W X Y Z A B C D E F G H I J
L L M N O P Q R S T U V W X Y Z A B C D E F G H I J K
M M N O P Q R S T U V W X Y Z A B C D E F G H I J K L
N N O P Q R S T U V W X Y Z A B C D E F G H I J K L M
O O P Q R S T U V W X Y Z A B C D E F G H I J K L M N
P P Q R S T U V W X Y Z A B C D E F G H I J K L M N O
Q Q R S T U V W X Y Z A B C D E F G H I J K L M N O P
R R S T U V W X Y Z A B C D E F G H I J K L M N O P Q
S S T U V W X Y Z A B C D E F G H I J K L M N O P Q R
T T U V W X Y Z A B C D E F G H I J K L M N O P Q R S
U U V W X Y Z A B C D E F G H I J K L M N O P Q R S T
V V W X Y Z A B C D E F G H I J K L M N O P Q R S T U
W W X Y Z A B C D E F G H I J K L M N O P Q R S T U V
X X Y Z A B C D E F G H I J K L M N O P Q R S T U V W
Y Y Z A B C D E F G H I J K L M N O P Q R S T U V W X
Z Z A B C D E F G H I J K L M N O P Q R S T U V W X Y
```

A tabula recta for use with an autokey cipher

An **autokey cipher** (also known as the **autoclave cipher**) is a cipher which incorporates the message (the plaintext) into the key. There are two forms of autokey cipher: *key autokey* and *text autokey* ciphers. A key-autokey cipher uses previous members of the keystream to determine the next element in the keystream. A text-autokey uses the previous message text to determine the next element in the keystream.

In modern cryptography, self-synchronizing stream ciphers are autokey ciphers.

12.1   History

The first autokey cipher was invented by Girolamo Cardano and contained a fatal defect. Like many autokey ciphers it used the plaintext to encrypt itself; however, since there was no additional key, it is no easier for the intended recipient to read the message than anyone else who knows that the cipher is being used.[1] A number of attempts were made by other cryptographers to produce a system that was neither trivial to break nor too difficult for the intended recipient to decipher. Eventually one was invented in 1564 by Giovan Battista Bellaso using a "reciprocal table" with five alphabets of his invention and another form was described in 1586 by Blaise de Vigenère with a similar reciprocal table of ten alphabets.

One popular form of autokey starts with a tabula recta, a square with 26 copies of the alphabet, the first line starting with 'A', the next line starting with 'B', etc., like the one above. In order to encrypt a plaintext, one locates the row with the first letter to be encrypted, and the column with the first letter of the key. The letter where the line and column cross is the ciphertext letter.

Giovan Battista Bellaso used the first letter of each word as a primer to start his text autokey. Blaise de Vigenère used as a primer an agreed-upon single letter of the alphabet.

The autokey cipher as used by the members of the American Cryptogram Association is in the way the key is generated. It starts with a relatively short keyword, and appends the message to it. So if the keyword is "QUEENLY", and the message is "ATTACK AT DAWN", the key would be "QUEENLYATTACKATDAWN" [2]

Plaintext: ATTACK AT DAWN... Key: QUEENL YA TTACK AT DAWN.... Ciphertext: QNXEPV YT WTWP...

The ciphertext message would therefore be "QNXEPVYTWTWP".

12.2   Cryptanalysis

Using an example message "meet at the fountain" encrypted with the keyword "KILT":[3]

plaintext: MEETATTHEFOUNTAIN (unknown) key: KILTMEETATTHEFOUN (unknown) ciphertext: WMPMMXXAEYHBRYOCA (known)

We try common words, bigrams, trigrams etc. in all possible positions in the key. For example, "THE":

ciphertext: WMP MMX XAE YHB RYO CA key: THE THE THE THE THE .. plaintext: DFL TFT ETA FAX YRK .. ciphertext: W MPM MXX AEY HBR YOC A key: . THE THE THE THE THE . plaintext: . TII TQT HXU OUN FHY . ciphertext: WM PMM XXA EYH BRY OCA key: .. THE THE THE THE THE plaintext: .. WFI EQW LRD IKU VVW

We sort the plaintext fragments in order of likelihood:

unlikely <-----------------> promising EQW DFL TFT ... ... ETA OUN FAX

We know that a correct plaintext fragment will also appear in the key, shifted right by the length of the keyword. Similarly our guessed key fragment ("THE") will also appear in the plaintext shifted left. So by guessing keyword lengths (probably between 3 and 12) we can reveal more plaintext and key.

Trying this with "OUN" (possibly after wasting some time with the others):

shift by 4: ciphertext: WMPMMXXAEYHBRYOCA key: ......ETA.THE.OUN plaintext: ......THE.OUN.AIN by 5: ciphertext: WMPMMXXAEYHBRYOCA key: .....EQW..THE..OU plaintext: .....THE..OUN..OG by 6: ciphertext: WMPMMXXAEYHBRYOCA key: ....TQT...THE...O plaintext: ....THE...OUN...M

We see that a shift of 4 looks good (both of the others have unlikely Qs), so we shift the revealed "ETA" back by 4 into the plaintext:

ciphertext: WMPMMXXAEYHBRYOCA key: ..LTM.ETA.THE.OUN plaintext: ..ETA.THE.OUN.AIN

We have a lot to work with now. The keyword is probably 4 characters long ("..LT"), and we have some of the message:

M.ETA.THE.OUN.AIN

Because our plaintext guesses have an effect on the key 4 characters to the left, we get feedback on correct/incorrect guesses, so we can quickly fill in the gaps:

MEETATTHEFOUNTAIN

The ease of cryptanalysis is thanks to the feedback from the relationship between plaintext and key. A 3-character guess reveals 6 more characters, which then reveal further characters, creating a cascade effect, allowing us to rule out incorrect guesses quickly.

12.3   Autokey in modern ciphers

Modern autokey ciphers use very different encryption methods, but they follow the same approach of using either key bytes or plaintext bytes to generate more key bytes. Most modern stream ciphers are based on pseudorandom number generators: the key is used to initialize the generator, and either key bytes or plaintext bytes are fed back into the generator to produce more bytes.

Some stream ciphers are said to be "self-synchronizing", because the next key byte usually depends only on the previous N bytes of the message. If a byte in the message is lost or corrupted, therefore, the key-stream will also be corrupted—but only until N bytes have been processed. At that point the keystream goes back to normal, and the rest of the message will decrypt correctly.

12.4   See also

- Chaocipher

12.5   Notes

[1] Kahn, David, *The Codebreakers*, revised edition, 1996, p. 144.

[2] "Autokey Calculator". Asecuritysite.com. Retrieved 2012-12-26.

[3] "Autokey Calculator". Asecuritysite.com. Retrieved 2012-12-26.

12.6   References

- Bellaso, Giovan Battista, *Il vero modo di scrivere in cifra con facilità, prestezza, et securezza di Misser Giovan Battista Bellaso, gentil'huomo bresciano*, Iacobo Britannico, Bressa 1564.

- Vigenère, Blaise de, *Traicté des chiffres ou secrètes manières d'escrire*, Abel l'Angelier, Paris 1586. ff. 46r-49v.

- LABRONICUS (Buonafalce, A), *Early Forms of the Porta Table*, "The Cryptogram", vol. LX n. 2, Wilbraham 1994.

- Buonafalce, Augusto, *Bellaso's Reciprocal Ciphers*, "Cryptologia" 30 (1):39-51, 2006.

- LABRONICUS (Buonafalce, A), *Vigenère and Autokey. An Update*, "The Cryptogram", vol. LXXIV n. 3, Plano 2008.

12.7   External links

- Secret Code Breaker - AutoKey Cipher Decoder and Encoder

- A Javascript implementation of the Autokey cipher

Chapter 13

Bacon's cipher

Bacon's cipher or the **Baconian cipher** is a method of steganography (a method of hiding a secret message as opposed to just a cipher) devised by Francis Bacon in 1605. A message is concealed in the presentation of text, rather than its content.

13.1   Cipher details

To encode a message, each letter of the plaintext is replaced by a group of five of the letters 'A' or 'B'. This replacement is a binary encoding and is done according to the alphabet of the Baconian cipher, shown below.

a AAAAA g AABBA n ABBAA t BAABA b AAAAB h AABBB o ABBAB u-v BAABB c AAABA i-j ABAAA p ABBBA w BABAA d AAABB k ABAAB q ABBBB x BABAB e AABAA l ABABA r BAAAA y BABBA f AABAB m ABABB s BAAAB z BABBB

Note: A second version of Bacon's cipher uses a unique code for each letter. In other words, *I* and *J* each has its own pattern.

The writer must make use of two different typefaces for this cipher. After preparing a false message with the same number of letters as all of the *A*s and *B*s in the real, secret message, two typefaces are chosen, one to represent *A*s and the other *B*s. Then each letter of the false message must be presented in the appropriate typeface, according to whether it stands for an *A* or a *B*.[1]

To decode the message, the reverse method is applied. Each "typeface 1" letter in the false message is replaced with an *A* and each "typeface 2" letter is replaced with a *B*. The Baconian alphabet is then used to recover the original message.

Any method of writing the message that allows two distinct representations for each character can be used for the Bacon Cipher. Bacon himself prepared a *Biliteral Alphabet*[2] for handwritten capital and small letters with each having two alternative forms, one to be used as *A* and the other as *B*. This was published as an illustrated plate in his *De Augmentis Scientiarum* (The Advancement of Learning).

Because any message of the right length can be used to carry the encoding, the secret message is effectively hidden in plain sight. The false message can be on any topic and thus can distract a person seeking to find the real message.

13.2   Baconian cipher example

The word 'steganography', encoded with padding, where text in italics represents "typeface 2" and standard text represents "typeface 1":

*T*o en*c*ode *a* message e*a*ch letter *of* the *plaint*ext *i*s replaced by *a* grou*p of f*i*v*e of *t*he lett*er*s '*A*' or '*B*'.

13.3   Bacon and Shakespeare

Some people have suggested that the plays attributed to William Shakespeare were in fact written by Francis Bacon, and that the published plays contain enciphered messages to that effect. Both Ignatius L. Donnelly and Elizabeth Wells Gallup attempted to find such messages by looking for the use of Bacon's cipher in early printed editions of the plays.

However, American cryptologists William and Elizebeth Friedman refuted the claims that the works of Shakespeare contain hidden ciphers that disclose Bacon's or any other candidate's secret authorship in their *The Shakespeare Ciphers Examined* (1957).

13.4   References

[1] Helen Fouché Gaines, *Cryptanalysis: a Study of Ciphers and Their Solutions* (1989), page 6]

[2] Biliteral can mean: "written in two different scripts", *Oxford English Dictionary*

13.5   Further reading

- William Friedman and Elizebeth Friedman, *The Shakespearean Ciphers Examined*, Cambridge University Press, 1957

13.6   External links

- How to Make Anything Signify Anything

- Tool to encode/decode Baconian ciphers

Chapter 14

Beaufort cipher

The **Beaufort cipher,** created by Sir Francis Beaufort, is a substitution cipher similar to the Vigenère cipher, with a slightly modified enciphering mechanism and tableau.[1] Its most famous application was in a rotor-based cipher machine, the Hagelin M-209.[2] The Beaufort cipher is based on the Beaufort square which is essentially the same as a Vigenère square but in reverse order starting with the letter "Z" in the first row,[3] where the first row and the last column serve the same purpose.[4]

14.1 Using the cipher

To encrypt, first choose the plaintext character from the top row of the tableau, call this column P. Secondly, travel down column P to the corresponding key Letter K. Finally, move directly left from the Key letter to the left edge of the tableau, the CipherText encryption of Plaintext P with Key K will be there.

For example if encrypting Plain text character "d" with Key "m" the steps would be:

1. find the column with "d" on the top,

2. travel down that column to find Key "m",

3. travel to the left edge of the tableau to find the Cipher-Text letter ("J" in this case).

To decrypt, the process is reversed. The Beaufort cipher is a reciprocal cipher, that is, Decryption and Encryption algorithms are the same.

14.2 Decrypting as a Vigenere cipher

Due to the similarities between the **Beaufort cipher** and the Vigenère cipher it is possible, after applying a transformation, to solve it as a Vigenère cipher. By replacing every letter in the ciphertext with its opposite letter (such that 'a' becomes 'z', 'b' becomes 'y' etc.) it can be solved like a Vigenère cipher.

14.3 Distinguished from 'variant Beaufort'

The Beaufort cipher should not be confused with the "variant Beaufort" cipher. In variant Beaufort, encryption is performed by performing the decryption step of the standard Vigenère cipher, and likewise decryption is performed by using Vigenère encryption.

14.4 References

[1] Franksen, Ole Immanuel, *Babbage and cryptography. Or, the mystery of Admiral Beaufort's cipher*. Mathematics and Computers in Simulation 35 (1993) 327-367

[2] Mollin, Richard A., *An Introduction to Cryptography*, page 100. Chapman & Hall/CRC, 2001

[3] Jörg Rothe (2006). *Complexity Theory and Cryptology: An Introduction to Cryptocomplexity*. Springer Science & Business Media. p. 164. ISBN 9783540285205.

[4] Arto Salomaa (2013). *Public-Key Cryptography: Volume 23 of Monographs in Theoretical Computer Science. An EATCS Series*. Springer Science & Business Media. p. 31. ISBN 9783662026274.

Chapter 15

Bifid cipher

In classical cryptography, the **bifid cipher** is a cipher which combines the Polybius square with transposition, and uses fractionation to achieve diffusion. It was invented around 1901 by Felix Delastelle.

15.1 Operation

First, a mixed alphabet Polybius square is drawn up:

1 2 3 4 5 1 B G W K Z 2 Q P N D S 3 I O A X E 4 F C L U M 5 T H Y V R

The message is converted to its coordinates in the usual manner, but they are written vertically beneath:

F L E E A T O N C E 4 4 3 3 3 5 3 2 4 3 1 3 5 5 3 1 2 3 2 5

They are then read out in rows:

4 4 3 3 3 5 3 2 4 3 1 3 5 5 3 1 2 3 2 5

Then divided up into pairs again, and the pairs turned back into letters using the square Worked example:

44 33 35 32 43 13 55 31 23 25 U A E O L W R I N S

In this way, each ciphertext character depends on two plaintext characters, so the bifid is a digraphic cipher, like the Playfair cipher. To decrypt, the procedure is simply reversed.

Longer messages are first broken up into blocks of fixed length, called the period. As shown above, the period is 5 so solve for 5 letters at a time. Each block is then encrypted separately. Statistical analysis to detect the period uses ciphertext letters. Since each letter corresponds to two numbers, it infers half the period, not the period directly. Thus, odd periods are more secure than even, because the statistical anomalies register both on half the period rounded down and rounded up.[1]

15.2 See also

- Other ciphers by Delastelle:
    - four-square cipher (related to Playfair)
    - trifid cipher (similar to bifid)

15.3 References

[1] http://practicalcryptography.com/cryptanalysis/ stochastic-searching/cryptanalysis-bifid-cipher/

15.4 External links

- Online Bifid Encipherer/Decipherer with polybius square generator

Chapter 16

Book cipher

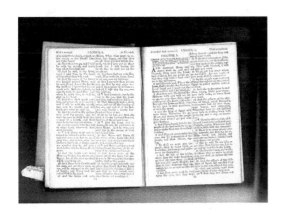

The King James Bible, a highly available publication suitable for the book cipher.

A **book cipher** is a cipher in which the key is some aspect of a book or other piece of text; books being common and widely available in modern times, users of book ciphers take the position that the details of the key are sufficiently well hidden from attackers in practice. It is typically essential that both correspondents not only have the same book, but the same edition.[1]

Traditionally book ciphers work by replacing words in the plaintext of a message with the location of words from the book being used. In this mode, book ciphers are more properly called codes.

This can have problems; if a word appears in the plaintext but not in the book, it cannot be encoded. An alternative approach which gets around this problem is to replace individual letters rather than words. One such method, used in the second Beale cipher, substitutes the first letter of a word in the book with that word's position. In this case, the book cipher is properly a cipher — specifically, a homophonic substitution cipher. However, if used often, this technique has the side effect of creating a larger ciphertext (typically 4 to 6 digits being required to encipher each letter or syllable) and increases the time and effort required to decode the message.

16.1 Choosing the key

The main strength of a book cipher is the key. The sender and receiver of encoded messages can agree to use any book or other publication available to both of them as the key to their cipher. Someone intercepting the message and attempting to decode it, unless they are a skilled cryptographer (see Security below), must somehow identify the key from a huge number of possibilities available. In the context of espionage, a book cipher has a considerable advantage for a spy in enemy territory. A conventional codebook, if discovered by the local authorities, instantly incriminates the holder as a spy and gives the authorities the chance of deciphering the code and sending false messages impersonating the agent. On the other hand a book, if chosen carefully to fit with the spy's cover story, would seem entirely innocuous. The drawback to a book cipher is that both parties have to possess an identical copy of the key. The book must not be of the sort that would look out of place in the possession of those using it and it must be of a type likely to contain any words required. Thus, for example, a spy wishing to send information about troop movements and numbers of armaments would be unlikely to find a cookery book or a romantic novel useful keys.

16.2 Using widely available publications

16.2.1 Dictionary

Another approach is to use a dictionary as the codebook. This guarantees that nearly all words will be found, and also makes it much easier to find a word when encoding. This approach was used by George Scovell for the Duke of Wellington's army in some campaigns of the Peninsular War. In Scovell's method, a codeword would consist of a number (indicating the page of the dictionary), a letter (indicating the column on the page), and finally a number indicating which entry of the column was meant. However, this approach also has a disadvantage: because entries are arranged in alphabetical order, so are the code numbers. This can give strong hints to the cryptanalyst unless the message is superenciphered. The wide distribution and availability of dictionaries also present a problem; it is likely that anyone trying to break such a code is also in possession of the dictionary which can be used to read the message.

16.2.2 Bible cipher

The Bible is a widely available book that is almost always printed with chapter and verse markings making it easy to find a specific string of text within it, making it particularly useful for this purpose; the widespread availability of concordances can ease the encoding process as well.

16.3 Security

Essentially, the code version of a "book cipher" is just like any other code, but one in which the trouble of preparing and distributing the codebook has been eliminated by using an existing text. However this means, as well as being attacked by all the usual means employed against other codes or ciphers, partial solutions may help the cryptanalyst to guess other codewords, or even to break the code completely by identifying the key text. This is, however, not the only way a book cipher may be broken. It is still susceptible to other methods of cryptanalysis, and as such is quite easily broken, even without sophisticated means, without the cryptanalyst having any idea what book the cipher is keyed to.[2]

If used carefully, the cipher version is probably much stronger, because it acts as a homophonic cipher with an extremely large number of equivalents. However, this is at the cost of a very large ciphertext expansion.

16.4 Examples

- A famous use of a book cipher is in the Beale ciphers, of which document no. 2 uses a (variant printing of) the United States Declaration of Independence as the key text.

- In the American Revolution, Benedict Arnold used a book cipher, sometimes known as the Arnold Cipher, which used Sir William Blackstone's *Commentaries on the Laws of England* as a key text.

- Book ciphers have consistently been used throughout the Cicada 3301 mystery.[3]

16.4.1 In fiction

- In *The Valley of Fear*, Sherlock Holmes decrypts a message enciphered with a book cipher by deducing which book had been used as a key text.

- The name of Ken Follett's World War II thriller *The Key to Rebecca* refers to a German spy in Cairo using Daphne du Maurier's novel *Rebecca* as the basis of a code.

- In *A Presumption of Death*, Lord Peter Wimsey, on assignment for British Intelligence in World War II Nazi-occupied Europe, uses a code based on the works of John Donne. The Germans, suspecting that an intelligence service in which Oxonians have a major role would choose a classical work of English literature, systematically try such works until hitting the right one and breaking the code, coming near to catching the spy. Wimsey then improvises a new code, based on an unpublished text known only to himself and his wife.

- Graham Greene's protagonists often use book codes. In *The Human Factor*, several books are used, and an edition of Charles Lamb's *Tales from Shakespeare* is used in *Our Man in Havana*.

- A book cipher plays an important role in the TV version of *Sharpe's Sword*. The key text is Voltaire's *Candide*.

- In the 2004 film *National Treasure*, an Ottendorf cipher is discovered on the back of the U. S. Declaration of Independence, using the "Silence Dogood" letters as the key text.

- The protagonists of the Matthew Reilly novel *The Six Sacred Stones* used a book cipher to send confidential messages to each other. The key text was the Harry Potter books, but the messages were sent *via a The Lord of the Rings* forum to make the key text harder to identify.

- In *Lost: Mystery of the Island*, a series of four jigsaw puzzles released in 2007, Ottendorf cipher was used on each puzzle's box to hide *spoilers* and reveal information about the show to the fans.

- "The Fisher King", a two-part episode of *Criminal Minds*, features an Ottendorf cipher brought to the Behavioral Analysis Unit by the UNSUB via Agent Hotchner's wife. The cypher was part of a larger puzzle to find a girl who had been missing for two years. The key text was *The Collector* by John Fowles.

- *Burn Notice* (episodes "Where There's Smoke" and "Center of the Storm", 2010): Michael Westen steals a Bible from a safe deposit box that is the code book of Simon. This becomes part of the season plot to track an organization starting wars for profit as Michael tries to arrange an interview with Simon.

- In the episode "The Blind Banker" of the BBC series *Sherlock*, Sherlock Holmes searches for a book that is the key to a cipher being used by Chinese Tong smugglers to communicate with their agents and with each other through graffiti messages;

- In the film *Unknown* (2011), Prof. Bressler's passwords are obscured by an Ottendorf cipher.

- In *The Unit* episode "Paradise Lost", Jonas Blane (aka Snake Doctor) uses a book code from the poem *Paradise Lost* to communicate to his wife, Molly, that he has arrived safely in Panama.

- In "The Good Soldier Švejk" by Jaroslav Hašek, the title character's commanding officers attempt to use a book cipher. Their attempts are undone, however, when it is revealed that the novel in question is composed of two volumes, and Švejk has delivered the first volume to the officers, thinking that they intended to read the novel, rather than the second, where the code is ciphered from.

- In *An Instance of the Fingerpost*, a historical mystery by Iain Pears, a book cipher conceals one character's family history and its relationship with the English Civil War.

- In John Le Carre's A Perfect Spy, the protagonist Magnus Pym uses a book cipher based on the German text Simplicissimus.

- In the movie *Manhunter*, Hannibal Lecter, who is in prison, communicates in a personal ad in a newspaper using a book code the police know is not what he says it is (he mentions verses in the Bible, but some of the chapter numbers are not valid.) The police later discover which book Lecter was actually using, and he has given the man the home address of an FBI profiler, Will Graham, and warned the man to kill Graham.

16.5   See also

- Running key cipher

- Codebook

16.6   References

[1] Changda Wang; Shiguang Ju (2008). "Book Cipher with Infinite Key Space". *2008 International Symposium on Information Science and Engineering*. p. 456. doi:10.1109/ISISE.2008.273. ISBN 978-0-7695-3494-7.

[2] Yardley, Herbert O. *The American Black Chamber* (Annapolis: Naval Institute Press, 2004; reprints original edition).

[3] Bell, Chris. "Cicada 3301 update: the baffling internet mystery is back". *Daily Telegraph*. Archived from the original on 7 January 2014.

Chapter 17

Thomas Brierley

Thomas Brierley was born on 16 July 1785 at Mellor, Lancashire United Kingdom to Joab Brierley and Betty Arnfield. He was also known as "Tommy" and some references call him "Didymus" - perhaps confusing him for an uncle of that name or as a common alternative to Thomas.

Thomas became a blockprinter at the Printworks mill in Strines Manchester England, a mill where calico, a type of textile was printed. Later as a carter he plied his trade between Ludworth and Disley.

17.1 Freemasonry

The Freemason Lodge of Union (originally a Lancashire Lodge of Union No.50) received its Warrant on 27 September 1788. The Lodge migrated from Manchester to Mellor in 1822 it met at the Devonshire Arms and several other hostelries in the locality before it shifted to the Shuttle Inn (renamed the George) at Ludworth. Returns to the Clerk of Peace between 1834 and 1841 show that the Lodge averaged about 20 members each meeting; chiefly miners and minor tradesmen.[1]

Thomas Brierley was a regular attendee (according to the records that exist between 1824 and 1830 and from 1840 to 1848). He was also Treasurer of the Royal Arch chapter (founded 1824). He was also a member of the Moon Lodge of benevolence, as well as other degrees including Mark and Rose Croix.[2]

His connection with Freemasonry is told in this anecdote:

When the Duke of Devonshire was Provincial Grandmaster for Derbyshire, Thomas and some friends walked to Chatsworth House which sat in a large Deer Park laid out by Capability Brown where they were refused admittance as the Duke was home. After a great deal of pertinacity, Thomas managed to get a servant to present a message, hastily written in cipher on a paper scrap. The Duke instantly came in person and showed his humble brother and his friends over the house and ordered lunch to be served to them.[2][3]

However, an extract from the Mirror of Literature and Amusement 1844 states that "The Duke of Devonshire allows all persons whatsoever to see the mansion and grounds every day of the year. Sundays not excepted, from 10 in the morning 'til 5 in the afternoon. The humblest individual is not only shown the whole, but the Duke has expressly ordered the waterworks to be played to everyone without exception. This is acting in the true spirit of great wealth and enlightened liberality; let us add also, the spirit of wisdom."

17.2 An early burial

Thomas seemed to have some periods of illness and had recourse to the sick funds of the society. A number of members complained and made unpleasant personal remarks, as apparently his illness coincided with a slack time at Strines Printworks. It is said that he was "an honourable man and this charge grieved him sore." (Other sources refer to him as one who was prone to display his membership of the masonic fraternity and to make it known that his worth was not sufficiently recognised.)

Either way, he had a stone coffin made by Azariah Ollerenshaw, a stonemason of local repute, and for which he lay down so that the coffin could be accurately cut for his body and head for a perfect fit. (Another source claims that the Duke, hearing that Thomas was ill, had the coffin made for him.)

The coffin was then placed, exposed on a previously purchased grave site at St. Thomas' Church, Mellor. The lid was carved with some Masonic symbols and underneath the words, "I am belied," referring to the accusations of feigned illness. It lay there for some years and because quite a tourist attraction. However, it eventually created too much unwanted attention for the vicar, Rev. Matthew Freeman, who ordered it to be buried in the grave (and it apparently still lies there just below the surface).

Not to be frustrated, Thomas had a memorial headstone prepared covered with 'cipher-writings' and ornate and masonic emblems which was placed over his grave before he died. Subsequently, there was talk of burying him in his stone coffin but it was found to be too heavy to remove to the house and it was not done to take the body to the coffin in the grave. He was buried in a wooden coffin presumably beside the stone coffin.[3][4][5][6]

17.3 Mystery

Thomas Brierley's memorial, Mellor (Photo: Mark Brierley)

The cipher on the headstone was presented as a mystery in books and newspaper articles right into the latter part of the 20th century. The headstone is actually written in five pig-pen variations. The text at the head of the stone says "Thomas Brierley made his ingress July 16th 1785, His

Progress was ____ Years And his Egress___". The headstone was never completed after his death (possibly because no one was interested and his father survived him only one more year and was of advanced age).

The cipher at the foot of the gravestone says "Holiness of the Lord". The Pigpen cipher was used by Freemasons in the 18th century to keep their records private and surprisingly the cipher on Thomas Brierley's grave seems to have a non-standard symbol for the letter "S". It is possible the variation in the cipher is a clue to or a key to documents that he dealt with as the treasurer.

However, at the time of its placement in the graveyard the common impression was that it contained the old charge against his fellows and it was stated to be purposefully written in Hebrew to defy objections to it being placed over the grave during Thomas' lifetime. Indeed, newspaper reports echoed this and one gentleman visiting the grave solemnly asserted it was Greek but when cornered in the subject admitted it was a kind of Greek that a university education had not acquainted him with.

According to some, Thomas Brierley fell to his death from the church tower, but other sources disagree so this story may be an urban legend. To add to the mystery, a bronze plaque was added to the stone in recent times with more cipher upon it, the cipher used being similar but not identical.

He is reported to have died in 1854 aged 69 years although Letters of Administration,[7] after his death, granted to his father Joab states that he died on 22 July 1855. He was interred in Mellor Churchyard.[8]

17.4 References

[1] Manton, James O. (1913). *Early Freemasonry in Derbyshire, with Especial Reference to the Tyrian Lodge, No. 253.* Manchester: Association for Masonic Research/Marsden & Co. pp. 18–19. ISBN 978-1171776307.

[2] *Masonic Square*, March 1987, pp. 22–23

[3] Wainwright, Joel. *Glimpses of Mellor.* pp. 14–15.

[4] *The North Cheshire Herald.* February 1882. Missing or empty |title= (help)

[5] Astle, William, ed. (1898). *Cheshire Notes & Queries.* **3**. pp. 113–117.

[6] *Transactions of the Lancashire & Cheshire Antiquarian Society.* **XV**: 188–189. 1897. Missing or empty |title= (help)

[7] Joab Brierley of Mellor applied for Letters of Administration of the Estate and Effects of Thomas Briarley late of Mellor, Labourer on 29 August 1855.

[8] Burial's Book, Parish of Mellor, entry #1653 26 July 1855
      aged 70 years "Thomas, the son of Joab and Betty Briarley,
      of Paradise"

Chapter 18

Caesar cipher

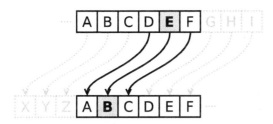

The action of a Caesar cipher is to replace each plaintext letter with a different one a fixed number of places down the alphabet. The cipher illustrated here uses a left shift of three, so that (for example) each occurrence of E in the plaintext becomes B in the ciphertext.

In cryptography, a **Caesar cipher**, also known as **Caesar's cipher**, the **shift cipher**, **Caesar's code** or **Caesar shift**, is one of the simplest and most widely known encryption techniques. It is a type of substitution cipher in which each letter in the plaintext is replaced by a letter some fixed number of positions down the alphabet. For example, with a left shift of 3, D would be replaced by A, E would become B, and so on. The method is named after Julius Caesar, who used it in his private correspondence.

The encryption step performed by a Caesar cipher is often incorporated as part of more complex schemes, such as the Vigenère cipher, and still has modern application in the ROT13 system. As with all single-alphabet substitution ciphers, the Caesar cipher is easily broken and in modern practice offers essentially no communication security.

18.1 Example

The transformation can be represented by aligning two alphabets; the cipher alphabet is the plain alphabet rotated left or right by some number of positions. For instance, here is a Caesar cipher using a left rotation of three places, equivalent to a right shift of 23 (the shift parameter is used as the key):

Plain: ABCDEFGHIJKLMNOPQRSTUVWXYZ Cipher:

XYZABCDEFGHIJKLMNOPQRSTUVW

When encrypting, a person looks up each letter of the message in the "plain" line and writes down the corresponding letter in the "cipher" line.

Plaintext: THE QUICK BROWN FOX JUMPS OVER THE LAZY DOG Ciphertext: QEB NRFZH YOLTK CLU GRJMP LSBO QEB IXWV ALD

Deciphering is done in reverse, with a right shift of 3.

The encryption can also be represented using modular arithmetic by first transforming the letters into numbers, according to the scheme, A = 0, B = 1,..., Z = 25.[1] Encryption of a letter x by a shift n can be described mathematically as,[2]

$$E_n(x) = (x + n) \mod 26.$$

Decryption is performed similarly,

$$D_n(x) = (x - n) \mod 26.$$

(There are different definitions for the modulo operation. In the above, the result is in the range 0...25. I.e., if $x+n$ or $x-n$ are not in the range 0...25, we have to subtract or add 26.)

The replacement remains the same throughout the message, so the cipher is classed as a type of *monoalphabetic substitution*, as opposed to *polyalphabetic substitution*.

18.2 History and usage

The Caesar cipher is named after Julius Caesar, who, according to Suetonius, used it with a shift of three to protect messages of military significance. While Caesar's was the first recorded use of this scheme, other substitution ciphers are known to have been used earlier.

> If he had anything confidential to say, he wrote it in cipher, that is, by so changing the

The Caesar cipher is named for Julius Caesar, who used an alphabet with a left shift of three.

order of the letters of the alphabet, that not a word could be made out. If anyone wishes to decipher these, and get at their meaning, he must substitute the fourth letter of the alphabet, namely D, for A, and so with the others.
— Suetonius, *Life of Julius Caesar* 56

His nephew, Augustus, also used the cipher, but with a right shift of one, and it did not wrap around to the beginning of the alphabet:

Whenever he wrote in cipher, he wrote B for A, C for B, and the rest of the letters on the same principle, using AA for Z.
— Suetonius, *Life of Augustus* 88

There is evidence that Julius Caesar used more complicated systems as well,[3] and one writer, Aulus Gellius, refers to a

(now lost) treatise on his ciphers:

There is even a rather ingeniously written treatise by the grammarian Probus concerning the secret meaning of letters in the composition of Caesar's epistles.
— Aulus Gellius, *Attic Nights 17.9.1–5*

It is unknown how effective the Caesar cipher was at the time, but it is likely to have been reasonably secure, not least because most of Caesar's enemies would have been illiterate and others would have assumed that the messages were written in an unknown foreign language.[4] There is no record at that time of any techniques for the solution of simple substitution ciphers. The earliest surviving records date to the 9th century works of Al-Kindi in the Arab world with the discovery of frequency analysis.[5]

A Caesar cipher with a shift of one is used on the back of the mezuzah to encrypt the names of God. This may be a holdover from an earlier time when Jewish people were not allowed to have mezuzot. The letters of the cryptogram themselves comprise a religiously significant "divine name" which Orthodox belief holds keeps the forces of evil in check.[6]

In the 19th century, the personal advertisements section in newspapers would sometimes be used to exchange messages encrypted using simple cipher schemes. Kahn (1967) describes instances of lovers engaging in secret communications enciphered using the Caesar cipher in *The Times*.[7] Even as late as 1915, the Caesar cipher was in use: the Russian army employed it as a replacement for more complicated ciphers which had proved to be too difficult for their troops to master; German and Austrian cryptanalysts had little difficulty in decrypting their messages.[8]

Caesar ciphers can be found today in children's toys such as secret decoder rings. A Caesar shift of thirteen is also performed in the ROT13 algorithm, a simple method of obfuscating text widely found on Usenet and used to obscure text (such as joke punchlines and story spoilers), but not seriously used as a method of encryption.[9]

A construction of 2 rotating disks with a Caesar cipher can be used to encrypt or decrypt the code.

The Vigenère cipher uses a Caesar cipher with a different shift at each position in the text; the value of the shift is defined using a repeating keyword. If the keyword is as long as the message, chosen random, never becomes known to anyone else, and is never reused, this is the one-time pad cipher, proven unbreakable. The conditions are so difficult they are, in practical effect, never achieved. Keywords shorter than the message (e.g., "Complete Victory" used by the Confederacy during the American Civil War), introduce a cyclic pattern that might be detected with a statistically advanced version of frequency analysis.[10]

In April 2006, fugitive Mafia boss Bernardo Provenzano was captured in Sicily partly because some of his messages, clumsily written in a variation of the Caesar cipher, were broken. Provenzano's cipher used numbers, so that "A" would be written as "4", "B" as "5", and so on.[11]

In 2011, Rajib Karim was convicted in the United Kingdom of "terrorism offences" after using the Caesar cipher to communicate with Bangladeshi Islamic activists discussing plots to blow up British Airways planes or disrupt their IT networks. Although the parties had access to far better encryption techniques (Karim himself used PGP for data storage on computer disks), they chose to use their own scheme(implemented in Microsoft Excel), rejecting a more sophisticated code program called Mujhaddin Secrets "because 'kaffirs', or non-believers, know about it, so it must be less secure". [12]

The animated series *Gravity Falls* uses the Caesar cipher as one of three different ciphers (the other two being Atbash and an A1Z26 cipher) during the end credits of the first six episodes.

18.3 Breaking the cipher

The Caesar cipher can be easily broken even in a ciphertext-only scenario. Two situations can be considered:

1. an attacker knows (or guesses) that some sort of simple substitution cipher has been used, but not specifically that it is a Caesar scheme;

2. an attacker knows that a Caesar cipher is in use, but does not know the shift value.

In the first case, the cipher can be broken using the same techniques as for a general simple substitution cipher, such as frequency analysis or pattern words.[13] While solving, it is likely that an attacker will quickly notice the regularity in the solution and deduce that a Caesar cipher is the specific algorithm employed.

In the second instance, breaking the scheme is even more straightforward. Since there are only a limited number of possible shifts (26 in English), they can each be tested in turn in a brute force attack.[14] One way to do this is to write out a snippet of the ciphertext in a table of all possible shifts[15] – a technique sometimes known as "completing the plain component".[16] The example given is for the ciphertext "EXXEGOEXSRGI"; the plaintext is instantly recognisable by eye at a shift of four. Another way of viewing this method is that, under each letter of the ciphertext,

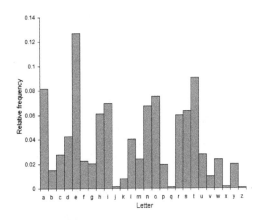

The distribution of letters in a typical sample of English language text has a distinctive and predictable shape. A Caesar shift "rotates" this distribution, and it is possible to determine the shift by examining the resultant frequency graph.

the entire alphabet is written out in reverse starting at that letter. This attack can be accelerated using a set of strips prepared with the alphabet written down in reverse order. The strips are then aligned to form the ciphertext along one row, and the plaintext should appear in one of the other rows.

Another brute force approach is to match up the frequency distribution of the letters. By graphing the frequencies of letters in the ciphertext, and by knowing the expected distribution of those letters in the original language of the plaintext, a human can easily spot the value of the shift by looking at the displacement of particular features of the graph. This is known as frequency analysis. For example, in the English language the plaintext frequencies of the letters E, T, (usually most frequent), and Q, Z (typically least frequent) are particularly distinctive.[17] Computers can also do this by measuring how well the actual frequency distribution matches up with the expected distribution; for example, the chi-squared statistic can be used.[18]

For natural language plaintext, there will, in all likelihood, be only one plausible decryption, although for extremely short plaintexts, multiple candidates are possible. For example, the ciphertext MPQY could, plausibly, decrypt to either "aden" or "know" (assuming the plaintext is in English); similarly, "ALIIP" to "dolls" or "wheel"; and "AFCCP" to "jolly" or "cheer" (see also unicity distance).

Multiple encryptions and decryptions provide no additional security. This is because two encryptions of, say, shift *A* and shift *B*, will be equivalent to an encryption with shift *A* + *B*. In mathematical terms, the encryption under various keys forms a group.[19]

18.4   Notes

[1] Luciano, Dennis; Gordon Prichett (January 1987). "Cryptology: From Caesar Ciphers to Public-Key Cryptosystems". *The College Mathematics Journal.* **18** (1): 2–17. doi:10.2307/2686311. JSTOR 2686311.

[2] Wobst, Reinhard (2001). *Cryptology Unlocked.* Wiley. p. 19. ISBN 978-0-470-06064-3.

[3] Reinke, Edgar C. (December 1992). "Classical Cryptography". *The Classical Journal.* **58** (3): 114.

[4] Pieprzyk, Josef; Thomas Hardjono; Jennifer Seberry (2003). *Fundamentals of Computer Security.* Springer. p. 6. ISBN 3-540-43101-2.

[5] Singh, Simon (2000). *The Code Book.* Anchor. pp. 14–20. ISBN 0-385-49532-3.

[6] Alexander Poltorak. "Mezuzah and Astrology". chabad.org. Retrieved 2008-06-13.

[7] Kahn, David (1967). *The Codebreakers.* pp. 775–6. ISBN 978-0-684-83130-5.

[8] Kahn, David (1967). *The Codebreakers.* pp. 631–2. ISBN 978-0-684-83130-5.

[9] Wobst, Reinhard (2001). *Cryptology Unlocked.* Wiley. p. 20. ISBN 978-0-470-06064-3.

[10] Kahn, David (1967). *The Codebreakers.* ISBN 978-0-684-83130-5.

[11] Leyden, John (2006-04-19). "Mafia boss undone by clumsy crypto". *The Register.* Retrieved 2008-06-13.

[12] "BA jihadist relied on Jesus-era encryption". *The Register.* 2011-03-22. Retrieved 2011-04-01.

[13] Beutelspacher, Albrecht (1994). *Cryptology.* Mathematical Association of America. pp. 9–11. ISBN 0-88385-504-6.

[14] Beutelspacher, Albrecht (1994). *Cryptology.* Mathematical Association of America. pp. 8–9. ISBN 0-88385-504-6.

[15] Leighton, Albert C. (April 1969). "Secret Communication among the Greeks and Romans". *Technology and Culture.* **10** (2): 139–154. doi:10.2307/3101474. JSTOR 3101474.

[16] Sinkov, Abraham; Paul L. Irwin (1966). *Elementary Cryptanalysis: A Mathematical Approach.* Mathematical Association of America. pp. 13–15. ISBN 0-88385-622-0.

[17] Singh, Simon (2000). *The Code Book.* Anchor. pp. 72–77. ISBN 0-385-49532-3.

[18] Savarese, Chris; Brian Hart (2002-07-15). "The Caesar Cipher". Retrieved 2008-07-16.

[19] Wobst, Reinhard (2001). *Cryptology Unlocked.* Wiley. p. 31. ISBN 978-0-470-06064-3.

18.5   Bibliography

- David Kahn, *The Codebreakers – The Story of Secret Writing,* Revised ed. 1996. ISBN 0-684-83130-9.

- F.L. Bauer, *Decrypted Secrets,* 2nd edition, 2000, Springer. ISBN 3-540-66871-3.

- Chris Savarese and Brian Hart, *The Caesar Cipher,* 1999

18.6   External links

- Weisstein, Eric W. "Caesar's Method". *MathWorld.*

Chapter 19

Chaocipher

The **Chaocipher** [1] is a cipher method invented by J. F. Byrne in 1918 and described in his 1953 autobiographical *Silent Years*.[2] He believed Chaocipher was simple, yet unbreakable. Byrne stated that the machine he used to encipher his messages could be fitted into a cigar box. He offered cash rewards for anyone who could solve it.

In May 2010 the Byrne family donated all Chaocipher-related papers and artifacts[3] to the National Cryptologic Museum in Ft. Meade, Maryland, USA. This led to the disclosure of the Chaocipher algorithm.[4]

19.1 How Chaocipher works

The Chaocipher system consists of two alphabets, with the "right" alphabet used for locating the plaintext letter while the other ("left") alphabet is used for reading the corresponding ciphertext letter. The underlying algorithm is related to the concept of dynamic substitution[5] whereby the two alphabets are slightly modified after each input plaintext letter is enciphered. This leads to nonlinear and highly diffused alphabets as encryption progresses.

Deciphering is identical to enciphering, with the ciphertext letter being located in the "left" alphabet while the corresponding plaintext letter being read from the "right" alphabet.

A detailed description of the Chaocipher algorithm is available[4] as well as discussions of the deciphered plaintexts [6] and the solution to Byrne's challenge.[7]

19.2 Points of interest

Henry E. Langen,[8] editor of *The Cryptogram* during that time, was quoted as saying "He did explain that the machine is made up somewhat like a typewriter with two revolving disks with the alphabets arranged along the periphery in a complete disorder ... With only two disks used, I am a bit confused as to how this can result in such utter chaotification of the plaintext message."

Until 2010 at least three people knew how it works: Byrne's son John, and two of the editors of *Cryptologia* to whom John confided the underlying method in 1990.[9]

19.3 See also

- Autokey cipher

19.4 References

[1] What is Chaocipher?, The Chaocipher Clearing House, retrieved August 8, 2010

[2] Byrne , J. F. 1953 . Silent Years: An Autobiography with Memoirs of James Joyce and Our Ireland . New York : Farrar, Straus, and Young (Reprinted in 1975 by Octagon Books, a division of Farrar, Straus, and Giroux).

[3] Chaocipher Machine and Papers National Cryptologic Museum, retrieved July 2, 2010

[4] Rubin, Moshe (July 2, 2010). "Chaocipher Revealed: The Algorithm" (PDF). Retrieved July 3, 2010.

[5] Substitution Cipher with Pseudo-Random Shuffling: The Dynamic Substitution Combiner. Ritter, T. 1990. Cryptologia. 14(4): 289-303. Retrieved July 2, 2010

[6] Rubin, Moshe (August 8, 2010). "Chaocipher Revealed: Deciphering Exhibit #1" (PDF). Retrieved August 9, 2010.

[7] Cowan, Mike (December 2010). "Chaocipher: Solving Exhibits 1 and 4" (PDF).

[8] Henry E. Langen biographical information, The Chaocipher Clearing House, retrieved July 2, 2010

[9] ?, ?. "The Tragic Story of J.F. Byrne." PurpleHunt.com. 1998. Aug 17, 2007.

19.5   Further Reading

- John F. Byrne's Chaocipher Revealed: An Historical and Technical Appraisal by Moshe Rubin, Cryptologia, Volume 35, Issue 4, October 2011

- Decoding Chaocipher Exhibits 2 & 3 by Esa Peuha (PDF). Retrieved April 23, 2014.

- Chaocipher Exhibit 5: History, Analysis, and Solution of Cryptologia's 1990 Challenge by Jeff Calof, Jeff Hill & Moshe Rubin, Cryptologia, Volume 38, Issue 1, January 2014, pages 1-25

19.6   External links

- The Chaocipher Clearing House - Basic resources and analyses for working on the Chaocipher

- The Crypto Forum - Discussion and analysis of the Chaocipher

- Cracking Chaocipher - A visual description of how Chaocipher works, and an explanation of cracking Exhibit 1

- Interesting ciphers and computer methods for solving - A review of Chaocipher.

- Famous Unsolved Codes and Ciphers - Elonka Dunin's famous site dedicated to unsolved codes and ciphers, including Chaocipher. Retrieved April 23, 2014

Chapter 20

Copiale cipher

Pages 16-17

The **Copiale cipher** is an encrypted manuscript consisting of 75,000 handwritten characters filling 105 pages in a bound volume.[1] Undeciphered for more than 260 years, the document was cracked in 2011 with the help of modern computer techniques. An international team consisting of Kevin Knight of the University of Southern California Information Sciences Institute and USC Viterbi School of Engineering, along with Beáta Megyesi and Christiane Schaefer of Uppsala University in Sweden, found the cipher to be an encrypted German text. The manuscript is a homophonic cipher that uses a complex substitution code, including symbols and letters, for its text and spaces.[2]

Previously examined by scientists at the German Academy of Sciences at Berlin in the 1970s, the cipher was thought to date from between 1760 and 1780.[3] Decipherment revealed that the document had been created in the 1730s by a secret society[1][2][4] called the "high enlightened (Hocherleuchtete) oculist order"[5] of Wolfenbüttel,[6] or Oculists.[5][7][8] The Oculists used sight as a metaphor for knowledge.[9]

A parallel manuscript is kept at the Staatsarchiv Wolfenbüttel.[5]

The Copiale cipher includes abstract symbols, as well as letters from Greek and most of the Roman alphabet. The only plain text in the book is "Copiales 3" at the end and "Philipp 1866" on the flyleaf. Philipp is thought to have been an owner of the manuscript.[5] The plain-text letters of the message were found to be encoded by accented Roman letters, Greek letters and symbols, with unaccented Roman letters serving only to represent spaces.

The researchers found that the initial 16 pages describe an Oculist initiation ceremony. The manuscript portrays, among other things, an initiation ritual in which the candidate is asked to read a blank piece of paper and, on confessing inability to do so, is given eyeglasses and asked to try again, and then again after washing the eyes with a cloth, followed by an "operation" in which a single eyebrow hair is plucked.[10][11]

20.1 Substitution cipher

The Copiale cipher is a substitution cipher. It is not a 1-for-1 substitution but rather a homophonic cipher: each ciphertext character stands for a particular plaintext character, but several ciphertext characters may encode the same plaintext character. For example, all the unaccented Roman characters encode a space. Seven ciphertext characters encode the single letter "e". In addition, some ciphertext characters stand for several characters or even a word. One ciphertext character ("†") encodes "sch", and another encodes the secret society's name.[5][10]

20.2 De-encryption method

A machine translation expert, Knight approached language translation as if all languages were ciphers, effectively treating foreign words as symbols for English words. His approach, which tasked an expectation-management algorithm with generating every possible match of foreign and English words, enabled the algorithm figured out a few words with each pass. A comparison with 80 lan-

41

guages confirmed that the original language was likely German, which the researchers had guessed based on the word "Philipp," a German spelling. Knight then used a combination of intuition and computing techniques to decipher most of the code in a few weeks. Megyesi later realized that a particular symbol meant "eye", and Schaefer connected that discovery to the Oculists.

20.3 The Oculists

The Oculists were a group of ophthalmologists led by Count Friedrich August von Veltheim, who died in April 1775. The Philipp 1866 Copiales 3 document, however, appears to suggest that the Oculists, or at least Count Veltheim, were a group of Freemasons who created the Oculist society in order to pass along the Masonic rites[7] which had recently been banned by Pope Clement XII.

20.4 See also

- List of ciphertexts
- Voynich manuscript

20.5 References

[1] "Computer Scientist Cracks Mysterious 'Copiale Cipher'". American Association for the Advancement of Science. October 25, 2011.

[2] *New York Times*: John Markoff, "How revolutionary tools cracked a 1700s code," October 24, 2011, retrieved October 25, 2011

[3] Forscher knacken deutschen Geheim-Code (at Bild.de)

[4] (the complete proceedings) or (the relevant presentation): Knight, Kevin, Megyesi, Beáta and Schaefer, Christiane "The Copiale Cipher," Proceedings of the 4th Workshop on building and using comparable corpora, pages 2-9, 49th Annual Meeting of the Association for Comparable Linguistics, 24 June 2011. Retrieved October 25, 2011

[5] Knight, Kevin, Megyesi, Beáta and Schaefer, Christiane (2011). "The Copiale Cipher". *Uppsala Universitet, Institutionen för lingvistik och filologi website*. Retrieved 2011-10-25. Includes images of the full text, as well as full translations in German and English.

[6] Henning, Aloys "Eine frühe Loge des 18. Jahrhunderts: 'Die Hocherleuchtete Oculisten-Gesellschaft' in Wolfenbüttel", in: Europa in der frühen Neuzeit, Festschrift für Günter Mühlpfordt 5, Aufklärung in Europa, hg. Erich Donnert, Köln/Weimar/Wien 1999, S. 65-82.

[7] Shactman, Noah (16 November 2012). "They Cracked This 250-Year-Old Code, and Found a Secret Society Inside". *wired.com*. Wired (magazine). Retrieved 2 November 2013.

[8] USC Scientist Cracks Mysterious "Copiale Cipher" on YouTube, on the official USC channel.

[9] https://www.wired.com/2012/11/ff-the-manuscript/

[10] Boyle, Alan (October 25, 2011). "Secret society's code cracked". MSNBC. Retrieved October 25, 2011.

[11] Waugh. Rob "How translation software helped crack 'unbreakable' code in 1866 secret society manuscript *Daily Mail, October 25, 2011*, Retrieved October 25, 2011

20.6 External links

- Knight, K; Megyesi, B; Schaefer, C (Nov 24, 2012). "The Copiale Cipher". *Project*. Uppsala Universitet: Beáta Megyesi.

  - "Deciphered German" (pdf). (German)
  - "English translation" (pdf).

Chapter 21

DRYAD

This article is about the enciphering system. For other uses, see Dryad (disambiguation).

The **DRYAD Numeral Cipher/Authentication System (KTC 1400 D)** is a simple, paper cryptographic system employed by the U.S. military for authentication and for encryption of short, numerical messages. Each unit with a radio is given a set of matching DRYAD code sheets. A single sheet is valid for a limited time (e.g. 6 hours), called a *cryptoperiod*.

KTV 14000

	ABC 0	DEF 1	GHJ 2	KI 3	MN 4	PQR 5	ST 6	UV 7	WX 8	YZ 9
A	ERSQ	WOJ	NKI	PB	YD	MTA	GU	HV	XF	LC
B	GJNH	ULF	EKA	OY	VB	STC	DI	QP	WR	XM
C	DAFH	CUB	TKM	OR	NE	GXQ	VY	IL	SP	JW
D	RMXF	IVO	TQY	WS	JP	LBO	CK	GE	HU	NA
E	IATL	DVO	SWX	MH	KQ	EYF	RN	BC	PU	JG
F	RCMX	AGO	TIE	NF	PH	YDB	QV	LK	UJ	SW
	ABC 0	DEF 1	GHJ 2	KI 3	MN 4	PQR 5	ST 6	UV 7	WX 8	YZ 9
G	TYKN	AHE	VUQ	IM	FD	RCW	BO	XP	JS	LG
H	AHOG	CKS	PNU	BR	DT	MYX	EQ	FL	VW	JI
I	OWGJ	SXC	DAP	RE	LY	QUF	MV	NB	TH	IK
J	YNAT	GBD	LOF	EJ	RS	MIK	WH	PQ	XU	VC
K	LYQE	UVN	JIC	HM	AQ	KTP	DW	OX	SR	FB
L	GQCN	HUI	SMR	JB	FO	XWY	VT	EA	KL	PO
	ABC 0	DEF 1	GHJ 2	KI 3	MN 4	PQR 5	ST 6	UV 7	WX 8	YZ 9
M	CLUR	TJN	VAF	EX	DW	QKH	MP	GB	YI	OS
N	RPJU	QHX	CTN	OW	MA	KBV	EL	IG	SO	FY
O	QTOY	XMK	AWN	RJ	EF	PLS	DV	HB	CI	UG
P	PWMR	IEJ	AOK	GH	TS	QYC	ON	BU	LF	VX
Q	JRDA	QFN	BOI	SM	WH	KCX	GP	VL	YT	EU
R	MPBR	WXC	VJD	UN	KG	HQF	SE	LI	AY	TO
	ABC 0	DEF 1	GHJ 2	KI 3	MN 4	PQR 5	ST 6	UV 7	WX 8	YZ 9
S	YPFV	DLU	QKT	HR	EO	ASI	CG	XN	MJ	WB
T	NCRT	DOG	UYX	BE	WJ	FSH	QP	LI	VM	AK
U	EBJR	IHV	YGL	AQ	NC	WPS	UX	KD	FO	TM
V	JOTC	VAB	DIR	FS	LW	QHU	EP	XY	KN	GM
W	AOCN	WJL	KDB	PI	RV	FGQ	UH	SM	XT	YE
X	SVHC	EML	YOA	GU	DK	FXI	JN	WT	PB	RQ
Y	EBOH	STL	FIM	GW	PY	JVA	UR	DN	KX	QC

A sample DRYAD cipher sheet

A DRYAD cipher sheet contains 25 lines or rows of scrambled letters. Each line is labeled by the letters A to Y in a column on the left of the page. Each row contains a random permutation of the letters A through Y. The letters in each row are grouped into 10 columns labeled 0 through 9. The columns under 0, 1, 2 and 5 have more letters than the other digits, which have just two each.

While crude, the DRYAD Numeral Cipher/Authentication System has the advantage of being fast, relatively easy and requires no extra equipment (such as a pencil). The presence of more cipher-text columns under the digits 0, 1, 2 and 5, is apparently intended to make ciphertext frequency analysis more difficult. But much of the security comes from keeping the cryptoperiod short.

DRYAD can be used in two modes, authentication or encryption.

21.1 Authentication

For authentication, a challenging station selects a letter at random from the left most column followed by a second (randomly selected) letter in the row of the first chosen letter. The station being challenged would then authenticate by picking the letter directly below the row and position of the second letter selected.[1][2]

For example, using the example cipher sheet to the right and the NATO phonetic alphabet, Jason could challenge Peggy by transmitting "authenticate Alpha Bravo". Peggy's correct response would then be "authenticate Yankee".

Another form used involves selecting the third letter to the right of the second letter chosen by the challenging station (Jason's "Bravo" letter). Both the directional offset (up, down, left or right) and numeral offset can be different values then the examples given here; but must be agreed upon and understood by both parties before authentication.

One problem presented is that an enemy impersonator has a one in 25 chance of guessing the correct response (one

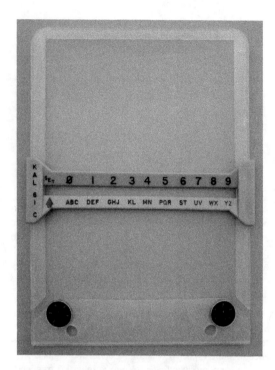

Holder for coding sheets with slide to facilitate use

21.3   See also

- BATCO — similar paper based tactical cipher used by the British forces
- M-94 — tactical cipher used in WWII
- Dryad — original meaning in mythology
- Polyalphabetic cipher
- Substitution cipher

21.4   References

[1] Army Field Manual 24-19, Chapter 5

[2] U.S. Army Field Manual FM 24-12, Chapter 7, Communications Security Operations

- Further explanation of the DRYAD Numeral Cipher/Authentication System
- U.S. Army Field Manual FM 24-35

in 24 if a letter is selected from the same row). A solution to this is for Jason to require Peggy to authenticate twice; lowering the impersonator's odds of guessing the correct response to one in 625. The downside to this method is reduced longevity of the current DRYAD page, since the page is getting twice as much use as a single-authentication scheme.

21.2   Encryption

The second mode is used to encrypt short numeric information (such as map coordinates or a new radio frequency). The coder selects two letters at random. The first selects a row in the current active page. The second letter is used as in the authentication mode, except the adjacent letter to the right is the one selected; and is called the "SET LETTER."

Numbers are enciphered one digit at a time. A ciphertext letter is chosen from the selected row in the column under the plain text digit. If the digit occurs more than once in the number, the coder is instructed to choose a different letter in the same column. All the digits in a single plaintext number are encoded from the same row. (There is also a provision for encoding letters associated with map grid coordinates.)

Chapter 22

Dvorak encoding

Dvorak encoding is a type of encoding based on the differences in layout of a QWERTY keyboard and a Dvorak keyboard. There is one main variation: One is achieved by typing in the Dvorak layout on a QWERTY keyboard, and the other is similarly achieved by typing in the QWERTY layout on a Dvorak keyboard. This effectively makes Dvorak encoding into a monoalphabetic substitution cipher like ROT13 and the Caesar Cipher, since each one character translates to one other character in a consistent pattern.

Several layers of Dvorak encoding may be added on top of each other for a variance of the translation table, which adds an obfuscating effect. The one where the Dvorak layout is used on a QWERTY keyboard can be added to the one where a QWERTY layout is used on a Dvorak keyboard, since they are not each other's opposites in terms of decoding. When decoding, the correct order of the severally applied translation tables must happen in the correct order. If encoding or decoding in one direction (for example, from Dvorak to QWERTY), it takes only 210 layers of encoding for the original Dvorak string to be encoded back to itself.[1]

Dvorak encoding, like other monoalphabetic encryption ciphers, is a very simple encoding and provides a very weak level of security. It may be useful in combination with other encodings. The security involved is in no way comparable to modern encryption algorithms which advocate security, and the advantages with this encoding can as such be summarised to encompass:

- Dvorak encoding is an unavoidable consequence of typing on a non-Dvorak keyboard using the Dvorak layout, for instance when using a software driver to compensate for the lack of rerouting of signals in the keyboard. This is the most common practice because it doesn't require a purchase of a special Dvorak keyboard.

- Dvorak encoding can be typed real-time by anyone proficient with the Dvorak keyboard layout, allowing for very fast encoding by hand.

- Dvorak encoding may make it harder for physically present surveillance to find out what the user is typing since it happens very fast. In some cases, it can even be hard for a physical keylogger to probably guess what is being written, but since most keyloggers save the logged data for later retrieval and analysis, the original cryptographic weakness of the encoding applies.

Variations in the use of left- and right-hand Dvorak keyboard layouts also provide an additional subset of encodings. The left and right variants are slightly better because the number keys are changed as well as the character keys – in this respect, the left-hand Dvorak encoding changes the most keys. Notably, the a and m keys never change in the default Dvorak keyboard layout.

22.1 Conversion table

Here is the translation from Qwerty to Dvorak (U.S. Simplified, Standard). Ordering is based on a US 104 Key keyboard from left to right, top row to bottom row, then shifted keys.

Qwerty: `1234567890-
=qwertyuiop[]\asdfghjkl;'zxcvbnm,./~!@#$%^&*()_+QWERTYUIOP{}|AS

Dvorak: `1234567890[]',.pyfgcrl/=\aoeuidhtns-
;qjkxbmwvz~!@#$%^&*(){}"<>PYFGCRL?+|AOEUIDHTNS_:
QJKXBMWVZ

Here are two simplified tables, ordered nearly-alphabetically and so the top one can be used in a regular expression pattern class (between brackets []).

Qwerty:][abcdefghijklmnopqrstuvwxyzABCDEFGHIJKLMNOPQRSTUV\
Dvorak: =/axje.uidchtnmbrl'poygk,qf;AXJE>UIDCHTNMBRL"POYGK<Q
s-wvz\protect\char"007B\relax\protect\char"007D\relax?
+S_WVZ][

and

Dvorak:][abcdefghijklmnopqrstuvwxyzABCDEFGHIJKLMNOPQRSTUV\
Qwerty: =-anihdyujgcvpmlsrxo;kf.,bt/ANIHDYUJGCVPMLSRXO:KF><B]

45

Note that the digits **0-9**, the letters **amAM**, and the symbols `` `~!@#$%^&*()\| `` are the same for both Qwerty and Dvorak Standard layouts. Symmetric pairs that convert the same in either direction include:] and **=**, **w** and **,**(comma), **W** and **<**. There is a cycle of 15 characters starting with **B** and of 14 characters starting with **C**. The reason text returns to its original after 210 conversions in the same direction is that 210 is the lowest common multiple of the cycle lengths 1, 2, 14, and 15.

22.2   Use in literature

In the hacker fiction book *Stealing the Network: How to Own an Identity*, a hacker by the name of Bl@ckToⅤⅤ3r effectively uses the Dvorak keyboard layout as a layer of confusion when intruders are trying to get into his computer.

22.3   See also

- dv - an open source command-line utility program for converting to and from 'Dvorak Encoding' written in C (programming language)

22.4   References

[1] "Dvorak Fun". Angela Gong. 2011-07-01. Archived from the original on October 2, 2012. Retrieved 2011-07-15.

- Keyser, Andrew (2006). "Dvorak Encoding". *Dvorak Encoding: A Simple Encoding Mechanism*. Retrieved 2006-03-19.

- Hatch, Brian; Moss, Jeff "Dark Tangent"; Beale, Jay; Long, Johnny "Google Hacker"; Eller, Riley "Caezar"; Alder, Raven "Elevator Ninja"; Parker, Tom; Mullen, Timothy "Thor"; Hurley, Chris; Russell, Ryan "Blue-Boar" (2005). *Stealing the Network: How to Own an Identity*. Syngress Publishing. ISBN 1-59749-006-7.

Chapter 23

Four-square cipher

The **four-square cipher** is a manual symmetric encryption technique.[1] It was invented by the famous French cryptographer Felix Delastelle.

The technique encrypts pairs of letters (*digraphs*), and thus falls into a category of ciphers known as polygraphic substitution ciphers. This adds significant strength to the encryption when compared with monographic substitution ciphers which operate on single characters. The use of digraphs makes the four-square technique less susceptible to frequency analysis attacks, as the analysis must be done on 676 possible digraphs rather than just 26 for monographic substitution. The frequency analysis of digraphs is possible, but considerably more difficult - and it generally requires a much larger ciphertext in order to be useful.

23.1 Using four-square

The four-square cipher uses four 5 by 5 (5x5) matrices arranged in a square. Each of the 5 by 5 matrices contains the letters of the alphabet (usually omitting "Q" or putting both "I" and "J" in the same location to reduce the alphabet to fit). In general, the upper-left and lower-right matrices are the "plaintext squares" and each contain a standard alphabet. The upper-right and lower-left squares are the "ciphertext squares" and contain a mixed alphabetic sequence.

To generate the ciphertext squares, one would first fill in the spaces in the matrix with the letters of a keyword or phrase (dropping any duplicate letters), then fill the remaining spaces with the rest of the letters of the alphabet in order (again omitting "Q" to reduce the alphabet to fit). The key can be written in the top rows of the table, from left to right, or in some other pattern, such as a spiral beginning in the upper-left-hand corner and ending in the center. The keyword together with the conventions for filling in the 5 by 5 table constitute the cipher key. The four-square algorithm allows for two separate keys, one for each of the two ciphertext matrices.

As an example, here are the four-square matrices for the keywords "example" and "keyword." The plaintext matrices are in lowercase and the ciphertext matrices are in caps to make this example visually more simple:

```
a b c d e E X A M P f g h i j L B C D F k l m n o G H I J
K p r s t u N O R S T v w x y z U V W Y Z K E Y W O a
b c d e R D A B C f g h i j F G H I J k l m n o L M N P S
p r s t u T U V X Z v w x y z
```

23.2 Algorithm

To encrypt a message, one would follow these steps:

- Split the payload message into digraphs. (*HELLO WORLD* becomes *HE LL OW OR LD*)

- Find the first letter in the digraph in the upper-left plaintext matrix.

```
a b c d e E X A M P f g h i j L B C D F k l m n o G H I J
K p r s t u N O R S T v w x y z U V W Y Z K E Y W O a
b c d e R D A B C f g h i j F G H I J k l m n o L M N P S
p r s t u T U V X Z v w x y z
```

- Find the second letter in the digraph in the lower-right plaintext matrix.

```
a b c d e E X A M P f g h i j L B C D F k l m n o G H I J
K p r s t u N O R S T v w x y z U V W Y Z K E Y W O a
b c d e R D A B C f g h i j F G H I J k l m n o L M N P S
p r s t u T U V X Z v w x y z
```

- The first letter of the encrypted digraph is in the same row as the first plaintext letter and the same column as the second plaintext letter. It is therefore in the upper-right ciphertext matrix.

```
a b c d e E X A M P f g h i j L B C D F k l m n o G H I J
K p r s t u N O R S T v w x y z U V W Y Z K E Y W O a
b c d e R D A B C f g h i j F G H I J k l m n o L M N P S
p r s t u T U V X Z v w x y z
```

- The second letter of the encrypted digraph is in the same row as the second plaintext letter and the same column as the first plaintext letter. It is therefore in the lower-left ciphertext matrix.

a b c d e E X A M P f g **h** i j L B C D **F** k l m n o G H I J
K **p** r s t u N O R S T v w x y z U V W Y Z K E **Y** W O a
b c d **e** R D A B C f g h i j F G H I J k l m n o L M N P S
p r s t u T U V X Z v w x y z

Using the four-square example given above, we can encrypt the following plaintext:

Plaintext: he lp me ob iw an ke no bi Ciphertext: FY GM KY HO BX MF KK KI MD

Here is the four-square written out again but blanking all of the values that aren't used for encrypting the first digraph "he" into "FY"

```
- - - - - - - - - - - - h - - - - - - F - - - - - - - - - - - - - - - - - - - -
- - - - - - - - - - - - Y - - - - - - e - - - - - - - - - - - - - - - - - - - -
- - - - - - - - - - - - - - - - - - - -
```

As can be seen clearly, the method of encryption simply involves finding the other two corners of a rectangle defined by the two letters in the plaintext digraph. The encrypted digraph is simply the letters at the other two corners, with the upper-right letter coming first.

Decryption works the same way, but in reverse. The ciphertext digraph is split with the first character going into the upper-right matrix and the second character going into the lower-left matrix. The other corners of the rectangle are then located. These represent the plaintext digraph with the upper-left matrix component coming first.

23.3   Four-square cryptanalysis

Like most pre-modern era ciphers, the four-square cipher can be easily cracked if there is enough text. Obtaining the key is relatively straightforward if both plaintext and ciphertext are known. When only the ciphertext is known, brute force cryptanalysis of the cipher involves searching through the key space for matches between the frequency of occurrence of digrams (pairs of letters) and the known frequency of occurrence of digrams in the assumed language of the original message.

Cryptanalysis of four-square generally involves pattern matching on repeated monographs. This is only the case when the two plaintext matrices are known. A four-square encipherment usually uses standard alphabets in these matrices but it is not a requirement. If this is the case, then certain words will always produce single-letter ciphertext repeats. For instance, the word MI LI TA RY will always produce the same ciphertext letter in the first and third po-

sitions regardless of the keywords used. Patterns like these can be cataloged and matched against single-letter repeats in the ciphertext. Candidate plaintext can then be inserted in an attempt to uncover the ciphertext matrices.

Unlike the Playfair cipher, a four-square cipher will not show reversed ciphertext digraphs for reversed plaintext digraphs (e.g. the digraphs AB BA would encrypt to some pattern XY YX in Playfair, but not in four-square). This, of course, is only true if the two keywords are different. Another difference between four-square and Playfair which makes four-square a stronger encryption is the fact that double letter digraphs will occur in four-square ciphertext.

By all measures, four-square is a stronger system for encrypting information than Playfair. However, it is more cumbersome because of its use of two keys, and, preparing the encryption/decryption sheet can be time consuming. Given that the increase in encryption strength afforded by four-square over Playfair is marginal and that both schemes are easily defeated if sufficient ciphertext is available, Playfair has become much more common.

A good tutorial on reconstructing the key for a four-square cipher can be found in chapter 7, "Solution to Polygraphic Substitution Systems," of Field Manual 34-40-2, produced by the United States Army.

23.4   References

[1] William Maxwell Bowers (1959). *Digraphic substitution: the Playfair cipher, the four square cipher*. American Cryptogram Association. p. 25.

23.5   See also

- Topics in cryptography

Chapter 24

Great Cipher

In the history of cryptography, the **Great Cipher** or *Grand Chiffre* was a nomenclator cipher developed by the Rossignols, several generations of whom served the French Crown as cryptographers. The Great Cipher was so named because of its excellence and because it was reputed to be unbreakable. Modified forms were in use by the French Peninsular army until the summer of 1811,[1] and after it fell out of current use many documents in the French archives were unreadable.

24.1 Historical background

Antoine Rossignol's cryptographic skills became known when in 1626 an encrypted letter was taken from a messenger leaving the city of Réalmont, controlled by the Huguenots and surrounded by the French army. The letter told that the Huguenots would not be able to hold on to the city for much longer, and by the end of the day Rossignol had successfully deciphered it. The French returned the letter with the deciphered message, forcing the Huguenots to surrender. He and his son, Bonaventure Rossignol, were soon appointed to prominent roles in the court.

Together, the two devised a code so strong it baffled cryptanalysts for centuries. Commandant Étienne Bazeries managed to break the cipher around 1893 over a period of three years, realizing that each number stood for a French syllable rather than single letters as traditional codes did. He guessed that a particular sequence of repeated numbers, 124-22-125-46-345, stood for *les ennemis* ("the enemies") and from that information was able to unravel the entire cipher.

24.1.1 The Man in the Iron Mask

In one of the encrypted letters between Louis XIV and his marshal Nicolas de Catinat appeared a possible solution to the mystery of the Man in the Iron Mask.[2] The letter concerned a general named Vivien de Bulonde who was to attack the Italian town of Cuneo but instead fled, fearing the arrival of the Austrians, and consequently put in serious danger the success of the entire French campaign in Piedmont. The letter said:

His Majesty knows better than any other person the consequences of this act, and he is also aware of how deeply our failure to take the place will prejudice our cause, a failure which must be repaired during the winter. His Majesty desires that you immediately arrest General Bulonde and cause him to be conducted to the fortress of Pignerole, where he will be locked in a cell under guard at night, and permitted to walk the battlement during the day with a 330 309.

The "330" and "309" codegroups appeared only once in the correspondence, so it is impossible to confirm what they stand for. Bazeries verified General Bulonde was disgraced and removed from command, so he reasoned 330 and 309 stood for *masque* and a full stop.[3] However, none of the cipher variants used in the Iron Mask period included *masque*, an unlikely word to include in the cipher's small repertory.[4]

24.2 Technical nature of the Cipher

The basis of the code cracked by Bazeries was a set of 587 numbers that stood for syllables.[5] There were other variations, and Louis XIV's overseas ministers were sent different code sheets that encrypted not only syllables but also letters and words.[6][7] To counter frequency analysis, some number sets were "nulls" meant to be ignored by the intended recipient. Others were traps, including a codegroup that meant to ignore the previous codegroup.[8]

As a nomenclator cipher, the Great Cipher replaced the names of key generals such as Auguste de Marmont, references to *les ennemis*, and other sensitive terms with

One of many nomenclators used to encode the Great Cipher.

24.4 Sources

- Kahn, David. "The Man in Iron Mask -- Encore et Efin, Cryptologically." Cryptologia, January 2005, Volume XXIX, Number 1.

- Singh, Simon. *The Code Book: The Science of Secrecy from Ancient Egypt to Quantum Cryptography.* New York: Anchor Books, 1999. ISBN 0-385-49532-3.

- Urban, Mark. "The Blockade of Ciudad Rodrigo, June to November 1811 - The Great Cipher." in *The Man Who Broke Napoleon's Codes.* Harper Perennial, 2003. ISBN 978-0-06-093455-2.

homophonic substitutions.[9] Code sheets included alternative digits to modify the gender or letter case,[10] so the rules of French composition held true to encryptions as well. Since *e* is the most commonly used letter in French, the Cipher typically allocated the most code numbers to writing this vowel: in one nomenclature, 131 out of 711 code numbers stood for *e*.[11]

24.3 References

[1] Urban 2004, p. 104

[2] Kahn, 2005, p. 45

[3] Kahn 2005, p. 45

[4] Kahn 2005, p. 46

[5] Singh

[6] Urban 2004, p. 104

[7] Urban, Mark (2001-08-25). "Wellington's lucky break | Education". London: The Guardian. Retrieved 2009-10-10.

[8] "[2.0] Refining The Art". Vectorsite.net. Retrieved 2009-10-10.

[9] Kahn 2005, p. 47

[10] Urban 2003, p. 111

[11] Urban 2004, p. 117

Chapter 25

Grille (cryptography)

Not to be confused with Grill (cryptology).

In the history of cryptography, a **grille cipher** was a technique for encrypting a plaintext by writing it onto a sheet of paper through a pierced sheet (of paper or cardboard or similar). The earliest known description is due to the polymath Girolamo Cardano in 1550. His proposal was for a rectangular stencil allowing single letters, syllables, or words to be written, then later read, through its various apertures. The written fragments of the plaintext could be further disguised by filling the gaps between the fragments with anodyne words or letters. This variant is also an example of steganography, as are many of the grille ciphers.

25.1 Cardan grille and variations

Main article: Cardan grille

The Cardan grille was invented as a method of secret writing. The word *cryptography* became the more familiar term for secret communications from the middle of the 17th century. Earlier, the word *steganography* was common. The other general term for secret writing was *cypher* - also spelt *cipher*. There is a modern distinction between cryptography and steganography

Sir Francis Bacon gave three fundamental conditions for ciphers. Paraphrased, these are:

1. a cipher method should not be difficult to use

2. it should not be possible for others to recover the plaintext (called 'reading the cipher')

3. in some cases, the presence of messages should not be suspected

It is difficult to fulfil all three conditions simultaneously. Condition 3 applies to steganography. Bacon meant that a cipher message should, in some cases, not appear to be a cipher at all. The original Cardan Grille met that aim.

Variations on the Cardano original, however, were not intended to fulfill condition 3 and generally failed to meet condition 2 as well. But, few if any ciphers have ever achieved this second condition, so the point is generally a cryptanalyst's delight whenever the grille ciphers are used.

The attraction of a grille cipher for users lies in its ease of use (condition 1). In short, it's very simple.

25.1.1 Single-letter grilles

Not all ciphers are used for communication with others: records and reminders may be kept in cipher for use of the author alone. A grille is easily usable for protection of brief information such as a key word or a key number in such a use.

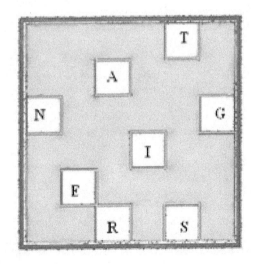

A cardboard grille with eight single-letter apertures.

51

In the example, a grille has eight irregularly placed (ideally randomly) holes – equal to the length of a key word TANG-IERS. The grille is placed on a gridded sheet (not required in actual practice) and the letters written in from top to bottom.

B	1	H	J	T	K
D	P	A	Q	U	2
N	3	U	N	9	G
F	E	O	I	I	8
V	E	A	O	7	T
O	M	R	6	S	L

A grid filled with random letters and numbers surrounding a key word entered from a grille.

Removing the grille, the grid is filled with random letters and numbers. Then, one hopes, only the possessor of the grille or a copy can read out the hidden letters or numbers – which could, for example, be the key to a polyalphabetic cipher such as that proposed around the same time by Giambattista della Porta.

The grille and the grid are kept separately. If there is only one copy of the grille and one of the grid, the loss of either results is the loss of both.

Clearly, in the case of communication by grille cipher, both sender and recipient must possess an identical copy of the grille. The loss of a grille leads to the probable loss of all secret correspondence encrypted with that grille. Either the messages cannot be read (i.e., decrypted) or someone else (with the lost grille) may be reading them.

A further use for such a grille has been suggested: it is a method of generating pseudo-random sequences from a pre-existing text. This view has been proposed in connection with the Voynich manuscript. It is an area of cryptography that David Kahn termed enigmatology and touches on the works of Dr John Dee and ciphers supposedly embedded in the works of Shakespeare proving that Francis Bacon wrote them, which William F. Friedman examined and discredited.[1]

25.1.2 Trellis ciphers

The Elizabethan spymaster Sir Francis Walsingham (1530–1590) is reported to have used a "trellis" to conceal the letters of a plaintext in communication with his agents. However, he generally preferred the combined code-cipher method known as a *nomenclator*, which was the practical state-of-the-art in his day. The trellis was described as a device with spaces that was reversible. It appears to have been a transposition tool that produced something much like the Rail fence cipher and resembled a chess board.

Cardano is not known to have proposed this variation, but he was a chess player who wrote a book on gaming, so the pattern would have been familiar to him. Whereas the ordinary Cardan grille has arbitrary perforations, if his method of cutting holes is applied to the white squares of a chess board a regular pattern results.

The encipherer begins with the board in the wrong position for chess. Each successive letter of the message is written in a single square. If the message is written vertically, it is taken off horizontally and vice versa.

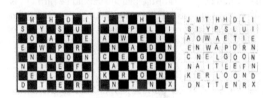

A trellis or chessboard cipher.

After filling in 32 letters, the board is turned through 90 degrees and another 32 letters written (note that flipping the board horizontally or vertically is the equivalent). Shorter messages are filled with null letters (i.e., padding). Messages longer than 64 letters require another turn of the board and another sheet of paper. If the plaintext is too short, each square must be filled up entirely with nulls.

J M T H H D L I S I Y P S L U I A O W A E T I E E N W A P D E N E N E L G O O N N A I T E E F N K E R L O O N D D N T T E N R X

This transposition method produces an invariant pattern and is not satisfactorily secure for anything other than cursory notes.

33, 5, 41, 13, 49, 21, 57, 29, 1, 37, 9, 45, 17, 53, 25, 61, 34, 6, 42, 14, 50, 22, 58, 30, 2, 38, 10, 46, 18, 54, 26, 62, 35, 7, 43, 15, 51, 23, 59, 31, 3, 39, 11, 47, 19, 55, 27, 63, 36, 8, 44, 16, 52, 24, 60, 32, 4, 40, 12, 48, 20, 56, 28, 64

A second transposition is needed to obscure the letters. Following the chess analogy, the route taken might be the knight's move. Or some other path can be agreed upon, such as a reverse spiral, together with a specific number of nulls to pad the start and end of a message.

25.1.3 Turning grilles

Rectangular Cardan grilles can be placed in four positions. The trellis or chessboard has only two positions, but it gave rise to a more sophisticated turning grille with four positions that can be rotated in two directions.

1	2	3	4	13	9	5	1
5	6	7	8	14	10	6	2
9	10	11	12	15	11	7	3
13	14	15	16	16	12	8	4
4	8	12	16	16	15	14	13
3	7	11	15	12	11	10	9
2	6	10	14	8	7	6	5
1	5	9	13	4	3	2	1

A Fleissner grille of dimensions 8x8 before the apertures are cut.

Baron Edouard Fleissner von Wostrowitz, a retired Austrian cavalry colonel, described a variation on the chess board cipher in 1880 and his grilles were adopted by the German army during World War I. These grilles are often named after Fleissner, although he took his material largely from a German work, published in Tübingen in 1809, written by Klüber who attributed this form of the grille to Cardano, as did Helen Fouché Gaines.[2]

Bauer notes that grilles were used in the 18th century, for example in 1745 in the administration of the Dutch Stadthouder William IV. Later, the mathematician C. F. Hindenburg studied turning grilles more systematically in 1796. '[they]are often called Fleissner grilles in ignorance of their historical origin.'

One form of the Fleissner (or Fleißner) grille makes 16 perforations in an 8x8 grid – 4 holes in each quadrant. If the squares in each quadrant are numbered 1 to 16, all 16 numbers must be used once only. This allows many variations in placing the apertures.

The grille has four positions – North, East, South, West.

Each position exposes 16 of the 64 squares. The encipherer places the grille on a sheet and writes the first 16 letters of the message. Then, turning the grille through 90 degrees, the second 16 are written, and so on until the grid is filled.

It is possible to construct grilles of different dimensions; however, if the number of squares in one quadrant is odd, even if the total is an even number, one quadrant or section must contain an extra perforation. Illustrations of the Fleissner grille often take a 6x6 example for ease of space; the number of apertures in one quadrant is 9, so three quadrants contain 2 apertures and one quadrant must have 3. There is no standard pattern of apertures: they are created by the user, in accordance with the above description, with the intention of producing a good mix.

The method gained wide recognition when Jules Verne used a turning grille as a plot device in his novel *Mathias Sandorf*, published in 1885. Verne had come across the idea in Fleissner's treatise *Handbuch der Kryptographie* which appeared in 1881.

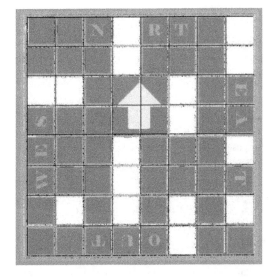

One of the many variations on a Fleissner grille which can be rotated clockwise or anticlockwise.

Fleissner Grilles were constructed in various sizes during World War I and were used by the German Army at the end of 1916.[3] Each grille had a different code name:- 5x5 ANNA; 6X6 BERTA; 7X7 CLARA; 8X8 DORA; 9X9 EMIL; 10X10 FRANZ. Their security was weak, and they were withdrawn after four months.

Another method of indicating the size of the grille in use was to insert a key code at the start of the cipher text: E = 5; F = 6 and so on. The grille can also be rotated in either direction and the starting position does not need to be NORTH. Clearly the working method is by arrangement between sender and receiver and may be operated in accordance with a schedule.

In the following examples, two cipher texts contain the same message. They are constructed from the example grille, beginning in the NORTH position, but one is formed by rotating the grille clockwise and the other anticlockwise. The ciphertext is then taken off the grid in horizontal lines - but it could equally be taken off vertically.

CLOCKWISE

ITIT ILOH GEHE TCDF LENS IIST FANB FSET EPES HENN URRE NEEN TRCG PR&I ODCT SLOE

ANTICLOCKWISE

LEIT CIAH GTHE TIDF LENB IIET FONS FSST URES NEDN EPRE HEEN TRTG PROI ONEC SL&C

In 1925 Luigi Sacco of the Italian Signals Corps began writing a book on ciphers which included reflections on the codes of the Great War, *Nozzioni di crittografia.* He observed that Fleissner's method could be applied to a fractionating cipher, such as a Delastelle Bifid or Four-Square, with considerable increase in security.

Grille ciphers are also useful device for transposing Chinese characters; they avoid the transcription of words into alphabetic or syllabic characters to which other ciphers (for example, substitution ciphers) can be applied.

After World War I, machine encryption made simple cipher devices obsolete, and grille ciphers fell into disuse except for amateur purposes. Yet, grilles provided seed ideas for transposition ciphers that are reflected in modern cryptography.

25.2 Unusual possibilities

25.2.1 The d'Agapeyeff cipher

The unsolved D'Agapeyeff cipher, which was set as a challenge in 1939, contains 14x14 dinomes and might be based on Sacco's idea of transposing a fractionated cipher text by means of a grille.

25.2.2 A Third-Party Grille: the crossword puzzle

The distribution of grilles, an example of the difficult problem of key exchange, can be eased by taking a readily-available third-party grid in the form of a newspaper crossword puzzle. Although this is not strictly a grille cipher, it resembles the chessboard with the black squares shifted and it can be used in the Cardan manner. The message

text can be written horizontally in the white squares and the ciphertext taken off vertically, or vice versa.

A crossword grid taken from a 1941 newspaper

CTATI ETTOL TTOEH RRHEI MUCKE SSEEL
AUDUE RITSC VISCH NREHE LEERD DTOHS ES-
DNN LEWAC LEONT OIIEA RRSET LLPDR EIVYT
ELTTD TOXEA E4TMI GIUOD PTRT1 ENCNE
ABYMO NOEET EBCAL LUZIU TLEPT SIFNT
ONUYK YOOOO

Again, following Sacco's observation, this method disrupts a fractionating cipher such as Seriated Playfair.

Crosswords are also a possible source of keywords. A grid of the size illustrated has a word for each day of the month, the squares being numbered.

25.3 Cryptanalysis

The original Cardano Grille was a literary device for gentlemen's private correspondence. Any suspicion of its use can lead to discoveries of hidden messages where no hidden messages exist at all, thus confusing the cryptanalyst. Letters and numbers in a random grid can take shape without substance. Obtaining the grille itself is a chief goal of the attacker.

But all is not lost if a grille copy can't be obtained. The later variants of the Cardano grille present problems which are common to all transposition ciphers. Frequency analysis will show a normal distribution of letters, and will suggest the language in which the plaintext was written.[4] The problem, easily stated though less easily accomplished, is to identify the transposition pattern and so decrypt the cipher-text. Possession of several messages written using the same grille is a considerable aid.

Gaines, in her standard work on hand ciphers and their cryptanalysis, gave a lengthy account of transposition ciphers, and devoted a chapter to the turning grille.[2]

25.4 See also

- Topics in cryptography

25.5 References

[1] Friedman, William F. (1957). *The Shakespearean Ciphers Examined*. Cambridge University Press.

[2] Fouché Gaines, Helen (1956) [1939]. *Cryptanalysis - a study of ciphers and their solution*. Dover. pp. 26–35. ISBN 0-486-20097-3.

[3] Kahn, David (1996). *The Codebreakers — The Comprehensive History of Secret Communication from Ancient Times to the Internet*. pp. 308–309. ISBN 0-684-83130-9.

[4] Pommerening, Klaus (2000). "Cryptology — Commentary on Verne's Mathias Sandorf". Retrieved 2013-11-15.

25.6 Further reading

- Richard Deacon, A *History of the British Secret Service*, Frederick Müller, London, 1969

- Luigi Sacco, *Nozzioni di crittografia*, privately printed, Rome, 1930; revised and reprinted twice as *Manuale di crittografia*

- Friedrich L. Bauer *Decrypted Secrets - Methods and Maxims of Cryptology*, Springer-Verlag, Berlin Heidelberg, 1997, ISBN 3-540-60418-9

25.7 External links

- Schneider, Matthias (2004-03-30). "The Turning Grille Toolset". Archived from the original on September 22, 2005. Retrieved 2006-05-30.

- Savard, John J. G. (1998). "Methods of Transposition". *A Cryptographic Compendium*. Retrieved 2013-11-15.

- "Grille". *Classic Cryptography*. ThinkQuest. Retrieved 2013-11-15.

- Matthews, Robert A. J. "Notes on the D'Agapeyeff Cipher". Retrieved 2013-11-15.

Chapter 26

Hill cipher

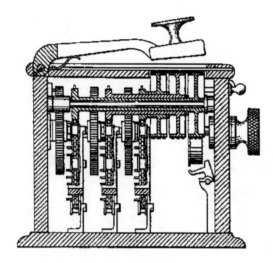

Hill's cipher machine, from figure 4 of the patent

In classical cryptography, the **Hill cipher** is a polygraphic substitution cipher based on linear algebra. Invented by Lester S. Hill in 1929, it was the first polygraphic cipher in which it was practical (though barely) to operate on more than three symbols at once. The following discussion assumes an elementary knowledge of matrices.

26.1   Operation

Each letter is represented by a number modulo 26. Often the simple scheme A = 0, B = 1, ..., Z = 25 is used, but this is not an essential feature of the cipher. To encrypt a message, each block of *n* letters (considered as an *n*-component vector) is multiplied by an invertible $n \times n$ matrix, again modulus 26. To decrypt the message, each block is multiplied by the inverse of the matrix used for encryption.

The matrix used for encryption is the cipher key, and it should be chosen randomly from the set of invertible $n \times n$ matrices (modulo 26). The cipher can, of course, be

adapted to an alphabet with any number of letters; all arithmetic just needs to be done modulo the number of letters instead of modulo 26.

Consider the message 'ACT', and the key below (or GYB-NQKURP in letters):

$$\begin{pmatrix} 6 & 24 & 1 \\ 13 & 16 & 10 \\ 20 & 17 & 15 \end{pmatrix}$$

Since 'A' is 0, 'C' is 2 and 'T' is 19, the message is the vector:

$$\begin{pmatrix} 0 \\ 2 \\ 19 \end{pmatrix}$$

Thus the enciphered vector is given by:

$$\begin{pmatrix} 6 & 24 & 1 \\ 13 & 16 & 10 \\ 20 & 17 & 15 \end{pmatrix} \begin{pmatrix} 0 \\ 2 \\ 19 \end{pmatrix} = \begin{pmatrix} 67 \\ 222 \\ 319 \end{pmatrix} \equiv \begin{pmatrix} 15 \\ 14 \\ 7 \end{pmatrix} \pmod{26}$$

which corresponds to a ciphertext of 'POH'. Now, suppose that our message is instead 'CAT', or:

$$\begin{pmatrix} 2 \\ 0 \\ 19 \end{pmatrix}$$

This time, the enciphered vector is given by:

$$\begin{pmatrix} 6 & 24 & 1 \\ 13 & 16 & 10 \\ 20 & 17 & 15 \end{pmatrix} \begin{pmatrix} 2 \\ 0 \\ 19 \end{pmatrix} \equiv \begin{pmatrix} 31 \\ 216 \\ 325 \end{pmatrix} \equiv \begin{pmatrix} 5 \\ 8 \\ 13 \end{pmatrix} \pmod{26}$$

which corresponds to a ciphertext of 'FIN'. Every letter has changed. The Hill cipher has achieved Shannon's diffusion, and an n-dimensional Hill cipher can diffuse fully across n symbols at once.

26.2 Decryption

In order to decrypt, we turn the ciphertext back into a vector, then simply multiply by the inverse matrix of the key matrix (IFKVIVVMI in letters). (There are standard methods to calculate the inverse matrix; see matrix inversion for details.) We find that, modulo 26, the inverse of the matrix used in the previous example is:

$$\begin{pmatrix} 6 & 24 & 1 \\ 13 & 16 & 10 \\ 20 & 17 & 15 \end{pmatrix}^{-1} \equiv \begin{pmatrix} 8 & 5 & 10 \\ 21 & 8 & 21 \\ 21 & 12 & 8 \end{pmatrix} \pmod{26}$$

Taking the previous example ciphertext of 'POH', we get:

$$\begin{pmatrix} 8 & 5 & 10 \\ 21 & 8 & 21 \\ 21 & 12 & 8 \end{pmatrix} \begin{pmatrix} 15 \\ 14 \\ 7 \end{pmatrix} \equiv \begin{pmatrix} 260 \\ 574 \\ 539 \end{pmatrix} \equiv \begin{pmatrix} 0 \\ 2 \\ 19 \end{pmatrix} \pmod{26}$$

which gets us back to 'ACT', just as we hoped.

We have not yet discussed two complications that exist in picking the encrypting matrix. Not all matrices have an inverse (see invertible matrix). The matrix will have an inverse if and only if its determinant is not zero. Also, in the case of the Hill Cipher, the determinant of the encrypting matrix must not have any common factors with the modular base. Thus, if we work modulo 26 as above, the determinant must be nonzero, and must not be divisible by 2 or 13. If the determinant is 0, or has common factors with the modular base, then the matrix cannot be used in the Hill cipher, and another matrix must be chosen (otherwise it will not be possible to decrypt). Fortunately, matrices which satisfy the conditions to be used in the Hill cipher are fairly common.

For our example key matrix:

$$\begin{vmatrix} 6 & 24 & 1 \\ 13 & 16 & 10 \\ 20 & 17 & 15 \end{vmatrix} \equiv 6(16 \cdot 15 - 10 \cdot 17) - 24(13 \cdot 15 - 10 \cdot 20) + 1(13 \cdot 17 - 16 \cdot 20)$$

So, modulo 26, the determinant is 25. Since this has no common factors with 26, this matrix can be used for the Hill cipher.

The risk of the determinant having common factors with the modulus can be eliminated by making the modulus prime. Consequently a useful variant of the Hill cipher adds 3 extra symbols (such as a space, a period and a question mark) to increase the modulus to 29.

26.3 Example

Let

$$K = \begin{pmatrix} 3 & 3 \\ 2 & 5 \end{pmatrix}$$

be the key and suppose the plaintext message is HELP. Then this plaintext is represented by two pairs

$$HELP \rightarrow \begin{pmatrix} H \\ E \end{pmatrix}, \begin{pmatrix} L \\ P \end{pmatrix} \rightarrow \begin{pmatrix} 7 \\ 4 \end{pmatrix}, \begin{pmatrix} 11 \\ 15 \end{pmatrix}$$

Then we compute

$$\begin{pmatrix} 3 & 3 \\ 2 & 5 \end{pmatrix} \begin{pmatrix} 7 \\ 4 \end{pmatrix} \equiv \begin{pmatrix} 7 \\ 8 \end{pmatrix} \pmod{26}, \text{ and}$$

$$\begin{pmatrix} 3 & 3 \\ 2 & 5 \end{pmatrix} \begin{pmatrix} 11 \\ 15 \end{pmatrix} \equiv \begin{pmatrix} 0 \\ 19 \end{pmatrix} \pmod{26}$$

and continue encryption as follows:

$$\begin{pmatrix} 7 \\ 8 \end{pmatrix}, \begin{pmatrix} 0 \\ 19 \end{pmatrix} \rightarrow \begin{pmatrix} H \\ I \end{pmatrix}, \begin{pmatrix} A \\ T \end{pmatrix}$$

The matrix K is invertible, hence K^{-1} exists such that $KK^{-1} = K^{-1}K = I_2$. The inverse of K can be computed by using the formula $\begin{pmatrix} a & b \\ c & d \end{pmatrix}^{-1} = (ad - bc)^{-1} \begin{pmatrix} d & -b \\ -c & a \end{pmatrix}$

This formula still holds after a modular reduction if a modular multiplicative inverse is used to compute $(ad - bc)^{-1}$. Hence in this case, we compute

$$K^{-1} \equiv 9^{-1} \begin{pmatrix} 5 & 23 \\ 24 & 3 \end{pmatrix} \equiv 3 \begin{pmatrix} 5 & 23 \\ 24 & 3 \end{pmatrix} \equiv \begin{pmatrix} 15 & 17 \\ 20 & 9 \end{pmatrix} \pmod{26}$$

$$HIAT \rightarrow \begin{pmatrix} H \\ I \end{pmatrix}, \begin{pmatrix} A \\ T \end{pmatrix} \rightarrow \begin{pmatrix} 7 \\ 8 \end{pmatrix}, \begin{pmatrix} 0 \\ 19 \end{pmatrix}$$

Then we compute

$$\begin{pmatrix} 15 & 17 \\ 20 & 9 \end{pmatrix} \begin{pmatrix} 7 \\ 8 \end{pmatrix} \equiv \begin{pmatrix} 7 \\ 4 \end{pmatrix} \pmod{26}, \text{ and}$$

$$\begin{pmatrix} 15 & 17 \\ 20 & 9 \end{pmatrix} \begin{pmatrix} 0 \\ 19 \end{pmatrix} \equiv \begin{pmatrix} 11 \\ 15 \end{pmatrix} \pmod{26}$$

Therefore

$$\begin{pmatrix} 7 \\ 4 \end{pmatrix}, \begin{pmatrix} 11 \\ 15 \end{pmatrix} \rightarrow \begin{pmatrix} H \\ E \end{pmatrix}, \begin{pmatrix} L \\ P \end{pmatrix} \rightarrow HELP.$$

26.4 Security

Unfortunately, the basic Hill cipher is vulnerable to a known-plaintext attack because it is completely linear. An opponent who intercepts n^2 plaintext/ciphertext character pairs can set up a linear system which can (usually) be easily solved; if it happens that this system is indeterminate, it is only necessary to add a few more plaintext/ciphertext pairs. Calculating this solution by standard linear algebra algorithms then takes very little time.

While matrix multiplication alone does not result in a secure cipher it is still a useful step when combined with other non-linear operations, because matrix multiplication can provide diffusion. For example, an appropriately chosen matrix can guarantee that small differences before the matrix multiplication will result in large differences after the matrix multiplication. Indeed, some modern ciphers use a matrix multiplication step to provide diffusion. For example, the MixColumns step in AES is a matrix multiplication. The function g in Twofish is a combination of non-linear S-boxes with a carefully chosen matrix multiplication (MDS).

26.4.1 Key size

The key size is the binary logarithm of the number of possible keys. There are 26^{n^2} matrices of dimension n × n. Thus $\log_2(26^{n^2})$ or about $4.7n^2$ is an upper bound on the key size of the Hill cipher using n × n matrices. This is only an upper bound because not every matrix is invertible and thus usable as a key. The number of invertible matrices can be computed via the Chinese Remainder Theorem. I.e., a matrix is invertible modulo 26 if and only if it is invertible both modulo 2 and modulo 13. The number of invertible n × n matrices modulo 2 is equal to the order of the general linear group $GL(n,\mathbf{Z}_2)$. It is

$$2^{n^2}(1-1/2)(1-1/2^2)\cdots(1-1/2^n).$$

Equally, the number of invertible matrices modulo 13 (i.e. the order of $GL(n,\mathbf{Z}_{13})$) is

$$13^{n^2}(1-1/13)(1-1/13^2)\cdots(1-1/13^n).$$

The number of invertible matrices modulo 26 is the product of those two numbers. Hence it is

$$26^{n^2}(1-1/2)(1-1/2^2)\cdots(1-1/2^n)(1-1/13)(1-1/13^2)\cdots(1-1/13^n).$$

Additionally it seems to be prudent to avoid too many zeroes in the key matrix, since they reduce diffusion. The net effect is that the effective keyspace of a basic Hill cipher is about $4.64n^2 - 1.7$. For a 5 × 5 Hill cipher, that is about 114 bits. Of course, key search is not the most efficient known attack.

26.5   Mechanical implementation

When operating on 2 symbols at once, a Hill cipher offers no particular advantage over Playfair or the bifid cipher, and in fact is weaker than either, and slightly more laborious to operate by pencil-and-paper. As the dimension increases, the cipher rapidly becomes infeasible for a human to operate by hand.

A Hill cipher of dimension 6 was implemented mechanically. Hill and a partner were awarded a patent (U.S. Patent 1,845,947) for this device, which performed a 6 × 6 matrix multiplication modulo 26 using a system of gears and chains.

Unfortunately the gearing arrangements (and thus the key) were fixed for any given machine, so triple encryption was recommended for security: a secret nonlinear step, followed by the wide diffusive step from the machine, followed by a third secret nonlinear step. (The much later Even-Mansour cipher also uses an unkeyed diffusive middle step). Such a combination was actually very powerful for 1929, and indicates that Hill apparently understood the concepts of a meet-in-the-middle attack as well as confusion and diffusion. Unfortunately, his machine did not sell.

26.6   See also

Other practical "pencil-and-paper" polygraphic ciphers include:

- Playfair cipher

- Bifid cipher

- Trifid cipher

26.7   References

- Lester S. Hill, Cryptography in an Algebraic Alphabet, *The American Mathematical Monthly* Vol.36, June–July 1929, pp. 306–312. (PDF)

- Lester S. Hill, Concerning Certain Linear Transformation Apparatus of Cryptography, *The American Mathematical Monthly* Vol.38, 1931, pp. 135–154.

- Jeffrey Overbey, William Traves, and Jerzy Wojdylo, On the Keyspace of the Hill Cipher, *Cryptologia*, Vol.29, No.1, January 2005, pp59–72. (CiteSeerX) (PDF)

26.8   External links

- "Hill Cipher Web App" implements the Hill cipher and shows the matrices involved

- "Hill Cipher Explained" illustrates the linear algebra behind the Hill Cipher

- "Hill's Cipher Calculator" outlines the Hill Cipher with a Web page

Chapter 27

Keyword cipher

A **keyword cipher** is a form of monoalphabetic substitution. A keyword is used as the key, and it determines the letter matchings of the cipher alphabet to the plain alphabet. Repeats of letters in the word are removed, then the cipher alphabet is generated with the keyword matching to A,B,C etc. until the keyword is used up, whereupon the rest of the ciphertext letters are used in alphabetical order, excluding those already used in the key.

Plaintext: A B C D E F G H I J K L M N O P Q R S T U V W X Y Z Encrypted: K R Y P T O S A B C D E F G H I J L M N Q U V W X Z

With KRYPTOS as the keyword, all As become Ks, all Bs become Rs and so on. Encrypting the message "knowledge is power" using the keyword "kryptos":

Plaintext: K N O W L E D G E I S P O W E R Encoded: D G H V E T P S T B M I H V T L

Only one alphabet is used here, so the cipher is monoalphabetic.

The best ways to attack a keyword cipher without knowing the keyword are through known-plaintext attack, frequency analysis and discovery of the keyword (often a cryptanalyst will combine all three techniques). Keyword discovery allows immediate decryption since the table can be made immediately.

27.1   References

Chapter 28

M-94

M-94 can also refer to a state trunkline in the U.S. state of Michigan. For the highway see, M-94 (Michigan highway)

The M-94 at the National Cryptologic Museum

The **M-94** was a piece of cryptographic equipment used by the United States army, consisting of several lettered discs arranged as a cylinder. The idea for the device was conceived by Colonel Parker Hitt and then developed by Major Joseph Mauborgne in 1917. Officially adopted in 1922, it remained in use until 1945, replaced by more complex and secure electromechanical rotor machines, particularly the M-209. The M-94 was also employed by the US Navy under the name **CSP 488**.

The device consisted of 25 aluminium discs attached to a four-and-a-half inch long rod, each disc containing the 26 letters of the Roman alphabet in scrambled order around its circumference (with the exception of the 17th disc, which began with the letters "ARMY OF THE US"). Each wheel had a different arrangement of the alphabet, and was stamped with an identifying number and letter; wheels were identified according to the letter following "A" on that wheel, from "B 1" to "Z 25". The wheels could be assembled on the rod in any order; the ordering used during encoding comprised the key. There were *25! (25 factorial) = 15,511,210,043,330,985,984,000,000* (more than 15 sep-

tillion) possible keys, which can be expressed as about an 84-bit key size.

Messages were encrypted 25 letters at a time. Turning the discs individually, the operator aligned the letters in the message horizontally. Then, any one of the remaining lines around the circumference of the cylinder was sent as the ciphertext. To decrypt, the wheels were turned until one line matched a 25 letter block of ciphertext. The plaintext would then appear on one of the other lines, which could be visually located easily, as it would be the only one likely to "read."

A variant, called a **strip cipher**, had each scrambled alphabet, repeated twice, printed on a metal strip that could be slid back and forth in a frame (see photo).

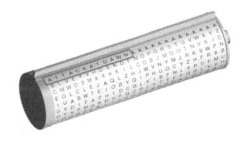

A wheel cipher being used to encode the phrase "ATTACK AT DAWN." One possible ciphertext is "CMWD SMXX KEIL."

The principle upon which the M-94/CSP-488 is based is at least as old as the 15th century, when the revolving wheel cryptograph was envisioned by Leone Battista Alberti. Thomas Jefferson independently invented a similar device in 1790, which had 36 disks.

Wheel ciphers could be broken, even in World War II, if enough ciphertext was intercepted. However, this took time and specialized skills, so the M-94 was still good enough for tactical communications. The DRYAD cipher currently in use by the U.S. military is not much more sophisticated.

28.1   See also

- Jefferson disk

28.2   External links

- DESCRIPTION OF CSP-488 a.k.a. M-94

- Jerry Proc's page on the M-94

- Pictures of the M-94

- *Instructions for the Cylindrical Cipher Device,* U.S. Navy, 1926

Chapter 29

Mirror writing

For the album by Jamie Woon, see Mirrorwriting.
Mirror writing is formed by writing in the direction that is

Mirror writing on the hood of an ambulance in the United Kingdom. The same word, "AMBULANCE", appears with identical typography, but reading in the normal direction, on the front of the vehicle near the top.

the reverse of the natural way for a given language, such that the result is the mirror image of normal writing: it appears normal when it is reflected in a mirror. It is sometimes used as an extremely primitive form of cipher. The most common modern usage of mirror writing can be found on the front of ambulances, where the word "AMBULANCE" is often written in very large mirrored text, so that drivers see the word the right way around in their rear-view mirror.

Research suggests that the ability to do mirror writing is probably inherited and caused by atypical language organization in the brain.[1] It is not known how many people in the population inherit the ability of mirror writing (an informal Australian newspaper experiment identified 10 true mirror-writers in a readership of 65,000[2]). Half of the children of

people with the ability inherit it. A higher proportion of left-handed people are better mirror writers than right-handed people, probably because it's more natural for a left-hander to write backwards.[3] 15% of left-handed people have the language centres in both halves of their brain. The cerebral cortex (thin layer of dense brain cells covering the whole brain) and motor homunculus (relates to voluntary movement) are affected by this causing them to be able to read and write backwards quite naturally.

In an experiment conducted by the Department of Neurosurgery at Hokkaido University School of Medicine in Sapporo, Japan, Scientists proposed that the origin of mirror writing comes from damage caused through accidental brain damage or neurological diseases, such as an essential tremor, Parkinson's disease, or spino-cerebellar degeneration. This hypothesis was proposed because these conditions affect a "neural mechanism that controls the higher cerebral function of writing via the thalamus."[4] Another study by the same university discovered that damage was not the only cause. The scientists observed that normal children exhibited signs of mirror writing while learning to write, thus concluding that currently there is no exact method for finding the true origin of mirror writing.

29.1 Notable examples

Leonardo da Vinci wrote most of his personal notes in mirror, only using standard writing if he intended his texts to be read by others. The purpose of this practice by Leonardo remains unknown, though several possible reasons have been suggested. For example, writing left handed from left to right would have been messy because the ink just put down would smear as his hand moved across it. Writing in reverse would prevent such smudging.

Matteo Zaccolini may have written his original four volume treatise on optics, color, and perspective in the early 17th century in mirror script.

Mirror writing calligraphy was popular in the Ottoman Em-

The notes on Leonardo da Vinci's famous Vitruvian Man image are in mirror writing.

Eighteenth century mirror writing in Ottoman calligraphy. Depicts the phrase Ali is the vicegerent of God *in both directions.*

pire during the 18th and 19th centuries among the Bektashi order, where it often carried mystical associations.[5] The origins of this mirror writing tradition may date to the pre-Islamic period in rock inscriptions of the western Arabian peninsula.[5]

Peep show images shown in a zograscope have headers in Mirror writing.

29.2   See also

- Boustrophedon

29.3   References

[1] Mathewson I. (2004). "Mirror writing ability is genetic and probably transmitted as a sex-linked dominant trait: it is hypothesised that mirror writers have bilateral language centres with a callosal interconnection". *Med Hypotheses.* **62** (5): 733–9. doi:10.1016/j.mehy.2003.12.039. PMID 15082098.

[2] News in Science - Mirror writing: my genes made me do it - 02/06/2004

[3] Schott, G. D. "Mirror Writing, Left-handedness, and Leftward Scripts". *Jama Network.* Retrieved 13 November 2014.

[4] Tashiro K, Matsumoto A, Hamada T, Moriwaka F (1987). "The aetiology of mirror writing: a new hypothesis". *J. Neurol.   Neurosurg.   Psychiatr.*   **50**:   1572–8. doi:10.1136/jnnp.50.12.1572. PMC 1032596. PMID 3437291.

[5] Library of Congress image bibliographic data. Retrieved 19 January 2009.

29.4   External links

- Media related to Mirror writings at Wikimedia Commons

- Mirror Writing a genetic trait

- Jay A. Gottfried, kruba sundar, Feyza Sancar, Anjan chatterjee. "Acquired mirror writing and reading: evidence for reflected graphemic representations" (PDF).

- Mirror writing: neurological reflections on an unusual phenomenon

Chapter 30

Mlecchita vikalpa

Mlecchita Vikalpa is one of the 64 arts listed in Vatsyayana's Kamasutra. The list appears in Chapter 3 of Part I of Kamasutra and Mlecchita Vikalpa appears as the 44th item in the list. The term Mlecchita Vikalapa has been translated into English as "the art of understanding writing in cypher, and the writing of words in a peculiar way".[1]

Mlecchita Vikalpa is the art of secret writing and secret communications. In *The Codebreakers*, a 1967 book by David Kahn about the history of cryptography, the reference to Mlecchita Vikalpa in Kamasutra is cited as proof of the prevalence of cryptographic methods in ancient India. Though Kamasutra does not have details of the methods by which people of that time practiced this particular form of art, later commentators of Kamasutra have described several methods. For example, Yasodhara in his Jayamangala commentaray on Kamasutra[2] gives descriptions of methods known by the names *Kautilya* and *Muladeviya*. The ciphers described in the Jayamangala commentary are substitution ciphers: in Kautiliyam the letter substitutions are based on phonetic relations, and Muladeviya is a simplified version of Kautiliyam. There are also references to other methods for secret communications like Gudhayojya, Gudhapada and Gudhavarna. Some modern writers on cryptography have christened the ciphers alluded to in the Kamasutra as *Kamasutra cipher* or *Vatsyayana cipher*.[3]

The exact date of the composition of Kamasutra has not been fixed. It is supposed that Vatsyayana must have lived between the first and sixth century CE. However, the date of the Jayamangla commentary has been fixed as between the tenth and thirteenth centuries CE.[1]

30.1 Kautiliya

This is a Mlecchita named after Kautilya, the author of the ancient Indian political treatise, the Arthashastra. In this system, the short and long vowels, the anusvara and the spirants are interchanged for the consonants and the conjuncts. The following table shows the substitutions used in the Kau-

tiliyam cipher. The characters not listed in the table are left unchanged.[4]

There is a simplified form of this scheme known by the name *Durbodha*.

30.2 Muladeviya

Another form of secret writing mentioned in Yasodhara's commentary on Kamasutra is known by the name *Muladeviya*. This existed both in the spoken form and in the written form. In the written form it is called *Gudhalekhya*. This form of secret communications were used by kings' spies as well as traders in various geographical locations in India. Also this form of secret communications has been popular among thieves and robbers.[4] However, there were variations in the actual scheme across the various geographical areas. For example, in the erstwhile Travancore Kingdom, spread over a part of present-day Kerala State in India, it was practiced under the name Mulabhadra with some changes from the schemes described by Yashodhara.

The cipher alphabet of Muladeviya consists of the reciprocal one specified in the table below.[4][5]

The great Indian epic Mahabharata contains an incident involving the use of this type of secret talking.[6] Duryodhana was planning to burn Pandavas alive and had made arrangements to send Pandavas to Varanavata. Vidura resorted to secret talk to warn Yudhishthira about the dangers in front of everybody present. Only Yudhishthira could understand the secret message. None others even suspected that it was a warning.

30.3   Gudhayojya

This is an elementary and trivial method for obscuring the true content of spoken messages and it is popular as a game among children. The idea is to add some unnecessary letters chosen randomly to the beginning or to the end of every word in a sentence. For example, to obscure the sentence "will visit you tonight" one may add the letters "dis" at the beginning of every word and convey the message as "diswill disvisit disyou distonight" the real content of which may not be intelligible to the uninitiated if pronounced rapidly.[4]

30.4   See also

- Mulabhadra

- Pig Latin

30.5   References

[1] Translators: Richard Burton, Bhagavanlal Indrajit, Shivaram Parashuram Bhide (January 18, 2009). *The Kama Sutra of Vatsyayana (Translated From The Sanscrit In Seven Parts With Preface,Introduction and Concluding Remarks)*. The Project Gutenberg. Retrieved 3 December 2015.

[2] David Kahn (December 1996). *The Codebreakers*. Simon and Schuster. p. 74. ISBN 9781439103555. Retrieved 25 November 2015.

[3] Simon Singh. "The Black Chamber". Retrieved 4 December 2015.

[4] Anil Baran Ganguly (1979). *Fine Arts of Ancient India*. Abhinav Publications. pp. 1678 – 170. Retrieved 4 December 2015.

[5] Friedrich L Brauer (2007). *Decrypted Secrets: Methods and Maxims of Cryptology*. Springer. p. 47. ISBN 978-3-540-24502-5.

[6] Anil Baran Ganguly (1979). *Fine Arts in Ancient India*. Abhinav Publications. p. 169. Retrieved 26 November 2015.

Chapter 31

Nihilist cipher

In the history of cryptography, the **Nihilist cipher** is a manually operated symmetric encryption cipher originally used by Russian Nihilists in the 1880s to organize terrorism against the tsarist regime. The term is sometimes extended to several improved algorithms used much later for communication by the First Chief Directorate with its spies.

31.1 Description

First the encipherer constructs a Polybius square using a mixed alphabet. This is used to convert both the plaintext and a keyword to a series of two digit numbers. These numbers are then added together in the normal way to get the ciphertext, with the key numbers repeated as required.

31.1.1 Example

Consider the Polybius square created using the keyword ZEBRAS:

with a plaintext of "DYNAMITE WINTER PALACE" and a key of RUSSIAN. This expands to:

PT: 23 55 41 15 35 32 45 12 53 32 41 45 12 14 43 15 34 15 22 12 KEY: 14 51 21 21 32 15 41 14 51 21 21 32 15 41 14 51 21 21 32 15 CT: 37 106 62 36 67 47 86 26 104 53 62 77 27 55 57 66 55 36 54 27

31.2 Nihilist cryptanalysis

Because each symbol in both plaintext and key is used as a whole number without any fractionation, the basic Nihilist cipher is little more than a numerical version of the Vigenère cipher, with multiple-digit numbers being the enciphered symbols instead of letters. As such, it can be attacked by very similar methods. An additional weakness is that the use of normal addition (instead of modular addition) leaks further information. For example, (assuming a

5 × 5 square) if a ciphertext number is greater than 100 then it is a certainty that both the plaintext and key came from the fifth row of the table.

31.3 Later variants or derivatives

During World War II, several Soviet spy rings communicated to Moscow Centre using two ciphers which are essentially evolutionary improvements on the basic Nihilist cipher. A very strong version was used by Max Clausen in Richard Sorge's network in Japan, and by Alexander Foote in the Lucy spy ring in Switzerland. A slightly weaker version was used by the *Rote Kapelle* network.

In both versions, the plaintext was first converted to digits by use of a straddling checkerboard rather than a Polybius square. This has the advantage of slightly compressing the plaintext, thus raising its unicity distance and also allowing radio operators to complete their transmissions quicker and shut down sooner. Shutting down sooner reduces the risk of the operator being found by enemy radio direction finders. Increasing the unicity distance increases strength against statistical attacks.

Clausen and Foote both wrote their plaintext in English, and memorized the 8 most frequent letters of English (to fill the top row of the checkerboard) through the mnemonic (and slightly menacing) phrase "a sin to err" (dropping the second "r"). The standard English straddling checkerboard has 28 characters and in this cipher these became "full stop" and "numbers shift". Numbers were sent by a numbers shift, followed by the actual plaintext digits in repeated pairs, followed by another shift. Then, similarly to the basic Nihilist, a digital additive was added in, which was called "closing". However a different additive was used each time, so finally a concealed "indicator group" had to be inserted to indicate what additive was used.

Unlike basic Nihilist, the additive was added by non-carrying addition (digit-wise addition modulo 10), thus producing a more uniform output which doesn't leak as much information. More importantly, the additive was generated not through a keyword, but by selecting lines at random from almanacs of industrial statistics. Such books were deemed dull enough to not arouse suspicion if an agent was searched (particularly as the agents' cover stories were as businessmen), and to have such high entropy density as to provide a very secure additive. Of course the figures from such a book are not actually uniformly distributed (there is an excess of "0" and "1" (see Benford's Law), and sequential numbers are likely to be somewhat similar), but nevertheless they have much higher entropy density than passphrases and the like; at any rate, in practice they seem never to have been successfully cryptanalysed.

The weaker version generated the additive from the text of a novel or similar book (at least one *Rote Kapelle* member used *The Good Soldier Schweik*) This text was converted to a digital additive using a technique similar to a straddling checkerboard.

The ultimate development along these lines was the VIC cipher, used in the 1950s by Reino Häyhänen. By this time, most Soviet agents were instead using one-time pads. However, despite the theoretical perfection of the one-time pad, in practice they *were* broken, while VIC was not.

31.4   See also

- Topics in cryptography

31.5   References

- David Kahn. *The Codebreakers*. 1968, 1974 edition Redwood Burn Ltd. pp 344, 368.

31.6   External links

- A JavaScript implementation of various Nihilist ciphers

Chapter 32

Null cipher

A **null cipher** is an ancient form of encryption where the plaintext is mixed with a large amount of non-cipher material. It would today be regarded as a simple form of steganography. Null ciphers can also be used to hide ciphertext, as part of a more complex system.

In classical cryptography a *null* is intended to confuse the cryptanalyst. Typically, a null will be a character which decrypts to obvious nonsense at the end of an otherwise intelligible phrase. In a null cipher, most of the characters may be nulls.

An example follows (Kipper 9):

> *News Eight Weather: Tonight increasing snow. Unexpected precipitation smothers eastern towns. Be extremely cautious and use snowtires especially heading east. The [highway is not] knowingly slippery. Highway evacuation is suspected. Police report emergency situations in downtown ending near Tuesday.*

Taking the first letter in each word successively yields the real message: "Newt is upset because he thinks he is President."

You can also choose to instead use the last letter of every word, or something like a pattern such as:

Susan sAys GaIl Lies. MAtt leTs Susan fEel joVial. Elated (or) aNgry?

Using the pattern (1,2,3,1,2,3 [each letter in each word]) gives the message: "Sail at seven."

32.1   See also

- Null encryption

32.2   References

- Kipper, Gregory Investigator's guide to steganography 2004 CRC Press LLC

- High Performance Enabled SSH/SCP (Pittsburgh Supercomputing Center) Retrieved 16-12-2008.

Chapter 33

Pig Latin

This article is about the language game. For the programming language, see Pig (programming tool).
Not to be confused with Dog Latin.

Pig Latin is a language game in which words in English are altered. The objective is to conceal the words from others not familiar with the rules. The reference to Latin is a deliberate misnomer, as it is simply a form of jargon, used only for its English connotations as a strange and foreign-sounding language.

33.1 Origins

Early mentions of pig Latin or hog Latin describe what we would today call dog Latin, a type of parody Latin. Examples of this predate even Shakespeare, whose 1598 play, *Love's Labour's Lost*, includes a reference to dog Latin:

An 1866 article describes a "hog latin" that has some similarities to current pig Latin. The article says, "He adds as many new letters as the boys in their 'hog latin,' which is made use of to mystify eavesdroppers. A boy asking a friend to go with him says, 'Wig-ge you-ge go-ge wig-ge me-ge?' The other, replying in the negative says, 'Noge, Ige woge.' "[2]

Another early mention of the name was in *Putnam's Magazine* in May 1869 "I had plenty of ammunition in reserve, to say nothing, Tom, of our pig Latin. 'Hoggibus, piggibus et shotam damnabile grunto,' and all that sort of thing," although the jargon is dog Latin.

The Atlantic January 1895 also included a mention of the subject: "They all spoke a queer jargon which they themselves had invented. It was something like the well-known 'pig Latin' that all sorts of children like to play with."

The modern version of pig Latin appears in a 1919 Columbia Records album containing what sounds like the modern variation, by a singer named Arthur Fields. The song, called Pig Latin Love, is followed by the subtitle "I-Yay Ove-Lay oo-yay earie-day".[3] The Three Stooges used it on multiple occasions, most notably *Tassels in the Air*, a 1938 short where Moe Howard attempts to teach Curley Howard how to use it, thereby conveying the rules to the audience. In an earlier (1934) episode, *Three Little Pigskins*, Larry Fine attempts to impress a woman with his skill in Pig Latin, but it turns out that she knows it, too. No explanation of the rules is given. A few months prior in 1934, in the *Our Gang* short film *Washee Ironee*, Spanky tries to speak to an Asian boy by using Pig Latin.[4]

A 1947 newspaper question and answer column describes the pig Latin as we understand it today. It describes moving the first letter to the end of a word and then adding "ay".[5]

33.2 Rules

For words that begin with consonant sounds, all letters before the initial vowel are placed at the end of the word sequence. Then, "ay" (some people just add "a") is added, as in the following examples:

- "pig" → "igpay"
- "banana" → "ananabay"
- "trash" → "ashtray"
- "happy" → "appyhay"
- "duck" → "uckday"
- "glove" → "oveglay"

For words that begin with vowel sounds, one just adds "way" to the end. Examples are:

- "eat" → "eatway"
- "omelet" → "omeletway"
- "are" → "areway"

Some people also follow this rule with words that begin with vowel sounds: only the first letter is moved to the end of the word, and then one just adds "way" after. Examples are:

- "egg" → "ggeway"

- "apple" → "ppleaway"

- "I" → "Iway"

33.3 In other languages

In the German-speaking area, varieties of Pig Latin include Kedelkloppersprook, which originated around Hamburg harbour, and Mattenenglisch that was used in the *Matte*, the traditional working-class neighborhood of Bern. Though Mattenenglisch has fallen out of use since the mid-20th century, it is still cultivated by voluntary associations. A characteristic of the Mattenenglisch Pig Latin is the complete substitution of the first vowel by *i*, in addition to the usual moving of the initial consonant cluster and the adding of *ee*.

The Swedish equivalent of Pig Latin is Fikonspråket ("Fig language" – see Language game § List of common language games).

French has the *loucherbem* (or *louchébem*, or *largonji*[6]) coded language, which supposedly was originally used by butchers (*boucher* in French).[7] In *loucherbem*, the leading consonant cluster is moved to the end of the word (as in Pig Latin) and replaced by an *L*, and then a suffix is added at the end of the word (*-oche*, *-em*, *-oque*, etc., depending on the word). Example: *combien* (how much) = *lombien-quès*. Similar coded languages are *verlan* and *langue de feu*. A few louchébem words have become usual French words: *fou* (crazy) = *loufoque*, *portefeuille* (wallet) = *larfeuille*, *en douce* (on the quiet) = *en loucedé*. Also similar is the widely used French argot *verlan*, in which the syllables of words are transposed, but without the addition of any further prefixes or suffixes.

Another equivalent of Pig Latin is used throughout the Slavic-speaking parts of the Balkans. It is called "Šatra" (/sha-tra/)or "Šatrovački" (/shatro-vachki/) and was used in crime-related and street language. For instance, the Balkan slang name for marihuana (trava - meaning "grass") turns to "vutra"; the Balkan slang name for cocaine (belo - meaning "white") turns to lobe, a pistol (pištolj) turns to štoljpi, bro (brate) turns to tebra. In the past few years it has become widely used between teenage immigrants in former Yugoslavian countries.

33.4 Notes

[1] **The Straight Dope:** What's the origin of pig Latin?

[2] Wakeman, George (1886). *Sound and Sense. The Galaxy: A Magazine of Entertaining Reading, Volume 1.* p. 638. Retrieved 13 December 2015.

[3] **I Always Wondered:** Where did Pig Latin come from? Consensus seems to be that the version of Pig Latin we know today, was born sometime in the 20th century. In 1919 Columbia records released an album with Arthur Fields singing "Pig Latin Love". The Subtitle "I-Yay Ove-Lay oo-yay earie-day" indicates that this is the modern form of Pig Latin we recognize today. I was able to scrounge up a photograph of the 1919 sheet music on eBay. Below the Pig Latin subtitle is the translation, "(I love you dearie)", suggesting that perhaps this form of Pig Latin hadn't taken root among the general public yet.

[4] https://www.youtube.com/watch?v=fcMWkY-Wlkk#t=10m35s

[5] "Answers to Questions - The Haskins' Service". *Reading Eagle*. 28 January 1947. p. 12. Retrieved 13 December 2015.

[6] "LARGONJI : Définition de LARGONJI". Cnrtl.fr. Retrieved 2014-03-10.

[7] Françoise Robert l'Argenton. *"Larlépem largomuche du louchébem. Parler l'argot du boucher"* (in French). Parlures argotiques. pp. 113–125. Retrieved 2014-03-10.

33.5 References

- Barlow, Jessica. 2001. Teen Titans Go! Episode - Obinray "Individual differences in the production of initial consonant sequences in Pig Latin." *Lingua* 111:667-696.

- Cowan, Nelson. 1989. "Acquisition of Pig Latin: A Case Study." *Journal of Child Language* 16.2:365-386.

- Day, R. 1973. "On learning 'secret languages.'" *Haskins Laboratories Status Report on Speech Research* 34:141-150.

- Haycock, Arthur. "Pig Latin." *American Speech* 8:3.81.

- McCarthy, John. 1991. "Reduplicative Infixation in Secret Languages" [*L'Infixation reduplicative dans les langages secrets*]. *Langages* 25.101:11-29.

- Vaux, Bert and Andrew Nevins. 2003. "Underdetermination in language games: Survey and analysis of Pig Latin dialects." Linguistic Society of America Annual Meeting, Atlanta.

33.6   External links

- Free English to Pig Latin translator utility

- Pig Latin translator at Fun translations

- Entiumgay – an AAT Pig Latin Font

- English to Pig Latin Translator

Chapter 34

Pigpen cipher

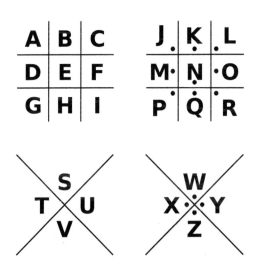

The pigpen cipher uses graphical symbols assigned according to a key similar to the above diagram.[1]

The **pigpen cipher** (alternately referred to as the **masonic cipher**, **Freemason's cipher**, **Napoleon cipher**, and **tic-tac-toe cipher**)[2][3] is a geometric simple substitution cipher, which exchanges letters for symbols which are fragments of a grid. The example key shows one way the letters can be assigned to the grid.

34.1   Security

The use of symbols instead of letters is no impediment to cryptanalysis, and this system is identical to that of other simple monoalphabetic substitution schemes. Due to the simplicity of the cipher, it is often included in children's books on ciphers and secret writing.[4]

34.2   History

The exact origin of the cipher is unknown, but records of this system have been found which go back to at least the 18th century. Variations of this cipher were used by both the Rosicrucian brotherhood[5] and the Freemasons, though the latter used it so often that the system is frequently called the Freemason's cipher. They began using it in the early 18th century to keep their records of history and rites private, and for correspondence between lodge leaders.[3][6][7] Tombstones of Freemasons can also be found which use the system as part of the engravings. One of the earliest stones in Trinity Church Cemetery in New York City, which opened in 1697, contains a cipher of this type which deciphers to "Remember death" (cf. "memento mori"). George Washington's army had documentation about the system, with a much more randomized form of the alphabet. And during the American Civil War, the system was used by Union prisoners in Confederate prisons.[5]

34.3   Variants

The core elements of this system are the grid and dots. Some systems use the X's, but even these can be rearranged. One commonly used method orders the symbols as shown in the above image: grid, grid, X, X. Another commonly used system orders the symbols as grid, X, grid, X. Another is grid, grid, grid, with each cell having a letter of the alphabet, and the last one having an "&" character. Letters from the first grid have no dot, letters from the second each have one dot, and letters from the third each have two dots. Another variation of this last one is called the Newark Cipher, which instead of dots uses one to three short lines which may be projecting in any length or orientation. This gives the illusion of a larger number of different characters than actually exist.[8]

Another system, used by the Rosicrucians, used a single grid of nine cells, and 1 to 3 dots in each cell or "pen".

73

So ABC would be in the top left pen, followed by DEF and GHI on the first line, then groups of JKL MNO PQR on the second, and STU VWX YZ on the third.[2][5] When enciphered, the location of the dot in each symbol (left, center, or right), would indicate which letter in that pen was represented.[1][5] More difficult systems use a non-standard form of the alphabet, such as writing it backwards in the grid, up and down in the columns,[4] or a completely randomized set of letters.

The Templar cipher is a method claimed to have been used by the Knights Templar. It uses a variant of a Maltese Cross.

34.4 Example

Using the Pigpen cipher key above, the message "X MARKS THE SPOT" is rendered in ciphertext as:

34.5 Notes

[1] Wrixon, pp. 182–183

[2] Barker, p. 40

[3] Wrixon, p. 27

[4] Gardner

[5] Pratt, pp. 142–143

[6] Kahn, 1967, p.~772

[7] Newton, 1998, p. 113

[8] *Glossary of Cryptography*

34.6 References

- Barker, Wayne G., ed. (1978). *The History of Codes and Ciphers in the United States Prior to World War I.* Aegean Park Press. ISBN 0-89412-026-3.

- Gardner, Martin (1972). *Codes, ciphers and secret writing.* ISBN 0-486-24761-9.

- Kahn, David (1967). *The Codebreakers. The Story of Secret Writing.* Macmillan.

- Kahn, David (1996). *The Codebreakers. The Story of Secret Writing.* Scribner. ISBN 0-684-83130-9.

- Newton, David E. (1998). "Freemason's Cipher". *Encyclopedia of Cryptology.* ISBN 0-87436-772-7.

- Pratt, Fletcher (1939). *Secret and Urgent: The story of codes and ciphers.* Aegean Park Press. ISBN 0-89412-261-4.

- Shulman, David; Weintraub, Joseph (1961). *A glossary of cryptography.* Crypto Press. p. 44.

- Wrixon, Fred B. (1998). *Codes, Ciphers, and other Cryptic & Clandestine Communication.* Black Dog & Leventhal Publishers, Inc. ISBN 1-57912-040-7.

34.7 External links

- The *Elian Script* is a similar grid-based cipher, used as art.

- Online Pigpen cipher tool for enciphering small messages.

- Cipher Code True Type Font

- Cryptii converts text in pigpen cipher and more.

Chapter 35

Playfair cipher

The Playfair system was invented by Charles Wheatstone, who first described it in 1854.

The **Playfair cipher** or **Playfair square** or **Wheatstone-Playfair cipher** or **Wheatstone cipher** is a manual symmetric encryption technique and was the first literal digram substitution cipher. The scheme was invented in 1854 by Charles Wheatstone, but bears the name of Lord Playfair who promoted the use of the cipher.

The technique encrypts pairs of letters (*bigrams* or *digrams*), instead of single letters as in the simple substitution cipher and rather more complex Vigenère cipher systems then in use. The Playfair is thus significantly harder to break since the frequency analysis used for simple substitution ciphers does not work with it. The frequency analysis of bigrams is possible, but considerably more difficult. With 600[1] possible bigrams rather than the 26 possible

monograms (single symbols, usually letters in this context), a considerably larger cipher text is required in order to be useful.

35.1 History

Lord Playfair, who heavily promoted its use.

It became known as the Playfair cipher after Lord Playfair, who heavily promoted its use, despite its invention by Wheatstone. The first recorded description of the Playfair cipher was in a document signed by Wheatstone on 26 March 1854.

It was rejected by the British Foreign Office when it was developed because of its perceived complexity. Wheatstone offered to demonstrate that three out of four boys in a nearby school could learn to use it in 15 minutes, but the Under Secretary of the Foreign Office responded, "That is very possible, but you could never teach it to attachés."

It was used for tactical purposes by British forces in the Second Boer War and in World War I and for the same purpose by the British and Australians during World War II. This was because Playfair is reasonably fast to use and requires no special equipment - just a pencil and some paper. A typical scenario for Playfair use was to protect important but non-critical secrets during actual combat e.g. the fact that an artillery barrage of smoke shells would commence within 30 minutes to cover soldiers' advance towards the next objective. By the time enemy cryptanalysts could decode such messages hours later, such information would be useless to them because it was no longer relevant.

During the Second World War, the Government of New Zealand used it for communication among New Zealand, the Chatham Islands, and the coastwatchers in the Pacific Islands.[2][3]

35.2   Superseded

Playfair is no longer used by military forces because of the advent of digital encryption devices. This cipher is now regarded as insecure for any purpose, because modern computers could easily break it within seconds.

The first published solution of the Playfair cipher was described in a 19-page pamphlet by Lieutenant Joseph O. Mauborgne, published in 1914.[4]

35.3   Description

The Playfair cipher uses a 5 by 5 table containing a key word or phrase. Memorization of the keyword and 4 simple rules was all that was required to create the 5 by 5 table and use the cipher.

To generate the key table, one would first fill in the spaces in the table with the letters of the keyword (dropping any duplicate letters), then fill the remaining spaces with the rest of the letters of the alphabet in order (usually omitting "Q" to reduce the alphabet to fit; other versions put both "I" and "J" in the same space). The key can be written in the top rows of the table, from left to right, or in some other pattern, such as a spiral beginning in the upper-left-hand corner and ending in the center. The keyword together with the conventions for filling in the 5 by 5 table constitute the cipher key.

To encrypt a message, one would break the message into

digrams (groups of 2 letters) such that, for example, "HelloWorld" becomes "HE LL OW OR LD", and map them out on the key table. If needed, append an uncommon monogram to complete the final digram. The two letters of the digram are considered as the opposite corners of a rectangle in the key table. Note the relative position of the corners of this rectangle. Then apply the following 4 rules, in order, to each pair of letters in the plaintext:

1. If both letters are the same (or only one letter is left), add an "X" after the first letter. Encrypt the new pair and continue. Some variants of Playfair use "Q" instead of "X", but any letter, itself uncommon as a repeated pair, will do.

2. If the letters appear on the same row of your table, replace them with the letters to their immediate right respectively (wrapping around to the left side of the row if a letter in the original pair was on the right side of the row).

3. If the letters appear on the same column of your table, replace them with the letters immediately below respectively (wrapping around to the top side of the column if a letter in the original pair was on the bottom side of the column).

4. If the letters are not on the same row or column, replace them with the letters on the same row respectively but at the other pair of corners of the rectangle defined by the original pair. The order is important – the first letter of the encrypted pair is the one that lies on the same **row** as the first letter of the plaintext pair.

To decrypt, use the INVERSE (opposite) of the last 3 rules, and the 1st as-is (dropping any extra "X"s, or "Q"s that do not make sense in the final message when finished).

There are several minor variations of the original Playfair cipher.[5]

35.4   Example

Using "playfair example" as the key (assuming that I and J are interchangeable), the table becomes (omitted letters in red):

P L A Y F I R E X M B C D G H K N O Q S T U V W Z

Encrypting the message "Hide the gold in the tree stump" (note the null "X" used to separate the repeated "E"s) :

HI DE TH EG OL DI NT HE TR EX ES TU MP ^ BM OD ZB XD NA BE KU DM UI XM MO UV IF

Thus the message "Hide the gold in the tree stump" becomes "BMODZ BXDNA BEKUD MUIXM MOUVI F". (Breaks included for ease of reading the cipher text.)

35.5 Clarification with picture

Assume one wants to encrypt the digram OR. There are five general cases:

35.6 Cryptanalysis

Like most classical ciphers, the Playfair cipher can be easily cracked if there is enough text. Obtaining the key is relatively straightforward if both plaintext and ciphertext are known. When only the ciphertext is known, brute force cryptanalysis of the cipher involves searching through the key space for matches between the frequency of occurrence of digrams (pairs of letters) and the known frequency of occurrence of digrams in the assumed language of the original message.[6]

Cryptanalysis of Playfair is similar to that of four-square and two-square ciphers, though the relative simplicity of the Playfair system makes identifying candidate plaintext strings easier. Most notably, a Playfair digraph and its reverse (e.g. AB and BA) will decrypt to the same letter pattern in the plaintext (e.g. RE and ER). In English, there are many words which contain these reversed digraphs such as REceivER and DEpartED. Identifying nearby reversed digraphs in the ciphertext and matching the pattern to a list of known plaintext words containing the pattern is an easy way to generate possible plaintext strings with which to begin constructing the key.

A different approach to tackling a Playfair cipher is the shotgun hill climbing method. This starts with a random square of letters. Then minor changes are introduced (i.e. switching letters, rows, or reflecting the entire square) to see if the candidate plaintext is more like standard plaintext than before the change (perhaps by comparing the digrams to a known frequency chart). If the new square is deemed to be an improvement, then it is adopted and then further mutated to find an even better candidate. Eventually, the plaintext or something very close is found to achieve a maximal score by whatever grading method is chosen. This is obviously beyond the range of typical human patience, but computers can adopt this algorithm to crack Playfair ciphers with a relatively small amount of text.

Another aspect of Playfair that separates it from four-square and two-square ciphers is the fact that it will never contain a double-letter digram, e.g. EE. If there are no double letter digrams in the ciphertext and the length of the message is long enough to make this statistically significant, it is very likely that the method of encryption is Playfair.

A good tutorial on reconstructing the key for a Playfair cipher can be found in chapter 7, "Solution to Polygraphic Substitution Systems," of Field Manual 34-40-2, produced by the United States Army. Another cryptanalysis of a Playfair cipher can be found in Chapter XXI of Helen Fouché Gaines, *Cryptanalysis / a study of ciphers and their solutions*.[7]

A detailed cryptanalysis of Playfair is undertaken in chapter 28 of Dorothy L. Sayers' mystery novel *Have His Carcase*. In this story, a Playfair message is demonstrated to be cryptographically weak, as the detective is able to solve for the entire key making only a few guesses as to the formatting of the message (in this case, that the message starts with the name of a city and then a date). Sayers' book includes a detailed description of the mechanics of Playfair encryption, as well as a step-by-step account of manual cryptanalysis.

The German Army, Air Force and Police used the **Double Playfair** system as a medium-grade cipher in WWII, but as they had broken the cipher early in WWI, they adapted it by introducing a second square from which the second letter of each bigram was selected, and dispensed with the keyword, placing the letters in random order. But with the German fondness for pro forma messages, they were broken at Bletchley Park. Messages were preceded by a sequential number, and numbers were spelled out. As the German numbers 1 (eins) to twelve (zwölf) contain all but eight of the letters in the Double Playfair squares, pro forma traffic was relatively easy to break (Smith, page 74-75)

35.7   Modern comparisons

Computer-run block ciphers work in a manner similar to Playfair's: they break the original message into blocks of characters and apply a complex mathematical transformation, based upon the key, to each of those blocks.

Naturally, modern ciphers are not restricted to upper-case, no-punctuation, J-less messages. Any form of data that can be stored on a computer can be encrypted with a modern cipher.

A modern block cipher can be run in a mode similar to that of Playfair, where the same block (in Playfair, a pair of letters) always encrypts to the same bit of ciphertext: in our example, CO will always come out as OW. Indeed, many poorly written encryption programs use just this technique, called Electronic Codebook, or ECB.[8]

More sophisticated implementation of a cipher will use one of many other modes. The most common is called Cipher Feedback Mode, or CFB.

CFB starts by encrypting something other than the message. This bit at the front of things is called an initialization vector, or IV. The IV need not be secret, but the same IV should never be re-used with the same encryption key.

First, encrypt the IV. Take the IV and combine it with the first block of the plaintext. With computers, this is done with a mathematical function called a binary XOR; a similar effect could be accomplished with Playfair by "adding" the two together: C + H = K; W + F = B. It is this value which is written to the ciphertext.

Next, take the result from the last step, encrypt it as normally, and add it to the next block from the plaintext. In this way, the encryption of each block depends upon the encryption of each preceding block.

Encrypt IV -> XOR (add) result with first block of plaintext -> write as ciphertext -> encrypt from previous -> XOR with next block of plaintext -> write as ciphertext -> repeat

The example encoded with Playfair modified in this way, using an IV of "AB" might look thus:

OKHKBGVF...

This process greatly increases the security of the encryption system. When done with computers, the speed of the processing of the encryption is not significantly hindered.

35.8   Use in modern crosswords

Advanced thematic cryptic crosswords like *The Listener* Crossword (published in the Saturday edition of the British newspaper *The Times*) occasionally incorporate Playfair ciphers.[9] Normally between 4 and 6 answers have to be entered into the grid in code, and the Playfair keyphrase is thematically significant to the final solution.

The cipher lends itself well to crossword puzzles, because the plaintext is found by solving one set of clues, while the ciphertext is found by solving others. Solvers can then construct the key table by pairing the digrams (it is sometimes possible to guess the keyword, but never necessary).

Use of the Playfair cipher is generally explained as part of the preamble to the crossword. This levels the playing field for those solvers who have not come across the cipher previously. But the way the cipher is used is always the same. The 25-letter alphabet used always contains Q and has I and J coinciding. The key table is always filled row by row.

35.9   In popular culture

- The novel *Have His Carcase* by Dorothy L. Sayers gives a blow-by-blow account of the cracking of a Playfair cipher.

- The World War 2 thriller *The Trojan Horse* by Hammond Innes conceals the formula for a new high-strength metal alloy using the Playfair cipher.

- In the film *National Treasure: Book of Secrets*, a treasure hunt clue is encoded as Playfair cipher.

- In the audio book *Rogue Angel : God of Thunder*, a Playfair cipher clue is used to send Anja Creed to Venice.

35.10   See also

- Topics in cryptography

35.11   Notes

[1] No duplicate letters are allowed, and one letter is omitted (Q) or combined (I/J), so the calculation is 600 = 25×24.

[2] "A History of Communications Security in New Zealand By Eric Mogon", Chapter 8

[3] "The History of Information Assurance (IA)". *Government Communications Security Bureau*. New Zealand Government. Retrieved 2011-12-24.

[4] Mauborgne, Joseph Oswald, *An Advanced Problem in Cryptography and Its Solution* (Fort Leavenwoth, Kansas: Army Service Schools Press, 1914).

[5] Gaines 1956, p. 201

[6] Gaines 1956, p. 201

[7] Gaines 1956, pp. 198–207

[8] Electronic codebook

[9] Listener crossword database

35.12 References

- Gaines, Helen Fouché (1956) [1939], *Cryptanalysis / a study of ciphers and their solutions*, Dover, ISBN 0-486-20097-3

- Smith, Michael *Station X: The Codebreakers of Bletchley Park* (1998, Channel 4 Books/Macmillan, London) ISBN 0-7522-2189-2

35.13 External links

- Online encrypting and decrypting Playfair with JavaScript

- Extract from some lecture notes on ciphers – Digraphic Ciphers: Playfair

- Playfair Cypher

- Cross platform implementation of Playfair cipher

Chapter 36

Poem code

The **poem code** is a simple, and insecure, cryptographic method which was used by SOE to communicate with their agents in Nazi-occupied Europe.

The method works by the sender and receiver pre-arranging a poem to use. The sender chooses a set number of words at random from the poem and gives each letter in the chosen words a number. The numbers are then used as a key for some cipher to conceal the plaintext of the message. The cipher used was often double transposition. To indicate to the receiver which words had been chosen an indicator group is sent at the start of the message.

36.1 Description

To encrypt a message, the agent would select words from the poem as the key. Every poem code message commenced with an indicator-group of five letters, which showed which five words of an agent's poem had been used to encrypt the message.

The words would be written sequentially, and their letters numbered to create a transposition key to encrypt a message. For example, if the words are YEO THOMAS IS A PAIN IN THE ARSE, then the transposition key is: 25 5 16, 23 8 17 13 1 20, 10 21, 2, 18 3 11 14, 12 15, 24 9 6, 4 19 22 7. These are the locations of the first appearances of A's, B, etc. in the sentence.

This defines a permutation which is used for encryption (25->1, 5->2 etc.). First, the plaintext message is arranged in columns. Then the columns are permuted, and then the rows are permuted.

For example, the text "THE OPERATION TO DEMOLISH THE BUNKER IS TOMORROW AT ELEVEN" would be written on grid paper as:

```
TPTTMSEKSOWLN
HEIOOHBETRAEA
ERODLTURORTVX
OANEIHNIMOEET
```

(The above transposition key requires longer messages which would have at least 25 columns and 25 rows).

As an additional security measure, the agent would add pre-arranged errors into the text as security checks. For example, there might be an intentional error in every 18th letter. This was to ensure that, if the agent was captured or the poem was found, the enemy might transmit without the security checks.

36.2 Analysis

The code's advantage is to provide relatively strong security while not requiring any codebook. The encryption process is error-prone and for security required messages at least 200 words long.

It is vulnerable to attacks. If one message is broken by any means (including threat, torture, or even cryptanalysis), future messages will be readable if the source poem has been identified. Since the poems used must be memorable for ease of use by an agent, there is a temptation to use well-known poems or poems from well-known poets. (e.g. SOE agents often used verses by Shakespeare, Racine, Tennyson, Molière, Keats, etc.).

If the agent used the same poem code words to send a number of messages, these words could be discovered easily by enemy cryptographers. If the words could be identified as coming from a famous poem or quotation, then all of the future traffic submitted in that poem code could be read. The German cryptologic units were successful in decoding many of the poems by searching through collections of poems.

The security check was usually not effective: if a code was used once intercepted and decoded, any security checks were revealed and could be tortured out from the agent.

36.3 Development

When Leo Marks was appointed codes officer of the Special Operations Executive (SOE) in London during World War II, he very quickly recognized the weakness of the technique, and the consequent damage to agents and to their organizations on the Continent, and began to press for changes. Eventually, the SOE began using original compositions (thus not in any published collection of poems from any poet) to give added protection (see *The Life That I Have*, an example). Frequently, the poems were humorous or overtly sexual to make them memorable ("Is de Gaulle's prick//Twelve inches thick//Can it rise//To the size//Of a proud flag-pole//And does the sun shine//From his arsehole?"). Another improvement was to use a new poem for each message, where the poem was written on fabric rather than memorized.

Gradually the SOE replaced the poem code with more secure methods. Worked-out Keys (WOKs) was the first major improvement - an invention of Marks'. WOKs are pre-arranged transposition keys given to the agents and which made the poem unnecessary. Each message would be encrypted on one key, which was written on special silk. They key was disposed off, by tearing a piece of the silk, when the message was sent.

A project of Marks', named by him "Operation Gift-Horse", was a deception scheme aimed to disguise the more secure WOK code traffic as poem code traffic, so that German cryptographers would think "Gift-Horsed" messages were easier to break than they actually were. This was done by adding false duplicate indicator groups to WOK-keys, to give the appearance that an agent had repeated the use of certain words of their code poem. The aim of Gift Horse was to waste the enemy's time, and was deployed prior to D-Day, when code traffic increased dramatically.

The poem code was ultimately replaced with the one-time pad, specifically the letter one-time pad (LOP). In LOP, the agent was provided with a string of letters and a substitution square. The plaintext was written under the string on the pad. The pairs of letters in each column (such as P,L) indicated a unique letter on the square (Q). The pad was never reused while the substitution square could be reused without loss of security. This enabled rapid and secure encoding of messages.

36.4 Bibliography

- *Between Silk and Cyanide* by Leo Marks, HarperCollins (1998) ISBN 0-00-255944-7; Marks was the Head of Codes at SOE and this book is an account of his struggle to introduce better encryption for use by field agents; it contains more than 20 previously unpublished code poems by Marks, as well as descriptions of how they were used and by whom.

36.5 See also

- Book cipher
- *The Life That I Have* (also known as *Yours*, arguably the most famous code poem)

Chapter 37

Polyalphabetic cipher

A **polyalphabetic cipher** is any cipher based on substitution, using multiple substitution alphabets. The Vigenère cipher is probably the best-known example of a polyalphabetic cipher, though it is a simplified special case. The Enigma machine is more complex but still fundamentally a polyalphabetic substitution cipher.

37.1 History

The Alberti cipher by Leon Battista Alberti around 1467 was believed to be the first polyalphabetic cipher. Alberti used a mixed alphabet to encrypt a message, but whenever he wanted to, he would switch to a different alphabet, indicating that he had done so by including an uppercase letter or a number in the cryptogram. For this encipherment Alberti used a decoder device, his *cipher disk*, which implemented a polyalphabetic substitution with mixed alphabets.

Although Alberti is usually considered the father of polyphabetic cipher, it has been claimed that polyalphabetic ciphers may have been developed by the Arab cryptologist Al Kindi 600 years before Alberti.[1] Johannes Trithemius—in his book *Polygraphiae libri sex* (Six books of polygraphia), which was published in 1518 after his death—invented a *progressive key* polyalphabetic cipher called the Trithemius cipher.[2] Unlike Alberti's cipher, which switched alphabets at random intervals, Trithemius switched alphabets for each letter of the message. He started with a tabula recta, a square with 26 alphabets in it (although Trithemius, writing in Latin, used 24 alphabets). Each alphabet was shifted one letter to the left from the one above it, and started again with A after reaching Z (see image).

Trithemius's idea was to encipher the first letter of the message using the first shifted alphabet, so A became B, B became C, etc. The second letter of the message was enciphered using the second shifted alphabet, etc. Alberti's cipher disk implemented the same scheme. It had two alphabets, one on a fixed outer ring, and the other on the rotating disk. A letter is enciphered by looking for that letter on the

	A	B	C	D	E	F	G	H	I	J	K	L	M	N	O	P	Q	R	S	T	U	V	W	X	Y	Z
A	A	B	C	D	E	F	G	H	I	J	K	L	M	N	O	P	Q	R	S	T	U	V	W	X	Y	Z
B	B	C	D	E	F	G	H	I	J	K	L	M	N	O	P	Q	R	S	T	U	V	W	X	Y	Z	A
C	C	D	E	F	G	H	I	J	K	L	M	N	O	P	Q	R	S	T	U	V	W	X	Y	Z	A	B
D	D	E	F	G	H	I	J	K	L	M	N	O	P	Q	R	S	T	U	V	W	X	Y	Z	A	B	C
E	E	F	G	H	I	J	K	L	M	N	O	P	Q	R	S	T	U	V	W	X	Y	Z	A	B	C	D
F	F	G	H	I	J	K	L	M	N	O	P	Q	R	S	T	U	V	W	X	Y	Z	A	B	C	D	E
G	G	H	I	J	K	L	M	N	O	P	Q	R	S	T	U	V	W	X	Y	Z	A	B	C	D	E	F
H	H	I	J	K	L	M	N	O	P	Q	R	S	T	U	V	W	X	Y	Z	A	B	C	D	E	F	G
I	I	J	K	L	M	N	O	P	Q	R	S	T	U	V	W	X	Y	Z	A	B	C	D	E	F	G	H
J	J	K	L	M	N	O	P	Q	R	S	T	U	V	W	X	Y	Z	A	B	C	D	E	F	G	H	I
K	K	L	M	N	O	P	Q	R	S	T	U	V	W	X	Y	Z	A	B	C	D	E	F	G	H	I	J
L	L	M	N	O	P	Q	R	S	T	U	V	W	X	Y	Z	A	B	C	D	E	F	G	H	I	J	K
M	M	N	O	P	Q	R	S	T	U	V	W	X	Y	Z	A	B	C	D	E	F	G	H	I	J	K	L
N	N	O	P	Q	R	S	T	U	V	W	X	Y	Z	A	B	C	D	E	F	G	H	I	J	K	L	M
O	O	P	Q	R	S	T	U	V	W	X	Y	Z	A	B	C	D	E	F	G	H	I	J	K	L	M	N
P	P	Q	R	S	T	U	V	W	X	Y	Z	A	B	C	D	E	F	G	H	I	J	K	L	M	N	O
Q	Q	R	S	T	U	V	W	X	Y	Z	A	B	C	D	E	F	G	H	I	J	K	L	M	N	O	P
R	R	S	T	U	V	W	X	Y	Z	A	B	C	D	E	F	G	H	I	J	K	L	M	N	O	P	Q
S	S	T	U	V	W	X	Y	Z	A	B	C	D	E	F	G	H	I	J	K	L	M	N	O	P	Q	R
T	T	U	V	W	X	Y	Z	A	B	C	D	E	F	G	H	I	J	K	L	M	N	O	P	Q	R	S
U	U	V	W	X	Y	Z	A	B	C	D	E	F	G	H	I	J	K	L	M	N	O	P	Q	R	S	T
V	V	W	X	Y	Z	A	B	C	D	E	F	G	H	I	J	K	L	M	N	O	P	Q	R	S	T	U
W	W	X	Y	Z	A	B	C	D	E	F	G	H	I	J	K	L	M	N	O	P	Q	R	S	T	U	V
X	X	Y	Z	A	B	C	D	E	F	G	H	I	J	K	L	M	N	O	P	Q	R	S	T	U	V	W
Y	Y	Z	A	B	C	D	E	F	G	H	I	J	K	L	M	N	O	P	Q	R	S	T	U	V	W	X
Z	Z	A	B	C	D	E	F	G	H	I	J	K	L	M	N	O	P	Q	R	S	T	U	V	W	X	Y

Tabula recta

outer ring, and encoding it as the letter underneath it on the disk. The disk started with A underneath B, and the user rotated the disk by one letter after encrypting each letter.

The cipher was trivial to break, and Alberti's machine implementation not much more difficult. *Key progression* in both cases was poorly concealed from attackers. Even Alberti's implementation of his polyalphabetic cipher was rather easy to break (the capitalized letter is a major clue to the cryptanalyst). For most of the next several hundred years, the significance of using multiple substitution alphabets was missed by almost everyone. Polyalphabetic substitution cipher designers seem to have concentrated on obscuring the choice of a few such alphabets (repeating as needed), not on the increased security possible by using many and never repeating any.

The principle (particularly Alberti's unlimited additional substitution alphabets) was a major advance—the most significant in the several hundred years since frequency analysis had been developed. A reasonable implementation would have been (and, when finally achieved, was) vastly harder to break. It was not until the mid-19th century (in Babbage's secret work during the Crimean War and Friedrich Kasiski's generally equivalent public disclosure some years later), that cryptanalysis of well-implemented polyalphabetic ciphers got anywhere at all.

37.2 Notes

[1] Maclean, Donald, *Al-Kindi*, retrieved 13 April 2012

[2] Johann Tritheim, *Polygraphiae libri sex* ... (Basel, Switzerland: Michael Furter and Adam Petri, 1518), *Liber quintus* (fifth book), pages 461-462; the *Recta transpositionis tabula* (square table of transpositions, or "Vigenère table") appears on page 463.

37.3 References

- Alberti, Leon Battista (1997), *A Treatise on Ciphers, trans. A. Zaccagnini. Foreword by David Kahn*, Torino: Galimberti

- Churchhouse, Robert (2002), *Codes and Ciphers: Julius Caesar, the Enigma and the Internet*, Cambridge: Cambridge University Press, ISBN 978-0-521-00890-7

- Gaines, Helen Fouché (1939), *Cryptanalysis*, Dover, ISBN 0-486-20097-3

37.4 See also

- Vigenère cipher
- Topics in cryptography

Chapter 38

Polybius square

In cryptography, the **Polybius square**, also known as the **Polybius checkerboard**, is a device invented by the Ancient Greek historian and scholar Polybius,[1] for fractionating plaintext characters so that they can be represented by a smaller set of symbols.

38.1 Basic form

The original square used the Greek alphabet, but can be used with any alphabet. In fact, it has also been used with Japanese hiragana (*see cryptography in Japan*). With the modern English alphabet, in typical form, it appears thus:

Each letter is then represented by its coordinates in the grid. For example, "BAT" becomes "12 11 44". Because 26 characters do not quite fit in a square, it is rounded down to the next lowest square number by combining two letters (usually C and K or sometimes I and J). (Polybius had no such problem because the Greek alphabet he was using had 24 letters). Alternatively, the ten digits could be added and 36 characters would be put into a 6 × 6 grid.

Such a larger grid might also be used for Cyrillic script (of which the most common alphabet variant has 33 letters, though some have fewer, and some up to 37).

38.2 Telegraphy and steganography

Polybius did not originally conceive of his device as a cipher so much as an aid to telegraphy; he suggested the symbols could be signalled by holding up pairs of sets of torches. It has also been used, in the form of the "knock code", to signal messages between cells in prisons by tapping the numbers on pipes or walls. In this form it is said to have been used by nihilist prisoners of the Russian Czars, and also by American prisoners of war in the Vietnam War. Arthur Koestler describes this code being used by political prisoners of Stalin in the 1930s in his anti-totalitarian novel *Darkness at Noon*. (Koestler had himself been a political prisoner in Spain during the Spanish Civil War.) Indeed it can be signalled in many simple ways (flashing lamps, blasts of sound, drums, smoke signals) and is much easier to learn than more sophisticated codes like the Morse code. However, it is also somewhat less efficient than the more complex codes.

The simple representation also lends itself to steganography. The figures from one to five can be indicated by knots in a string, stitches on a quilt, letters squashed together before a wider space, or many other simple ways.

38.3 Cryptography

The Polybius cipher can be used with a keyword like the Playfair cipher. By itself the Polybius square is not terribly secure, even if used with a mixed alphabet. The pairs of digits, taken together, just form a simple substitution in which the symbols happen to be pairs of digits. In this sense it is just another encoding which can be cracked with simple frequency analysis. However a Polybius square offers the possibility of fractionation, leading toward Claude E. Shannon's confusion and diffusion. As such, it is a useful component in several ciphers such as the ADFGVX cipher, the Nihilist cipher, and the bifid cipher.

Polybius was responsible for a useful tool in telegraphy which allowed letters to be easily signaled using a numerical system. This idea also lends itself to cryptographic manipulation and steganography.

38.4 See also

- Fryctoria
- Punnett square
- Straddling checkerboard
- Tap code

- Topics in cryptography

38.5 References

[1] Hist. X.45.6 ff.

Chapter 39

Rail fence cipher

"Rail fence" redirects here. For the actual fence, see split-rail fence.

The **rail fence cipher** (also called a zigzag cipher) is a form of transposition cipher. It derives its name from the way in which it is encoded.

39.1 Method

In the rail fence cipher, the plaintext is written downwards and diagonally on successive "rails" of an imaginary fence, then moving up when we reach the bottom rail. When we reach the top rail, the message is written downwards again until the whole plaintext is written out. The message is then read off in rows. For example, if we have 3 "rails" and a message of 'WE ARE DISCOVERED. FLEE AT ONCE', the cipherer writes out:

```
W . . . E . . . C . . R . . L . . T . . . E . E . R . D . S . O
. E . E . F . E . A . O . C . . . A . . . I . . . V . . . D . . . E . .
. N . .
```

Then reads off to get the ciphertext:

WECRL TEERD SOEEF EAOCA IVDEN

39.2 Problems with the rail fence cipher

The rail fence cipher is not very strong; the number of practical keys (the number of rails) is small enough that a cryptanalyst can try them all by hand.

39.3 Zigzag cipher

The term zigzag cipher may refer to the rail fence cipher as described above. However, it may also refer to a different type of cipher system that looks like a zigzag line going from the top of the page to the bottom. As described in Fletcher Pratt's *Secret and Urgent*, it is "written by ruling a sheet of paper in vertical columns, with a letter at the head of each column. A dot is made for each letter of the message in the proper column, reading from top to bottom of the sheet. The letters at the head of the columns are then cut off, the ruling erased and the message of dots sent along to the recipient, who, knowing the width of the columns and the arrangement of the letters at the top, reconstitutes the diagram and reads what it has to say."[1]

39.4 See also

- Transposition cipher
- Scytale

39.5 References

[1] Pratt, Fletcher (1939). *Secret and Urgent: The story of codes and ciphers*. Aegean Park Press. pp. 143–144. ISBN 0-89412-261-4.

- Helen Fouché Gaines, *Cryptanalysis, a study of ciphers and their solution*, Dover, 1956, ISBN 0-486-20097-3

39.6 External links

- American Cryptogram Association - Railfence
- cipher online
- The Railfence Cipher

Chapter 40

Rasterschlüssel 44

Rasterschlüssel 44 (RS 44) was a manual cipher system, used by the German Wehrmacht during the Second World War.

The cipher was designed by the astronomer and sometime cryptographer Dr. Drh.c.mult Walter Fricke while working as a conscript in Section IIb, of Group 2 of OKW/Chi and introduced in March 1944 and Allied forces codebreakers had considerable difficulties in breaking it.

Cryptanalysis, if successful, generally required a 40 letter crib (known plaintext) and some two weeks, making the tactical information outdated before it could be exploited. The combination of strength and ease of use made RS 44 an ideal hand cipher.

40.1 Design

The cipher is a transposition based grille cipher, consisting of a grid with 25 columns and 24 rows. Each row contains 10 randomly placed white cells (to be filled with text) and 15 black cells.

The columns are labeled with shuffled digraphs and numbers and the rows with dipgraphs. The key sheet also contains two letter substitution alphabets to encode place names, prior to encryption, and a letter conversion alphabet to encode digraphs.

The text is written in the grid, starting from a randomly chosen position, row by row, from left to right. The ciphertext is taken column by column, following the numbering of the columns. The first column to be taken is calculated from the minutes of the message time, the letter count of the message text and the randomly chosen column of the start cell.

The message key contains the start position of the text in the grid, designated by the column and header dipgraphs. The digraphs for the message key are encoded with the letter conversion table and then included in the message header.

The secret variable start cell and first column ensure a unique transposition for each message, making multiple anagramming very difficult.

40.2 Sources

- Schlüsselanleitung zum Rasterschlüssel 44 (RS 44) Retrieved from the Foundation for German communication and related technologies

- Rasterschlüssel 44 - The Epitome of hand Field Ciphers Cryptologia, Volume 28, Issue 2, 2004

40.3 External links

- Rasterschlüssel 44 on Cipher Machines and Cryptology

- Rasterschlüssel 44 on Interesting Ciphers

Chapter 41

Reihenschieber

The **Reihenschieber** (English: Row Slider) was a hand cipher system used by the German Bundeswehr. It was developed during 1957 and used until the early 1960s, although information about the system was released publicly only in 1992. The system was used to encrypt high-grade messages.

The device consists of a frame on which a set of "rods" are clipped: plastic square sticks containing a sequence of digits (0-9) and dots on each face. 10 rods are used, chosen out of a set of 26.

The Reihenschieber generated a stream of pseudo-random digits. These digits are then used to navigate through a number of printed tables to create a polyalphabetic cipher.

41.1   See also

- Topics in cryptography

41.2   References

- Michael van der Meulen: Reihenschieber, in *Cryptologia*, Vol. 20(2), 1996, pp 141–154.

41.3   External links

- Information and a photograph — by Jerry Proc

Chapter 42

Reservehandverfahren

Reservehandverfahren (RHV) (English: Reserve Hand Procedure) was a German Naval World War II hand-cipher system used as a backup method when no working Enigma machine was available.[1]

The cipher had two stages: a transposition followed by bigram substitution. In the transposition stage, the cipher clerk would write out the plaintext into a "cage" — a shape on a piece of paper. Pairs of letters were then substituted using a set of bigram tables.[2]

The Reservehandverfahren cipher was first solved at Bletchley Park in June 1941 by means of documents captured from U-boat *U-110* the previous month. Thereafter it was solved using cryptanalysis for over three years. Some 1,400 signals were read during that period. The section working on RHV was headed by historian Sir John H. Plumb. The decrypts were sometimes useful in themselves for the intelligence that they contained, but were more important as a source for cribs for solving Naval Enigma.[2]

A Mediterranean variant was known as **Schlüssel Henno**, which was first tackled — unsuccessfully — in May 1943. It wasn't until after a capture of cipher documents from a raid on Mykonos in April 1944 that the Naval Section was able to read Henno. With over 1,000 signals a month, up to 30 people were assigned to solve the messages. A separate version of RHV existed for U-boats to use, called RHV Offizier. Only six messages in RHV Offizier were broken at Bletchley, three by James Hogarth. The work was abandoned in August 1944 after it was found the intelligence value of the decrypts was "rather disappointing".[3]

42.1 See also

- Werftschlüssel

42.2 Sources

[1] The Enigma General Procedure Manual, 1940

[2] Hugh Sebag-Montefiore, *Enigma: Battle for the Code*, 2000, pp. 213–214.

[3] Christoper Morris, "Navy Ultra's Poor Relations", pp. 238–239, in F. H. Hinsley and Alan Stripp, *The Codebreakers: The Inside Story of Bletchley Park*, 1993.

42.3 External links

- A detailed description of the German Reservehandverfahren (R.H.V.) M.Dv.Nr. 929/1

- Scanned cover of a 1940 Reservehandverfahren manual

- The Archives of German technical Manuals 1900-1945 (includes the Reservehandverfahren manual)

Chapter 43

ROT13

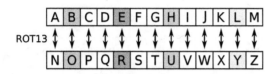

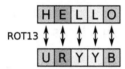

ROT13 replaces each letter by its partner 13 characters further along the alphabet. For example, HELLO becomes URYYB (or, reversing, URYYB becomes HELLO again).

ROT13 ("**rotate by 13 places**", sometimes hyphenated **ROT-13**) is a simple letter substitution cipher that replaces a letter with the letter 13 letters after it in the alphabet. ROT13 is a special case of the Caesar cipher, developed in ancient Rome.

Because there are 26 letters (2×13) in the basic Latin alphabet, ROT13 is its own inverse; that is, to undo ROT13, the same algorithm is applied, so the same action can be used for encoding and decoding. The algorithm provides virtually no cryptographic security, and is often cited as a canonical example of weak encryption.[1]

ROT13 is used in online forums as a means of hiding spoilers, punchlines, puzzle solutions, and offensive materials from the casual glance. ROT13 has been described as the "Usenet equivalent of a magazine printing the answer to a quiz upside down".[2] ROT13 has inspired a variety of letter and word games on-line, and is frequently mentioned in newsgroup conversations.

43.1 Description

Applying ROT13 to a piece of text merely requires examining its alphabetic characters and replacing each one by

the letter 13 places further along in the alphabet, wrapping back to the beginning if necessary.[3] A becomes N, B becomes O, and so on up to M, which becomes Z, then the sequence continues at the beginning of the alphabet: N becomes A, O becomes B, and so on to Z, which becomes M. Only those letters which occur in the English alphabet are affected; numbers, symbols, whitespace, and all other characters are left unchanged. Because there are 26 letters in the English alphabet and 26 = 2 × 13, the ROT13 function is its own inverse:[3]

$$\mathrm{ROT}_{13}(\mathrm{ROT}_{13}(x)) \;=\; x \text{ for any basic Latin-alphabet text } x.$$

In other words, two successive applications of ROT13 restore the original text (in mathematics, this is sometimes called an *involution*; in cryptography, a *reciprocal cipher*).

The transformation can be done using a lookup table, such as the following:

For example, in the following joke, the punchline has been obscured by ROT13:

Why did the chicken cross the road? Gb trg gb gur bgure fvqr!

Transforming the entire text via ROT13 form, the answer to the joke is revealed:

Jul qvq gur puvpxra pebff gur ebnq? To get to the other side!

A second application of ROT13 would restore the original.

43.2 Usage

ROT13 was in use in the net.jokes newsgroup by the early 1980s.[4] It is used to hide potentially offensive jokes, or to obscure an answer to a puzzle or other spoiler.[3][5] A shift of thirteen was chosen over other values, such as three as in the original Caesar cipher, because thirteen is the value for which encoding and decoding are equivalent, thereby allowing the convenience of a single command for both.[5] ROT13 is typically supported as a built-in feature to news-reading software.[5] Email addresses are also sometimes encoded with ROT13 to hide them from less sophisticated spam bots.[6] It is also used to circumvent email screening and spam filtering. By obscuring an email's content, the screening algorithm is unable to identify the email as, for instance, a security risk, and allows it into the recipient's in-box.

ROT13 is an example of the encryption algorithm known as a Caesar cipher, attributed to Julius Caesar in the 1st century BC.[7]

In encrypted, normal, English-language text of any significant size, ROT13 is recognizable from some letter/word patterns. The words "n", "V" (capitalized only), and "gur" (ROT13 for "a", "I", and "the"), and words ending in "yl" ("ly") are examples.

ROT13 is not intended to be used where secrecy is of any concern—the use of a constant shift means that the encryption effectively has no key, and decryption requires no more knowledge than the fact that ROT13 is in use. Even without this knowledge, the algorithm is easily broken through frequency analysis.[3] Because of its utter unsuitability for real secrecy, ROT13 has become a catchphrase to refer to any conspicuously weak encryption scheme; a critic might claim that "56-bit DES is little better than ROT13 these days". Also, in a play on real terms like "double DES", the terms "double ROT13", "ROT26", or "2ROT13" crop up with humorous intent, including a spoof academic paper "On the 2ROT13 Encryption Algorithm".[8] As applying ROT13 to an already ROT13-encrypted text restores the original plaintext, ROT26 is equivalent to no encryption at all. By extension, triple-ROT13 (used in joking analogy with 3DES) is equivalent to regular ROT13.

In December 1999, it was found that Netscape Communicator used ROT13 as part of an insecure scheme to store email passwords.[9] In 2001, Russian programmer Dimitry Sklyarov demonstrated that an eBook vendor, New Paradigm Research Group (NPRG), used ROT13 to encrypt their documents; it has been speculated that NPRG may have mistaken the ROT13 toy example—provided with the Adobe eBook software development kit—for a serious encryption scheme.[10] Windows XP uses ROT13 on some of its registry keys.[11] ROT13 is also used in the Unix fortune program to encrypt potentially offensive dicta.

43.3 Letter games and net culture

ROT13 provides an opportunity for letter games. Some words will, when transformed with ROT13, produce another word. Examples of 7-letter pairs in the English language are *abjurer* and *nowhere*, and *Chechen* and *purpura*. Other examples of words like these are shown in the table.[12] The pair *gnat* and *tang* is an interesting example which are both ROT13 reciprocals and (taken together) a palindrome.

The 1989 International Obfuscated C Code Contest (IOCCC) included an entry by Brian Westley. Westley's computer program can be encoded in ROT13 or reversed and still compiles correctly. Its operation, when executed, is either to perform ROT13 encoding on, or to reverse its input.[13]

The newsgroup alt.folklore.urban coined a word—*furrfu*—that was the ROT13 encoding of the frequently encoded utterance "sheesh". "Furrfu" evolved in mid-1992 as a response to postings repeating urban myths on alt.folklore.urban, after some posters complained that "Sheesh!" as a response to newcomers was being overused.[14]

43.4 Variants

ROT5 is a practice similar to ROT13 that applies to numeric digits (0 to 9). ROT13 and ROT5 can be used together in the same message (ROT13.5).

ROT47 is a derivative of ROT13 which, in addition to scrambling the basic letters, also treats numbers and common symbols. Instead of using the sequence A–Z as the alphabet, ROT47 uses a larger set of characters from the common character encoding known as ASCII. Specifically, the 7-bit printable characters, excluding space, from decimal 33 '!' through 126 '~', 94 in total, taken in the order of the numerical values of their ASCII codes, are rotated by 47 positions, without special consideration of case. For example, the character A is mapped to p, while a is mapped to 2. The use of a larger alphabet produces a more thorough obfuscation than that of ROT13; for example, a telephone number such as +1-415-839-6885 is not obvious at first sight from the scrambled result Z\c`d\gbh\eggd. On the other hand, because ROT47 introduces numbers and symbols into the mix without discrimination, it is more immediately obvious that the text has been enciphered.

Example:

The Quick Brown Fox Jumps Over The Lazy Dog.

enciphers to

%96 "F:4< qC@H? u@I yF>AD ~G6C %96 {2KJ s@8]

The GNU C library, a set of standard routines available for use in computer programming, contains a function—**memfrob()**[15]—which has a similar purpose to ROT13, although it is intended for use with arbitrary binary data. The function operates by combining each byte with the binary pattern 00101010 (42) using the exclusive or (XOR) operation. This effects a simple XOR cipher. Like ROT13, XOR (and therefore memfrob()) is self-reciprocal, and provides a similar, virtually absent, level of security.

43.5 Implementation

The ROT13 and ROT47 are fairly easy to implement using the Unix terminal application tr; to encrypt the string "The Quick Brown Fox Jumps Over The Lazy Dog" in ROT13:

$ # Map upper case A-Z to N-ZA-M and lower case a-z to n-za-m $ echo "The Quick Brown Fox Jumps Over The Lazy Dog" | tr 'A-Za-z' 'N-ZA-Mn-za-m' Gur Dhvpx Oebja Sbk Whzcf Bire Gur Ynml Qbt

and the same string for ROT47:

$ echo "The Quick Brown Fox Jumps Over The Lazy Dog" | tr '\!-~' 'P-~\!-O' %96 "F:4< qC@H? u@I yF>AD ~G6C %96 {2KJ s@8

In Emacs, one can ROT13 the buffer or a selection with the following commands:[16]

M-x toggle-rot13-mode M-x rot13-other-window M-x rot13-region

and in the Vim text editor, one can ROT13 a selection with the command:[17]

g?

43.6 See also

- Cryptanalysis

43.7 References

[1] Christopher Swenson (17 March 2008). *Modern Cryptanalysis: Techniques for Advanced Code Breaking*. John Wiley & Sons. p. 5. ISBN 9780470135938.

[2] Horrocks, Bruce (28 June 2003). "UCSM Cabal Circular #207-a". *Usenet group uk.comp.sys.mac (Message ID UZ36hgCSoh$+EwqG@nodomain.nodomain.us)*. Retrieved 17 September 2007.

[3] Schneier, Bruce (1996). *Applied Cryptography* (Second ed.). John Wiley & Sons. p. 11. ISBN 0-471-11709-9.

[4] Early uses of ROT13 found in the Google USENET archive date back to 8 October 1982, posted to the net.jokes newsgroup .

[5] Raymond, Eric S. (ed.) (29 December 2003). "ROT13". *The Jargon File, 4.4.7*. Retrieved 19 September 2007.

[6] Ferner, Matt. "How to Hide Email Addresses From Spam Bots". PracticalEcommerce. Retrieved 12 June 2014.

[7] Kahn, David. *The Codebreakers: The Story of Secret Writing*. New York: Macmillan. ISBN 0-684-83130-9.

[8] "On the 2ROT13 Encryption Algorithm" (PDF). Prüfziffernberechnung in der Praxis. 25 September 2004. Retrieved 20 September 2007.

[9] Hollebeek, Tim; Viega, John. "Bad Cryptography in the Netscape Browser: A Case Study". Reliable Software Technologies. Retrieved 28 August 2014.

[10] Perens, Bruce (1 September 2001). "Dimitry Sklyarov: Enemy or friend?". ZDNet News. Retrieved 3 February 2011.

[11] Ferri, Vic (4 January 2007). "The Count Keys in the Windows Registry". ABC: All 'Bout Computers. Retrieved 20 September 2007.

[12] De Mulder, Tom. "ROT13 Words". *Furrfu!*. Retrieved 19 September 2007.

[13] Westley, Brian (1989). "westley.c". *IOCCC*. Retrieved 13 August 2007.

[14] "Furrfu". Foldoc. 25 October 1995. Retrieved 3 October 2016.

[15] "5.10 Trivial Encryption". *The GNU C Library Reference Manual*. Free Software Foundation. 3 December 2006. Retrieved 20 September 2007.

[16] Emacs manual

[17] Best of VIM Tips, gVIM's Key Features zzapper

43.8 External links

- ROT13.com—Simply decode ROT13 text by copy/paste

- Leet Key - Firefox Addon—Leet Key is a Firefox add-on that encodes and decodes ROT13 text (among other text transformations)

- Bookmark to encode/decode ROT13 text—Use this bookmark to encode/decode selected text on a web page using ROT13

Chapter 44

Running key cipher

In classical cryptography, the **running key cipher** is a type of polyalphabetic substitution cipher in which a text, typically from a book, is used to provide a very long keystream. Usually, the book to be used would be agreed ahead of time, while the passage to be used would be chosen randomly for each message and secretly indicated somewhere in the message.

44.1 Example

The text used is *The C Programming Language* (1978 edition), and the *tabula recta* is the tableau. The plaintext is "Flee at once".

Page 63, line 1 is selected as the running key:

> errors can occur in several places. A label has...

The running key is then written under the plaintext:

The message is then sent as "JCVSR LQNPS". However, unlike a Vigenère cipher, the message is extended, the key is not repeated; the key text itself is used as the key. If the message is extended, such as, "Flee at once. We are discovered", then the running key continues as before:

To determine where to find the running key, a fake block of five ciphertext characters is subsequently added, with three denoting the page number, and two the line number, using A=0, B=1 etc. to encode digits. Such a block is called an **indicator block**. The indicator block will be inserted as the second last of each message. (It should be noted that many other schemes are possible for hiding indicator blocks.) Thus page 63, line 1 encodes as "AGDAB" (06301).

This yields a final message of "JCVSR LQNPS YGUIM QAWXS AGDAB MECTO".

44.2 Variants

Modern variants of the running key cipher often replace the traditional *tabula recta* with bitwise exclusive or, operate on whole bytes rather than alphabetic letters, and derive their running keys from large files. Apart from possibly greater entropy density of the files, and the ease of automation, there is little practical difference between such variants and traditional methods.

44.2.1 Permutation generated running keys

A more compact running key can be used if one combinatorially generates text using several start pointers (or combination rules). For example, rather than start at one place (a single pointer), one could use several start pointers and xor together the streams to form a new running key, similarly skip rules can be used. What is exchanged then is a series of pointers to the running key book and/or a series of rules for generating the new permuted running key from the initial key text. (These may be exchanged via public key encryption or in person. They may also be changed frequently without changing the running key book).

44.2.2 Ciphertext appearing to be plaintext

Traditional ciphertext appears to be quite different from plaintext. To address this problem, one variant outputs "plaintext" words instead of "plaintext" letters as the ciphertext output. This is done by creating an "alphabet" of words (in practice multiple words can correspond to each ciphertext output character). The result is a ciphertext output which looks like a long sequence of plaintext words (the process can be nested). Theoretically, this is no different from using standard ciphertext characters as output. However, plaintext-looking ciphertext may result in a "human in the loop" to try to mistakenly interpret it as decoded plaintext.

An example would be BDA (Berkhoff deflater algorithm), each ciphertext output character has at least one noun, verb, adjective and adverb associated with it. (E.g. (at least) one of each for every ASCII character). Grammatically plausible sentences are generated as ciphertext output. Decryption requires mapping the words back to ASCII, and then decrypting the characters to the real plaintext using the running key. Nested-BDA will run the output through the reencryption process several times, producing several layers of "plaintext-looking" ciphertext - each one potentially requiring "human-in-the-loop" to try to interpret its non-existent semantic meaning.

44.2.3 Gromark cipher

The "Gromark cipher" ("Gronsfeld cipher with mixed alphabet and running key") uses a running numerical key formed by adding successive pairs of digits.[1] The VIC cipher uses a similar lagged Fibonacci generator.

44.3 Security

If the running key is truly random, never reused, and kept secret, the result is a one-time pad, a method that provides perfect secrecy (reveals no information about the plaintext). However, if (as usual) the running key is a block of text in a natural language, security actually becomes fairly poor, since that text will have non-random characteristics which can be used to aid cryptanalysis. As a result, the entropy per character of both plaintext and running key is low, and the combining operation is easily inverted.

To attack the cipher, a cryptanalyst runs guessed probable plaintexts along the ciphertext, subtracting them out from each possible position. When the result is a chunk of something intelligible, there is a high probability that the guessed plain text is correct for that position (as either actual plaintext, or part of the running key). The 'chunk of something intelligible' can then often be extended at either end, thus providing even more probable plaintext - which can in turn be extended, and so on. Eventually it is likely that the source of the running key will be identified, and the jig is up.

There are several ways to improve the security. The first and most obvious is to use a secret mixed alphabet tableau instead of a *tabula recta*. This does indeed greatly complicate matters but it is not a complete solution. Pairs of plaintext and running key characters are far more likely to be high frequency pairs such as 'EE' rather than, say, 'QQ'. The skew this causes to the output frequency distribution is smeared by the fact that it is quite possible that 'EE' and 'QQ' map to the same ciphertext character, but nevertheless the distribution is not flat. This may enable the cryptanalyst to deduce part of the tableau, then proceed as before (but with gaps where there are sections missing from the reconstructed tableau).

Another possibility is to use a key text that has more entropy per character than typical English. For this purpose, the KGB advised agents to use documents like almanacs and trade reports, which often contain long lists of random-looking numbers.

Another problem is that the keyspace is surprisingly small. Suppose that there are 100 million key texts that might plausibly be used, and that on average each has 11 thousand possible starting positions. To an opponent with a massive collection of possible key texts, this leaves possible a brute force search of the order of 2^{40}, which by computer cryptography standards is a relatively easy target. (See permutation generated running keys above for an approach to this problem).

44.4 Confusion

Because both ciphers classically employed novels as part of their key material, many sources confuse the book cipher and the running key cipher. They are really only very distantly related. The running key cipher is a polyalphabetic substitution, the book cipher is a homophonic substitution. Perhaps the distinction is most clearly made by the fact that a running cipher would work best of all with a book of random numbers, whereas such a book (containing no text) would be useless for a book cipher.

44.5 See also

- Polyalphabetic substitution

- Substitution cipher

- Book cipher

- Topics in cryptography

44.6 References

[1] American Cryptogram Association. "The ACA and You". 2016.

Chapter 45

Scytale

For other uses, see Scytale (disambiguation).

In cryptography, a **scytale** (/ˈskɪtəli:/, rhymes ap-

A scytale

proximately with Italy; also transliterated **skytale**, Greek σκυτάλη "baton") is a tool used to perform a transposition cipher, consisting of a cylinder with a strip of parchment wound around it on which is written a message. The ancient Greeks, and the Spartans in particular, are said to have used this cipher to communicate during military campaigns.

The recipient uses a rod of the same diameter on which the parchment is wrapped to read the message. It has the advantage of being fast and not prone to mistakes—a necessary property when on the battlefield. It can, however, be easily broken. Since the strip of parchment hints strongly at the method, the ciphertext would have to be transferred to something less suggestive, somewhat reducing the advantage noted.

45.1 Encrypting

Suppose the rod allows one to write four letters around in a circle and five letters down the side of it. The plaintext could be: "Help me I am under attack".

To encrypt, one simply writes across the leather:

```
| | | | | | | H | E | L | P | M | | |__| E | I | A | M | U |__|
| | N | D | E | R | A | | | T | T | A | C | K | | | | | | | |
```

so the ciphertext becomes, "HENTEIDTLAEAPMRC-MUAK" after unwinding.

45.2 Decrypting

To decrypt, all one must do is wrap the leather strip around the rod and read across. The ciphertext is: "HENTEIDT-LAEAPMRCMUAK" Every fifth letter will appear on the same line, so the plaintext becomes:

HELPM EIAMU NDERA TTACK

After inserting spaces, the message is revealed: "Help me I am under attack".

45.3 History

From indirect evidence, the scytale was first mentioned by the Greek poet Archilochus, who lived in the 7th century BC. Other Greek and Roman writers during the following centuries also mentioned it, but it was not until Apollonius of Rhodes (middle of the 3rd century BC) that a clear indication of its use as a cryptographic device appeared. A description of how it operated is not known from before Plutarch (50-120 AD):

The dispatch-scroll is of the following character. When the ephors send out an admiral or a general, they make two round pieces of wood exactly alike in length and thickness, so that each corresponds to the other in its dimensions, and keep one themselves, while they give the other to their envoy. These pieces of wood they call scytalae. Whenever, then, they wish to send some secret and important message, they make a scroll of parchment

long and narrow, like a leathern strap, and wind it round their scytale, leaving no vacant space thereon, but covering its surface all round with the parchment. After doing this, they write what they wish on the parchment, just as it lies wrapped about the scytale; and when they have written their message, they take the parchment off and send it, without the piece of wood, to the commander. He, when he has received it, cannot otherwise get any meaning out of it,--since the letters have no connection, but are disarranged,--unless he takes his own scytale and winds the strip of parchment about it, so that, when its spiral course is restored perfectly, and that which follows is joined to that which precedes, he reads around the staff, and so discovers the continuity of the message. And the parchment, like the staff, is called scytale, as the thing measured bears the name of the measure.
—Plutarch, *Lives* (Lysander 19), ed. Bernadotte Perrin.

Due to difficulties in reconciling the description of Plutarch with the earlier accounts, and circumstantial evidence such as the cryptographic weakness of the device, several authors have suggested that the scytale was used for conveying messages in plaintext and that Plutarch's description is mythological.[1]

45.4 Message Authentication Hypothesis

An alternative hypothesis is that the scytale was used for message authentication rather than encryption.[2] Only if the sender wrote the message around a scytale of the same diameter as the receiver's would the receiver be able to read it. It would therefore be difficult for enemy spies to inject false messages into the communication between two commanders.

45.5 See also

- Caesar cipher

45.6 References

[1] Kelly 1998, pp. 244–260

[2] Russel, Frank (1999). *Information Gathering in Classical Greece*. U. Michigan Press. p. 117. ISBN 0-472-11064-0.

45.7 Further reading

- Kelly, Thomas (July 1998). "The Myth of the Skytale". *Cryptologia*. **22**: 244–260. doi:10.1080/0161-119891886902.

- Collard, Brigitte (2004). "Les Langages Secrets Dans l'Antiquité Gréco-Romaine" (in French). Universite Catholique de Louvain. (English: Secret Languages in Graeco-Roman Antiquity)

Chapter 46

Substitution cipher

In cryptography, a **substitution cipher** is a method of encoding by which units of plaintext are replaced with ciphertext, according to a fixed system; the "units" may be single letters (the most common), pairs of letters, triplets of letters, mixtures of the above, and so forth. The receiver deciphers the text by performing the inverse substitution.

Substitution ciphers can be compared with transposition ciphers. In a transposition cipher, the units of the plaintext are rearranged in a different and usually quite complex order, but the units themselves are left unchanged. By contrast, in a substitution cipher, the units of the plaintext are retained in the same sequence in the ciphertext, but the units themselves are altered.

There are a number of different types of substitution cipher. If the cipher operates on single letters, it is termed a **simple substitution cipher**; a cipher that operates on larger groups of letters is termed **polygraphic**. A **monoalphabetic cipher** uses fixed substitution over the entire message, whereas a **polyalphabetic cipher** uses a number of substitutions at different positions in the message, where a unit from the plaintext is mapped to one of several possibilities in the ciphertext and vice versa.

46.1 Simple substitution

Substitution of single letters separately—**simple substitution**—can be demonstrated by writing out the alphabet in some order to represent the substitution. This is termed a **substitution alphabet**. The cipher alphabet may be shifted or reversed (creating the Caesar and Atbash ciphers, respectively) or scrambled in a more complex fashion, in which case it is called a *mixed alphabet* or *deranged alphabet*. Traditionally, mixed alphabets may be created by first writing out a keyword, removing repeated letters in it, then writing all the remaining letters in the alphabet in the usual order.

Using this system, the keyword "zebras" gives us the following alphabets:

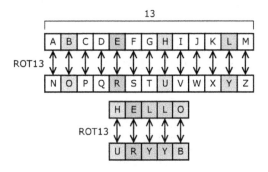

ROT13 is a Caesar cipher, a type of substitution cipher. In ROT13, the alphabet is rotated 13 steps.

A message of

flee at once. we are discovered!

enciphers to

SIAA ZQ LKBA. VA ZOA RFPBLUAOAR!

Traditionally, the ciphertext is written out in blocks of fixed length, omitting punctuation and spaces; this is done to help avoid transmission errors and to disguise word boundaries from the plaintext. These blocks are called "groups", and sometimes a "group count" (i.e., the number of groups) is given as an additional check. Five-letter groups are traditional, dating from when messages used to be transmitted by telegraph:

SIAAZ QLKBA VAZOA RFPBL UAOAR

If the length of the message happens not to be divisible by five, it may be padded at the end with "nulls". These can be any characters that decrypt to obvious nonsense, so the receiver can easily spot them and discard them.

The ciphertext alphabet is sometimes different from the plaintext alphabet; for example, in the pigpen cipher, the ciphertext consists of a set of symbols derived from a grid. For example:

X MARKS THE SPOT

Such features make little difference to the security of a scheme, however – at the very least, any set of strange symbols can be transcribed back into an A-Z alphabet and dealt with as normal.

In lists and catalogues for salespeople, a very simple encryption is sometimes used to replace numeric digits by letters.

Example: MAT would be used to represent 120.

46.1.1 Security for simple substitution ciphers

A disadvantage of this method of derangement is that the last letters of the alphabet (which are mostly low frequency) tend to stay at the end. A stronger way of constructing a mixed alphabet is to perform a columnar transposition on the ordinary alphabet using the keyword, but this is not often done.

Although the number of possible keys is very large ($26! \approx 2^{88.4}$, or about 88 bits), this cipher is not very strong, and is easily broken. Provided the message is of reasonable length (see below), the cryptanalyst can deduce the probable meaning of the most common symbols by analyzing the frequency distribution of the ciphertext—frequency analysis. This allows formation of partial words, which can be tentatively filled in, progressively expanding the (partial) solution (see frequency analysis for a demonstration of this). In some cases, underlying words can also be determined from the pattern of their letters; for example, *attract*, *osseous*, and words with those two as the root are the only common English words with the pattern *ABBCADB*. Many people solve such ciphers for recreation, as with cryptogram puzzles in the newspaper.

According to the unicity distance of English, 27.6 letters of ciphertext are required to crack a mixed alphabet simple substitution. In practice, typically about 50 letters are needed, although some messages can be broken with fewer if unusual patterns are found. In other cases, the plaintext can be contrived to have a nearly flat frequency distribution, and much longer plaintexts will then be required by the user.

46.2 Homophonic substitution

An early attempt to increase the difficulty of frequency analysis attacks on substitution ciphers was to disguise plaintext letter frequencies by **homophony**. In these ciphers, plaintext letters map to more than one ciphertext symbol. Usually, the highest-frequency plaintext symbols

The forged nomenclator message used in the Babington Plot

are given more equivalents than lower frequency letters. In this way, the frequency distribution is flattened, making analysis more difficult.

Since more than 26 characters will be required in the ciphertext alphabet, various solutions are employed to invent larger alphabets. Perhaps the simplest is to use a numeric substitution 'alphabet'. Another method consists of simple variations on the existing alphabet; uppercase, lowercase, upside down, etc. More artistically, though not necessarily more securely, some homophonic ciphers employed wholly invented alphabets of fanciful symbols.

One variant is the **nomenclator**. Named after the public official who announced the titles of visiting dignitaries, this cipher combines a small codebook with large homophonic substitution tables. Originally the code was restricted to the names of important people, hence the name of the cipher; in later years it covered many common words and place names as well. The symbols for whole words (*codewords* in modern parlance) and letters (*cipher* in modern parlance) were not distinguished in the ciphertext. The Rossignols' Great Cipher used by Louis XIV of France was one; after it went out of use, messages in French archives were unbroken for several hundred years.

Nomenclators were the standard fare of diplomatic correspondence, espionage, and advanced political conspiracy from the early fifteenth century to the late eighteenth century; most conspirators were and have remained less cryptographically sophisticated. Although government intelligence cryptanalysts were systematically breaking nomenclators by the mid-sixteenth century, and superior systems had been available since 1467, the usual response to cryptanalysis was simply to make the tables larger. By the late eighteenth century, when the system was beginning to die out, some nomenclators had 50,000 symbols.

Nevertheless, not all nomenclators were broken; today, cryptanalysis of archived ciphertexts remains a fruitful area of historical research.

The Beale ciphers are another example of a homophonic cipher. This is a story of buried treasure that was described in 1819–21 by use of a ciphered text that was keyed to the Declaration of Independence. Here each ciphertext character was represented by a number. The number was determined by taking the plaintext character and finding a word in the Declaration of Independence that started with that character and using the numerical position of that word in the Declaration of Independence as the encrypted form of that letter. Since many words in the Declaration of Independence start with the same letter, the encryption of that character could be any of the numbers associated with the words in the Declaration of Independence that start with that letter. Deciphering the encrypted text character X (which is a number) is as simple as looking up the Xth word of the Declaration of Independence and using the first letter of that word as the decrypted character.

Another homophonic cipher was described by Stahl[2][3] and was one of the first attempts to provide for computer security of data systems in computers through encryption. Stahl constructed the cipher in such a way that the number of homophones for a given character was in proportion to the frequency of the character, thus making frequency analysis much more difficult.

The book cipher and straddling checkerboard are types of homophonic cipher.

Francesco I Gonzaga, Duke of Mantua, is the one who use the earliest example of Homophonic Substitution cipher in 1401 for correspondence with one Simone de Crema.[4][5]

46.3 Polyalphabetic substitution

Main article: Polyalphabetic cipher

Polyalphabetic substitution ciphers were first described in 1467 by Leone Battista Alberti in the form of disks. Johannes Trithemius, in his book *Steganographia* (Ancient Greek for "hidden writing") introduced the now more standard form of a *tableau* (see below; ca. 1500 but not pub-

lished until much later). A more sophisticated version using mixed alphabets was described in 1563 by Giovanni Battista della Porta in his book, *De Furtivis Literarum Notis* (Latin for "On concealed characters in writing").

In a polyalphabetic cipher, multiple cipher alphabets are used. To facilitate encryption, all the alphabets are usually written out in a large table, traditionally called a *tableau*. The tableau is usually 26×26, so that 26 full ciphertext alphabets are available. The method of filling the tableau, and of choosing which alphabet to use next, defines the particular polyalphabetic cipher. All such ciphers are easier to break than once believed, as substitution alphabets are repeated for sufficiently large plaintexts.

One of the most popular was that of Blaise de Vigenère. First published in 1585, it was considered unbreakable until 1863, and indeed was commonly called *le chiffre indéchiffrable* (French for "indecipherable cipher").

In the Vigenère cipher, the first row of the tableau is filled out with a copy of the plaintext alphabet, and successive rows are simply shifted one place to the left. (Such a simple tableau is called a *tabula recta*, and mathematically corresponds to adding the plaintext and key letters, modulo 26.) A keyword is then used to choose which ciphertext alphabet to use. Each letter of the keyword is used in turn, and then they are repeated again from the beginning. So if the keyword is 'CAT', the first letter of plaintext is enciphered under alphabet 'C', the second under 'A', the third under 'T', the fourth under 'C' again, and so on. In practice, Vigenère keys were often phrases several words long.

In 1863, Friedrich Kasiski published a method (probably discovered secretly and independently before the Crimean War by Charles Babbage) which enabled the calculation of the length of the keyword in a Vigenère ciphered message. Once this was done, ciphertext letters that had been enciphered under the same alphabet could be picked out and attacked separately as a number of semi-independent simple substitutions - complicated by the fact that within one alphabet letters were separated and did not form complete words, but simplified by the fact that usually a *tabula recta* had been employed.

As such, even today a Vigenère type cipher should theoretically be difficult to break if mixed alphabets are used in the tableau, if the keyword is random, and if the total length of ciphertext is less than 27.6 times the length of the keyword. These requirements are rarely understood in practice, and so Vigenère enciphered message security is usually less than might have been.

Other notable polyalphabetics include:

- The Gronsfeld cipher. This is identical to the Vigenère except that only 10 alphabets are used, and so the "keyword" is numerical.

- The Beaufort cipher. This is practically the same as the Vigenère, except the *tabula recta* is replaced by a backwards one, mathematically equivalent to ciphertext = key - plaintext. This operation is *self-inverse*, whereby the same table is used for both encryption and decryption.

- The autokey cipher, which mixes plaintext with a key to avoid periodicity.

- The running key cipher, where the key is made very long by using a passage from a book or similar text.

Modern stream ciphers can also be seen, from a sufficiently abstract perspective, to be a form of polyalphabetic cipher in which all the effort has gone into making the keystream as long and unpredictable as possible.

46.4   Polygraphic substitution

In a polygraphic substitution cipher, plaintext letters are substituted in larger groups, instead of substituting letters individually. The first advantage is that the frequency distribution is much flatter than that of individual letters (though not actually flat in real languages; for example, 'TH' is much more common than 'XQ' in English). Second, the larger number of symbols requires correspondingly more ciphertext to productively analyze letter frequencies.

To substitute *pairs* of letters would take a substitution alphabet 676 symbols long ($26^2 = 676$). In the same *De Furtivis Literarum Notis* mentioned above, della Porta actually proposed such a system, with a 20 x 20 tableau (for the 20 letters of the Italian/Latin alphabet he was using) filled with 400 unique glyphs. However the system was impractical and probably never actually used.

The earliest practical **digraphic cipher** (pairwise substitution), was the so-called Playfair cipher, invented by Sir Charles Wheatstone in 1854. In this cipher, a 5 x 5 grid is filled with the letters of a mixed alphabet (two letters, usually I and J, are combined). A digraphic substitution is then simulated by taking pairs of letters as two corners of a rectangle, and using the other two corners as the ciphertext (see the Playfair cipher main article for a diagram). Special rules handle double letters and pairs falling in the same row or column. Playfair was in military use from the Boer War through World War II.

Several other practical polygraphics were introduced in 1901 by Felix Delastelle, including the bifid and four-square ciphers (both digraphic) and the trifid cipher (probably the first practical trigraphic).

The Hill cipher, invented in 1929 by Lester S. Hill, is a polygraphic substitution which can combine much larger groups of letters simultaneously using linear algebra. Each letter is treated as a digit in base 26: A = 0, B =1, and so on. (In a variation, 3 extra symbols are added to make the basis prime.) A block of n letters is then considered as a vector of n dimensions, and multiplied by a n x n matrix, modulo 26. The components of the matrix are the key, and should be random provided that the matrix is invertible in $\mathbb{Z}_{26}^n$ (to ensure decryption is possible). A mechanical version of the Hill cipher of dimension 6 was patented in 1929.[6]

The Hill cipher is vulnerable to a known-plaintext attack because it is completely linear, so it must be combined with some non-linear step to defeat this attack. The combination of wider and wider weak, linear diffusive steps like a Hill cipher, with non-linear substitution steps, ultimately leads to a substitution-permutation network (e.g. a Feistel cipher), so it is possible – from this extreme perspective – to consider modern block ciphers as a type of polygraphic substitution.

46.5   Mechanical substitution ciphers

Between circa World War I and the widespread availability of computers (for some governments this was approximately the 1950s or 1960s; for other organizations it was a decade or more later; for individuals it was no earlier than 1975), mechanical implementations of polyalphabetic substitution ciphers were widely used. Several inventors had similar ideas about the same time, and rotor cipher machines were patented four times in 1919. The most important of the resulting machines was the Enigma, especially in the versions used by the German military from approximately 1930. The Allies also developed and used rotor machines (e.g., SIGABA and Typex).

All of these were similar in that the substituted letter was chosen electrically from amongst the huge number of possible combinations resulting from the rotation of several letter disks. Since one or more of the disks rotated mechanically with each plaintext letter enciphered, the number of alphabets used was substantially more than astronomical. Early versions of these machine were, nevertheless, breakable. William F. Friedman of the US Army's SIS early found vulnerabilities in Hebern's rotor machine, and GC&CS's Dillwyn Knox solved versions of the Enigma machine (those without the "plugboard") well before WWII began. Traffic protected by essentially all of the German military Enigmas was broken by Allied cryptanalysts, most notably those at Bletchley Park, beginning with the German Army variant used in the early 1930s. This version was broken by inspired mathematical insight by Marian Rejewski in Poland.

No messages protected by the SIGABA and Typex machines were ever, so far as is publicly known, broken.

46.6 The one-time pad

Main article: One-time pad

One type of substitution cipher, the one-time pad, is quite special. It was invented near the end of WWI by Gilbert Vernam and Joseph Mauborgne in the US. It was mathematically proven unbreakable by Claude Shannon, probably during WWII; his work was first published in the late 1940s. In its most common implementation, the one-time pad can be called a substitution cipher only from an unusual perspective; typically, the plaintext letter is combined (not substituted) in some manner (e.g., XOR) with the key material character at that position.

The one-time pad is, in most cases, impractical as it requires that the key material be as long as the plaintext, *actually* random, used once and *only* once, and kept entirely secret from all except the sender and intended receiver. When these conditions are violated, even marginally, the one-time pad is no longer unbreakable. Soviet one-time pad messages sent from the US for a brief time during WWII used non-random key material. US cryptanalysts, beginning in the late 40s, were able to, entirely or partially, break a few thousand messages out of several hundred thousand. (See Venona project)

In a mechanical implementation, rather like the Rockex equipment, the one-time pad was used for messages sent on the Moscow-Washington *hot line* established after the Cuban missile crisis.

46.7 Substitution in modern cryptography

Substitution ciphers as discussed above, especially the older pencil-and-paper hand ciphers, are no longer in serious use. However, the cryptographic concept of substitution carries on even today. From a sufficiently abstract perspective, modern bit-oriented block ciphers (e.g., DES, or AES) can be viewed as substitution ciphers on an enormously large binary alphabet. In addition, block ciphers often include smaller substitution tables called S-boxes. See also substitution-permutation network.

46.8 Substitution ciphers in popular culture

- Sherlock Holmes breaks a substitution cipher in "The Adventure of the Dancing Men". There, the cipher remained undeciphered for years if not decades; not due to its difficulty, but because no one suspected it to be a code, instead considering it childish scribblings.

- The Al Bhed language in *Final Fantasy X* is actually a substitution cipher, although it is pronounced phonetically (i.e. "you" in English is translated to "oui" in Al Bhed, but is pronounced the same way that "oui" is pronounced in French).

- The Minbari's alphabet from the *Babylon 5* series is a substitution cipher from English.

- The language in *Starfox Adventures: Dinosaur Planet* spoken by native Saurians and Krystal is also a substitution cipher of the English alphabet.

- The television program *Futurama* contained a substitution cipher in which all 26 letters were replaced by symbols and called "Alien Language". This was deciphered rather quickly by the die hard viewers by showing a "Slurm" ad with the word "Drink" in both plain English and the Alien language thus giving the key. Later, the producers created a second alien language that used a combination of replacement and mathematical Ciphers. Once the English letter of the alien language is deciphered, then the numerical value of that letter (0 for "A" through 25 for "Z" respectively) is then added (modulo 26) to the value of the previous letter showing the actual intended letter. These messages can be seen throughout every episode of the series and the subsequent movies.

- At the end of every season 1 episode of the cartoon series *Gravity Falls*, during the credit roll, there is one of three simple substitution ciphers: A −3 Caesar cipher (hinted by "3 letters back" at the end of the opening sequence), an Atbash cipher, or a letter-to-number simple substitution cipher. The season 1 finale encodes a message with all three. In the second season, Vigenère ciphers are used in place of the various monoalphabetic ciphers, each using a key hidden within the its episode.

- In the Artemis Fowl series by Eoin Colfer there are three substitution ciphers; Gnommish, Centaurean and Eternean, which run along the bottom of the pages or are somewhere else within the books.

- In *Bitterblue*, the third novel by Kristin Cashore, substitution ciphers serve as an important form of coded communication.

- In the 2013 video game *BioShock Infinite*, there are substitution ciphers hidden throughout the game in which the player must find code books to help decipher them and gain access to a surplus of supplies.

46.9   See also

- Ban (unit) with Centiban Table

- Copiale cipher

- Dvorak encoding

- Leet

- Vigenère cipher

- Topics in cryptography

46.10   References

[1] David Crawford / Mike Esterl, *At Siemens, witnesses cite pattern of bribery*, The Wall Street Journal, January 31, 2007: "Back at Munich headquarters, he [Michael Kutschenreuter, a former Siemens-Manager] told prosecutors, he learned of an encryption code he alleged was widely used at Siemens to itemize bribe payments. He said it was derived from the phrase "Make Profit," with the phrase's 10 letters corresponding to the numbers 1-2-3-4-5-6-7-8-9-0. Thus, with the letter A standing for 2 and P standing for 5, a reference to "file this in the APP file" meant a bribe was authorized at 2.55 percent of sales. - A spokesman for Siemens said it has no knowledge of a "Make Profit" encryption system."

[2] Stahl, Fred A., *On Computational Security*, University of Illinois, 1974

[3] Stahl, Fred A. "A homophonic cipher for computational cryptography", afips, pp. 565, 1973 Proceedings of the National Computer Conference, 1973

[4] David Salomon. Coding for Data and Computer Communications. Springer, 2005.

[5] Fred A. Stahl. "A homophonic cipher for computational cryptography" Proceedings of the national computer conference and exposition (AFIPS '73), pp. 123–126, New York, USA, 1973.

[6] "Message Protector patent US1845947".   February 14, 1929. Retrieved November 9, 2013.

46.11   External links

- quipqiup An automated tool for solving simple substitution ciphers both with and without known word boundaries.

- CrypTool Exhaustive free and open-source e-learning tool to perform and break substititution ciphers and many more.

- Substitution Cipher Toolkit Application that can - amongst other things - decrypt texts encrypted with substitution cipher *automatically*

- SCB Cipher Solver A monoalphabetic cipher cracker.

- Monoalphabetic Cipher Implementation for Encrypting File (C Language).

- Substitution cipher implementation with Caesar and Atbash ciphers (Java)

- Online simple substitution implementation (Flash)

- Online simple substitution implementation for MAKEPROFIT code (CGI script: Set input in URL, read output in web page)

- Monoalphabetic Substitution Breaking A Monoalphabetic Encryption System Using a Known Plaintext Attack

- http://cryptoclub.math.uic.edu/substitutioncipher/sub2.htm

Chapter 47

Tabula recta

```
 |A B C D E F G H I J K L M N O P Q R S T U V W X Y Z
A|A B C D E F G H I J K L M N O P Q R S T U V W X Y Z
B|B C D E F G H I J K L M N O P Q R S T U V W X Y Z A
C|C D E F G H I J K L M N O P Q R S T U V W X Y Z A B
D|D E F G H I J K L M N O P Q R S T U V W X Y Z A B C
E|E F G H I J K L M N O P Q R S T U V W X Y Z A B C D
F|F G H I J K L M N O P Q R S T U V W X Y Z A B C D E
G|G H I J K L M N O P Q R S T U V W X Y Z A B C D E F
H|H I J K L M N O P Q R S T U V W X Y Z A B C D E F G
I|I J K L M N O P Q R S T U V W X Y Z A B C D E F G H
J|J K L M N O P Q R S T U V W X Y Z A B C D E F G H I
K|K L M N O P Q R S T U V W X Y Z A B C D E F G H I J
L|L M N O P Q R S T U V W X Y Z A B C D E F G H I J K
M|M N O P Q R S T U V W X Y Z A B C D E F G H I J K L
N|N O P Q R S T U V W X Y Z A B C D E F G H I J K L M
O|O P Q R S T U V W X Y Z A B C D E F G H I J K L M N
P|P Q R S T U V W X Y Z A B C D E F G H I J K L M N O
Q|Q R S T U V W X Y Z A B C D E F G H I J K L M N O P
R|R S T U V W X Y Z A B C D E F G H I J K L M N O P Q
S|S T U V W X Y Z A B C D E F G H I J K L M N O P Q R
T|T U V W X Y Z A B C D E F G H I J K L M N O P Q R S
U|U V W X Y Z A B C D E F G H I J K L M N O P Q R S T
V|V W X Y Z A B C D E F G H I J K L M N O P Q R S T U
W|W X Y Z A B C D E F G H I J K L M N O P Q R S T U V
X|X Y Z A B C D E F G H I J K L M N O P Q R S T U V W
Y|Y Z A B C D E F G H I J K L M N O P Q R S T U V W X
Z|Z A B C D E F G H I J K L M N O P Q R S T U V W X Y
```

Tabula recta

In cryptography, the **tabula recta** (from Latin *tabula rēcta*) is a square table of alphabets, each row of which is made by shifting the previous one to the left. The term was invented by the German author and monk Johannes Trithemius[1] in 1508, and used in his **Trithemius cipher**.

47.1 Trithemius cipher

The Trithemius was published by Johannes Trithemius in his book *Polygraphia*, which is credited with being the first published work on cryptology.

Trithemius used the *tabula recta* to define a polyalphabetic cipher, which was equivalent to Leon Battista Alberti's cipher disk except that the alphabets are not mixed. The *tabula recta* is often referred to in discussing pre-computer ciphers, including the Vigenère cipher and Blaise de Vigenère's less well-known autokey cipher. All polyalphabetic ciphers based on Caesar ciphers can be described in terms of the *tabula recta*.

It uses a letter square with the 26 letters of the alphabet following 26 rows of additional letters, each shifted once to the left. This creates 26 different Caesar ciphers.[2]

The resulting ciphertext appears as a random string or block of data. However, the letter frequencies are just shifted: If e is the most frequent letter in the cleartext and the shift is 3, then h will be the most frequent letter in the ciphertext. Especially if a person is aware that this method is being used, it becomes easy to break. The cipher is vulnerable to attack because it lacks a key, which is said to break Kerckhoffs's principle, a rule of cryptology.[2]

47.1.1 Improvements

In 1553, an important extension to Trithemius's method was developed by Giovan Battista Bellaso called the Vigenère cipher.[3] Bellaso added a key to switch cipher alphabets every letter. This method was misattributed to Blaise de Vigenère, who published a similar autokey cipher in 1586.

47.2 Usage

Each alphabet is shifted one letter to the left from the one above it. This forms 26 rows of shifted alphabets, ending with Z (as shown in image).

Data is encrypted by switching each letter of the message with the letter directly below, using the first shifted alphabet. The next letter is switched by using the second shifted alphabet, and this continues until you have encrypted the entire message.[4]

In order to encrypt a plaintext, one locates the row with the first letter to be encrypted, and the column with the first letter of the key. The letter where the line and column cross is the ciphertext letter.

Programmatically, the cipher is computable, assigning $A = 0, B = 1...$, then the encryption process is $ciphertext =$

$(plaintext + key)(\mod 26)$. Decryption follows the same process, exchanging ciphertext and plaintext. key may be defined as the value of a letter from a companion cipher-text in a running key cipher, a constant for a Caesar cipher, or a zero-based counter with some period in Trithemius's usage.[4]

47.3 References

47.3.1 Citations

[1] Sabrina Rosas, Data privacy, page 63

[2] Salmon, Data privacy, page 63

[3] Salomon, Coding for data, page 249

[4] Kahn, page 136

47.3.2 Sources

- Salomon, David (2005). *Coding for Data and Computer Communications*. Springer. ISBN 0-387-21245-0.

- Salomon, David (2003). *Data privacy and security*. Springer. ISBN 0-387-00311-8.

- King, Francis X. (1989). *Modern Ritual Magic: The Rise of Western Occultism* (2nd ed.). Prism Press. ISBN 1-85327-032-6.

- Kahn, David (1996). *The Codebreakers*. Simon and Schuster. ISBN 0-684-83130-9.

Chapter 48

Tap code

The **tap code**, sometimes called the **knock code**, is a way to encode text messages on a letter-by-letter basis in a very simple way. The message is transmitted using a series of tap sounds, hence its name.

The tap code has been commonly used by prisoners to communicate with each other. The method of communicating is usually by tapping either the metal bars, pipes, or the walls inside a cell.

48.1 Design

The tap code is based on a Polybius square using a 5×5 grid of letters representing all the letters of the Latin alphabet, except for K, which is represented by C.

The listener only needs to discriminate the timing of the taps to isolate letters.

Each letter is communicated by tapping two numbers

- the first designating the row
- the second designating the column

For example, to specify the letter "B", one taps once, pauses, and then taps twice.

Or to communicate the word "water", the cipher would be the following (the pause between each number in a pair is smaller than the pause between letters):

The letter "X" is used to break up sentences, and "K" for acknowledgements.

Because of the difficulty and length of time required for specifying a single letter, prisoners often devise abbreviations and acronyms for common items or phrases, such as "GN" for *Good night*, or "GBU" for *God bless you*.[1]

By comparison, Morse code is harder to send by tapping or banging because it requires the ability to create two differently sounding taps (representing the *dits* and *dahs* of Morse code). A Morse code novice would also need to keep a "cheat sheet" until he or she remembers every letter's code, which the captors would likely confiscate. Tap code can be more easily decoded in one's head by mentally using the table. For example, if you hear four knocks, you would think A... F... L... Q as the count increased; then after the pause, you hear three knocks and think Q... R... S to arrive at the letter S.

48.2 History

The origins of this encoding go back to the Polybius square of Ancient Greece. As the "knock code", a Cyrillic script version is said to have been used by nihilist prisoners of the Russian czars.[2] The knock code is featured in Arthur Koestler's classic 1941 work *Darkness at Noon*.[3]

United States prisoners of war during the Vietnam War are most known for having used the tap code. It was introduced in June 1965 by four POWs held in the Hỏa Lò Prison "Hanoi Hilton" prison: Captain Carlyle "Smitty" Harris, Lieutenant Phillip Butler, Lieutenant Robert Peel, and Lieutenant Commander Robert Shumaker.[1] Harris had heard of the tap code being used by prisoners in World War II[4] and remembered a United States Air Force instructor who had discussed it as well.[1]

In Vietnam, the tap code became a very successful way for otherwise isolated prisoners to communicate.[4] POWs would use the tap code in order to communicate to each other between cells in a way which the guards would be unable to pick up on. They used it to communicate everything from what questions interrogators were asking (in order for everyone to stay consistent with a deceptive story), to who was hurt and needed others to donate meager food rations. It was easy to teach and newly arrived prisoners became fluent in it within a few days.[5][6] It was even used when prisoners were sitting next to each other but not allowed to talk, by tapping on anothers' thigh.[6] By overcoming isolation with the tap code, prisoners were able to maintain a chain of command and keep up morale.[4]

48.3   References

[1] "'Return with Honor': The Tap Code". *American Experience*. PBS. 1999. Retrieved 2008-04-08.

[2] David Kahn, *The Codebreakers – The Story of Secret Writing*. 1967. ISBN 978-0-684-83130-5.

[3] Koestler, Arthur, *Darkness at Noon* (1941). Translated by Daphne Hardy. See page 19 of the Bantam Publishing paperback, 1981 printing for more info.

[4] Staff Sgt. Jason Tudor (1998-03-18). "Vets, Flyers discuss ideology, time in POW camps". Air Force News Service. Retrieved 2008-04-08.

[5] McCain, John; Mark Salter (1999). *Faith of My Fathers*. Random House. pp. 211–12. ISBN 0-375-50191-6.

[6] Brace, Ernest C. (1988). *A Code to Keep: The true story of America's longest held civilian prisoner of war in Vietnam*. St. Martin's Press. pp. 171–72, 187–88. ISBN 0-7090-3560-8.

48.4   External links

- Online Tap Code Encoder/Decoder

- Russian Prison Tap Codes

- http://www.premioceleste.it/opera/ido:260668/ Artist An Degrida's Tap Code artistic illustration

Chapter 49

Templar cipher

The **Templar cipher** is an encoding method which has been claimed to have been used by the Masonic Knights Templar.

It is a variant of the Masonic "Pigpen cipher", based on variations of a Maltese Cross shape (instead of on a # grid shape). I and J are the same in Templar cipher.

49.1 Key

49.2 References

49.3 External links

- http://freemasonry.bcy.ca/texts/templars_cipher. html

Chapter 50

Transposition cipher

In cryptography, a **transposition cipher** is a method of encryption by which the positions held by units of plaintext (which are commonly characters or groups of characters) are shifted according to a regular system, so that the ciphertext constitutes a permutation of the plaintext. That is, the order of the units is changed (the plaintext is reordered). Mathematically a bijective function is used on the characters' positions to encrypt and an inverse function to decrypt.

Following are some implementations.

50.1   Rail Fence cipher

The Rail Fence cipher is a form of transposition cipher that gets its name from the way in which it is encoded. In the rail fence cipher, the plaintext is written downwards on successive "rails" of an imaginary fence, then moving up when we get to the bottom. The message is then read off in rows. For example, using three "rails" and a message of 'WE ARE DISCOVERED. FLEE AT ONCE', the cipherer writes out:

```
W . . . E . . . C . . . R . . . L . . . T . . . E . E . R . D . S . O
. E . E . F . E . A . O . C . . . A . . . I . . . V . . . D . . . E . .
. N . .
```

Then reads off:

WECRL TEERD SOEEF EAOCA IVDEN

(The cipherer has broken this ciphertext up into blocks of five to help avoid errors. This is a common technique used to make the cipher more easily readable. The spacing is not related to spaces in the plaintext and so does not carry any information about the plaintext.)

The rail fence cipher was used by the ancient Greeks in the scytale, a mechanical system of producing a transposition cipher. The system consisted of a cylinder and a ribbon that was wrapped around the cylinder. The message to be encrypted was written on the coiled ribbon. The letters of the original message would be rearranged when the ribbon was uncoiled from the cylinder. However, the message was easily decrypted when the ribbon was recoiled on a cylinder of the same diameter as the encrypting cylinder.[1]

50.2   Route cipher

In a route cipher, the plaintext is first written out in a grid of given dimensions, then read off in a pattern given in the key. For example, using the same plaintext that we used for rail fence:

W R I O R F E O E E E S V E L A N J A D C E D E T C X

The key might specify "spiral inwards, clockwise, starting from the top right". That would give a cipher text of:

EJXCTEDECDAEWRIORFEONALEVSE

Route ciphers have many more keys than a rail fence. In fact, for messages of reasonable length, the number of possible keys is potentially too great to be enumerated even by modern machinery. However, not all keys are equally good. Badly chosen routes will leave excessive chunks of plaintext, or text simply reversed, and this will give cryptanalysts a clue as to the routes.

A variation of the route cipher was the Union Route Cipher, used by Union forces during the American Civil War. This worked much like an ordinary route cipher, but transposed whole words instead of individual letters. Because this would leave certain highly sensitive words exposed, such words would first be concealed by code. The cipher clerk may also add entire null words, which were often chosen to make the ciphertext humorous.

50.3   Columnar transposition

In a columnar transposition, the message is written out in rows of a fixed length, and then read out again column by column, and the columns are chosen in some scrambled order. Both the width of the rows and the permutation of the columns are usually defined by a keyword. For example, the keyword ZEBRAS is of length 6 (so the rows are of length 6), and the permutation is defined by the alphabetical order of the letters in the keyword. In this case, the order would be "6 3 2 4 1 5".

In a regular columnar transposition cipher, any spare spaces are filled with nulls; in an irregular columnar transposition cipher, the spaces are left blank. Finally, the message is read off in columns, in the order specified by the keyword. For example, suppose we use the keyword ZEBRAS and the message WE ARE DISCOVERED. FLEE AT ONCE. In a regular columnar transposition, we write this into the grid as follows:

6 3 2 4 1 5 W E A R E D I S C O V E R E D F L E E A T
O N C E Q K J E U

Providing five nulls (QKJEU) at the end. The ciphertext is then read off as:

EVLNE ACDTK ESEAQ ROFOJ DEECU WIREE

In the irregular case, the columns are not completed by nulls:

6 3 2 4 1 5 W E A R E D I S C O V E R E D F L E E A T
O N C E

This results in the following ciphertext:

EVLNA CDTES EAROF ODEEC WIREE

To decipher it, the recipient has to work out the column lengths by dividing the message length by the key length. Then he can write the message out in columns again, then re-order the columns by reforming the key word.

In a variation, the message is blocked into segments that are the key length long and to each segment the same permutation (given by the key) is applied. This is equivalent to a columnar transposition where the read-out is by rows instead of columns.

Columnar transposition continued to be used for serious purposes as a component of more complex ciphers at least into the 1950s.

50.4 Double transposition

A single columnar transposition could be attacked by guessing possible column lengths, writing the message out in its columns (but in the wrong order, as the key is not yet known), and then looking for possible anagrams. Thus to make it stronger, a double transposition was often used. This is simply a columnar transposition applied twice. The same key can be used for both transpositions, or two different keys can be used.

As an example, we can take the result of the irregular columnar transposition in the previous section, and perform a second encryption with a different keyword, STRIPE, which gives the permutation "564231":

5 6 4 2 3 1 E V L N A C D T E S E A R O F O D E E C
W I R E E

As before, this is read off columnwise to give the ciphertext:

CAEEN SOIAE DRLEF WEDRE EVTOC

If multiple messages of exactly the same length are encrypted using the same keys, they can be anagrammed simultaneously. This can lead to both recovery of the messages, and to recovery of the keys (so that every other message sent with those keys can be read).

During World War I, the German military used a double columnar transposition cipher, changing the keys infrequently. The system was regularly solved by the French, naming it Übchi, who were typically able to quickly find the keys once they'd intercepted a number of messages of the same length, which generally took only a few days. However, the French success became widely known and, after a publication in *Le Matin*, the Germans changed to a new system on 18 November 1914.[2]

During World War II, the double transposition cipher was used by Dutch Resistance groups, the French Maquis and the British Special Operations Executive (SOE), which was in charge of managing underground activities in Europe.[3] It was also used by agents of the American Office of Strategic Services[4] and as an emergency cipher for the German Army and Navy.

Until the invention of the VIC cipher, double transposition was generally regarded as the most complicated cipher that an agent could operate reliably under difficult field conditions.

50.5 Myszkowski transposition

A variant form of columnar transposition, proposed by Émile Victor Théodore Myszkowski in 1902, requires a keyword with recurrent letters. In usual practice, subsequent occurrences of a keyword letter are treated as if the next letter in alphabetical order, *e.g.,* the keyword TOMATO yields a numeric keystring of "532164."

In Myszkowski transposition, recurrent keyword letters are numbered identically, TOMATO yielding a keystring of "432143."

4 3 2 1 4 3 W E A R E D I S C O V E R E D F L E E A T
O N C E

Plaintext columns with unique numbers are transcribed

downward; those with recurring numbers are transcribed left to right:

ROFOA CDTED SEEEA CWEIV RLENE

50.6 Disrupted transposition

In a disrupted transposition, certain positions in a grid are blanked out, and not used when filling in the plaintext. This breaks up regular patterns and makes the cryptanalyst's job more difficult.

50.7 Grilles

Main article: Grille (cryptography)

Another form of transposition cipher uses *grilles*, or physical masks with cut-outs. This can produce a highly irregular transposition over the period specified by the size of the grille, but requires the correspondents to keep a physical key secret. Grilles were first proposed in 1550, and were still in military use for the first few months of World War One.

50.8 Scytale

A cipher from ancient Greek times that was used to make encryptions. The device used to make these ciphers was a rod with a polygon base, which was wrapped in paper. People then, could write on the paper horizontally. When the paper was removed from the device, it would make a strip of letters that seemed randomized. The only way to read the message would be to have a Scytale machine of your own.

50.9 Detection and cryptanalysis

Since transposition does not affect the frequency of individual symbols, simple transposition can be easily detected by the cryptanalyst by doing a frequency count. If the ciphertext exhibits a frequency distribution very similar to plaintext, it is most likely a transposition. This can then often be attacked by anagramming—sliding pieces of ciphertext around, then looking for sections that look like anagrams of English words, and solving the anagrams. Once such anagrams have been found, they reveal information about the transposition pattern, and can consequently be extended.

Simpler transpositions also often suffer from the property that keys very close to the correct key will reveal long sections of legible plaintext interspersed by gibberish. Consequently, such ciphers may be vulnerable to optimum seeking algorithms such as genetic algorithms.[5]

A detailed description of the cryptanalysis of a German transposition cipher can be found in chapter 7 of Herbert Yardley's "The American Black Chamber."

50.10 Combinations

Transposition is often combined with other techniques such as evaluation methods. For example, a simple substitution cipher combined with a columnar transposition avoids the weakness of both. Replacing high frequency ciphertext symbols with high frequency plaintext letters does not reveal chunks of plaintext because of the transposition. Anagramming the transposition does not work because of the substitution. The technique is particularly powerful if combined with fractionation (see below). A disadvantage is that such ciphers are considerably more laborious and error prone than simpler ciphers.

50.11 Fractionation

Transposition is particularly effective when employed with fractionation - that is, a preliminary stage that divides each plaintext symbol into several ciphertext symbols. For example, the plaintext alphabet could be written out in a grid, then every letter in the message replaced by its co-ordinates (see Polybius square and Straddling checkerboard). Another method of fractionation is to simply convert the message to Morse code, with a symbol for spaces as well as dots and dashes.

When such a fractionated message is transposed, the components of individual letters become widely separated in the message, thus achieving Claude E. Shannon's diffusion. Examples of ciphers that combine fractionation and transposition include the bifid cipher, the trifid cipher, the ADFGVX cipher and the VIC cipher.

Another choice would be to replace each letter with its binary representation, transpose that, and then convert the new binary string into the corresponding ASCII characters. Looping the scrambling process on the binary string multiple times before changing it into ASCII characters would likely make it harder to break. Many modern block ciphers use more complex forms of transposition related to this simple idea.

50.12 See also

- Substitution cipher

- Ban (unit)

- Topics in cryptography

50.13 Notes

[1] Smith, Laurence Dwight (1955) [1943], *Cryptography / The Science of Secret Writing*, New York: Dover, pp. 16, 92–93

[2] Kahn, pp. 301-304.

[3] Kahn, pp. 535 and 539.

[4] Kahn, p. 539.

[5] DOI:10.1080/0161-119391867863 Robert A. J. Matthews pages 187-201

50.14 References

- Kahn, David. The Codebreakers: The Story of Secret Writing. Rev Sub. Scribner, 1996.

- Yardley, Herbert. The American Black Chamber. Bobbs-Merrill, 1931.

Chapter 51

Trifid cipher

In classical cryptography, the **Trifid cipher** is a cipher invented around 1901 by Felix Delastelle, which extends the concept of the Bifid cipher to a third dimension, allowing each symbol to be fractionated into 3 elements instead of two.

While the Bifid uses the Polybius square to turn each symbol into coordinates on a 5×5 (or 6×6) square, the trifid turns them into coordinates on a $3 \times 3 \times 3$ cube.

As with the bifid, this is then combined with transposition to achieve diffusion.

However a higher degree of diffusion is achieved because each output symbol depends on 3 input symbols instead of two.

Thus the Trifid was the first practical trigraphic substitution.

51.1 Operation

Several variants probably exist of the Trifid cipher, and there are known Cyrillic variations of it as well.

Below is one example but most decoders work slightly differently.

All Trifid systems use TABLE,ROW,COLUMN or some variation of it.

The principle remains the same but the result will be completely different.

The Dutch version of this page has another example. And there are also different ways to fill out a keyword in the tables: spread out horizontally or fill up one table first.

First, a mixed alphabet cubic analogue of the Polybius square is drawn up:

In theory, the message is then converted to its coordinates in this grid; in practice, it is more convenient to write the triplets of trits out in a table, like so:

Then the coordinates are written out vertically beneath the message:

T R E A T Y E N D S B O E R W A R . 2 1 3 3 2 1 3 3 2
1 1 1 3 1 2 3 1 3 3 1 1 3 3 1 1 1 2 3 2 3 1 1 2 3 1 1 3 2 1 2
3 3 1 2 2 3 3 1 1 2 3 2 2 3

They are then read out in rows:

2 1 3 3 2 1 3 3 2 1 1 1 3 1 2 3 1 3 3 1 1 3 3 1 1 1 2 3 2 3 1
1 2 3 1 1 3 2 1 2 3 3 1 2 2 3 3 1 1 2 3 2 2 3

Then divided up into triplets again, and the triplets turned back into letters using the table:

213 321 332 111 312 313 311 331 112 323 112 311 321
233 122 331 123 223 **M U A F N . E Q R K R E U T X
Q B W**

In this way, each ciphertext character depends on three plaintext characters, so the trifid is a trigraphic cipher. To decrypt, the procedure is simply reversed.

51.2 Dimensions

As the bifid concept is extended to higher dimensions, we are much less free in our choice of parameters.

Since $2^3 = 8 < 26 < 27 = 3^3$, our cube needs to have a side length of at least three in order to fit in the 26 letters of the alphabet. But if we go even to 4, then our symbol set would have $4^3 = 64$ symbols, which is probably too much for classical cryptography. Thus, the trifid is only ever implemented with a $3 \times 3 \times 3$ cube, and each coordinate is indicated by a trinary digit, or trit. Incidentally, note that since this gives us 27 symbols, we will have one extra. In the example above, the period or full-stop was used.

If we increase the dimensions further to four, noting that $2^4 = 16 < 26$, we still need a side length of 3 - giving a symbol set of size $3^4 = 81$, far more than we need. If we go one step further, to five dimensions, then we only need a side length of 2, since $2^5 = 32 > 26$. But such a binary encoding - 5 bits - is what occurs in Baudot code for telegraphic purposes. Breaking letters into bits and manipulating the bits individually is the hallmark of modern cryp-

112

tography. Thus, in a sense, the trifid cipher can be thought to stand on the border between classical cryptography's ancient Polybius square, and the binary manipulations of the modern world.

51.3 See also

Other ciphers by Delastelle:

- Four-square cipher (related to Playfair)
- Bifid cipher (similar to Trifid)

Chapter 52

Two-square cipher

The **Two-square cipher**, also called **double Playfair**, is a manual symmetric encryption technique .[1] It was developed to ease the cumbersome nature of the large encryption/decryption matrix used in the four-square cipher while still being slightly stronger than the (single-square) Playfair cipher.

The technique encrypts pairs of letters (*digraphs*), and thus falls into a category of ciphers known as polygraphic substitution ciphers. This adds significant strength to the encryption when compared with monographic substitution ciphers which operate on single characters. The use of digraphs makes the two-square technique less susceptible to frequency analysis attacks, as the analysis must be done on 676 possible digraphs rather than just 26 for monographic substitution. The frequency analysis of digraphs is possible, but considerably more difficult - and it generally requires a much larger ciphertext in order to be useful.

52.1 Using two-square

The two-square cipher comes in two varieties - horizontal and vertical. The vertical two-square uses two 5 by 5 matrices one above the other. The horizontal two-square has the two 5 by 5 matrices side by side. Each of the 5 by 5 matrices contains the letters of the alphabet (usually omitting "Q" or putting both "I" and "J" in the same location to reduce the alphabet to fit). The alphabets in both squares are generally mixed alphabets, each based on some keyword or phrase.

To generate the 5 by 5 matrices, one would first fill in the spaces in the matrix with the letters of a keyword or phrase (dropping any duplicate letters), then fill the remaining spaces with the rest of the letters of the alphabet in order (again omitting "Q" to reduce the alphabet to fit). The key can be written in the top rows of the table, from left to right, or in some other pattern, such as a spiral beginning in the upper-left-hand corner and ending in the center. The keyword together with the conventions for filling in the 5 by 5 table constitute the cipher key. The two-square algorithm

allows for two separate keys, one for each matrix.

As an example, here are the vertical two-square matrices for the keywords "example" and "keyword:"

E X A M P L B C D F G H I J K N O R S T U V W Y Z
K E Y W O R D A B C F G H I J L M N P S T U V X Z

52.2 Algorithm

Encryption using two-square is basically the same as the system used in four-square, except that the plaintext and ciphertext digraphs use the same matrixes.

To encrypt a message, one would Follow these steps:

- Split the payload message into digraphs. (*help me obi wan kenobi* becomes *he lp me ob iw an ke no bi*)

- For a vertical two-square, the first character of both plaintext and ciphertext digraphs uses the top matrix, while the second character uses the bottom.

- For a horizontal two-square, the first character of both digraphs uses the left matrix, while the second character uses the right.

- Find the first letter in the digraph in the upper/left text matrix.

E X A M *P* L B C D F G H I J K N O R S T U V W Y Z
K E Y W O R D A B C F G H I J L M N P S T U V X Z

- Find the second letter in the digraph in the lower/right plaintext matrix.

E X A M *P* L B C D F G H I J K N O R S T U V W Y Z
K E Y W O R D A B C F G H I J L M N *P* S T U V X Z

- A rectangle is defined by the two plaintext characters and the opposite corners define the ciphertext digraph.

114

E X A M P **L** B C **D** F G H I J K N O R S T U V W Y Z
K E Y W O R D A B C F G H I J **L** M N **P** S T U V X Z

Using the vertical two-square example given above, we can encrypt the following plaintext:

Plaintext: he lp me ob iw an ke no bi Ciphertext: HE DL XW SD JY AN HO TK DG

Here is the same two-square written out again but blanking all of the values that aren't used for encrypting the digraph "LP" into "DL"

- - - - - L - - D -
- L - - P - - - - - -

The rectangle rule used to encrypt and decrypt can be seen clearly in this diagram. The method for decrypting is identical to the method for encryption.

Just like Playfair (and unlike four-square), there are special circumstances when the two letters in a digraph are in the same column for vertical two-square or in the same row for horizontal two-square. For vertical two-square, a plaintext digraph that ends up with both characters in the same column gives the same digraph in the ciphertext. For horizontal two-square, a plaintext digraph with both characters in the same row gives (by convention) that digraph with the characters reversed in the ciphertext. In cryptography this is referred to as a transparency. (The horizontal version is sometimes called a reverse transparency.) Notice in the above example how the digraphs "HE" and "AN" mapped to themselves. A weakness of two-square is that about 20% of digraphs will be transparencies.

E X A M P L B C D F G **H** I J K N O R S T U V W Y Z
K **E** Y W O R D A B C F G H I J L M N P S T U V X Z

52.3 Two-square cryptanalysis

Like most pre-modern era ciphers, the two-square cipher can be easily cracked if there is enough text. Obtaining the key is relatively straightforward if both plaintext and ciphertext are known. When only the ciphertext is known, brute force cryptanalysis of the cipher involves searching through the key space for matches between the frequency of occurrence of digraphs (pairs of letters) and the known frequency of occurrence of digraphs in the assumed language of the original message.

Cryptanalysis of two-square almost always revolves around the transparency weakness. Depending on whether vertical or horizontal two-square was used, either the ciphertext or the reverse of the ciphertext should show a significant number of plaintext fragments. In a large enough ciphertext sample, there are likely to be several transparent digraphs in a row, revealing possible word fragments. From these word fragments the analyst can generate candidate plaintext strings and work backwards to the keyword.

A good tutorial on reconstructing the key for a two-square cipher can be found in chapter 7, "Solution to Polygraphic Substitution Systems," of Field Manual 34-40-2, produced by the United States Army.

52.4 References

[1] "TICOM I-20 Interrogation of SonderFuehrer Dr Fricke of OKW/CHI". *sites.google.com*. NSA. 28 June 1945. p. 2. Retrieved 29 August 2016.

52.5 See also

- Topics in cryptography

- Playfair cipher

Chapter 53

VIC cipher

The **VIC cipher** was a pencil and paper cipher used by the Soviet spy Reino Häyhänen, codenamed "VICTOR".

If the cipher were to be given a modern technical name, it would be known as a "straddling bipartite monoalphabetic substitution superenciphered by modified double transposition."[1] However, by general classification it is part of the Nihilist family of ciphers.

It was arguably the most complex hand-operated cipher ever seen, when it was first discovered. The initial analysis done by the American National Security Agency (NSA) in 1953 did not absolutely conclude that it was a hand cipher, but its placement in a hollowed out 5c coin implied it could be broken by pencil and paper. The VIC cipher remained unbroken until more information about its structure was available.

Although certainly not as complex or secure as modern computer operated stream ciphers or block ciphers, in practice messages protected by it resisted all attempts at cryptanalysis by at least the NSA from its discovery in 1953 until Häyhänen's defection in 1957.

53.1 A revolutionary leap

The VIC cipher can be regarded as the evolutionary pinnacle of the Nihilist cipher family.

The VIC cipher has several important integrated components, including mod 10 chain addition, a lagged Fibonacci generator (a recursive formula used to generate a sequence of pseudorandom digits), a straddling checkerboard, and a disrupted double transposition.

Until the discovery of VIC, it was generally thought that a double transposition alone was the most complex cipher an agent, as a practical matter, could use as a field cipher.

53.2 History

During World War II, several Soviet spy rings communicated to Moscow Centre using two ciphers which are essentially evolutionary improvements on the basic Nihilist cipher. A very strong version was used by Max Clausen in Richard Sorge's network in Japan, and by Alexander Foote in the Lucy spy ring in Switzerland. A slightly weaker version was used by the *Rote Kapelle* network.

In both versions, the plaintext was first converted to digits by use of a straddling checkerboard rather than a Polybius square. This has the advantage of slightly compressing the plaintext, thus raising its unicity distance and also allowing radio operators to complete their transmissions quicker and shut down sooner. Shutting down sooner reduces the risk of the operator being found by enemy radio direction finders. Increasing the unicity distance increases strength against statistical attacks.

Clausen and Foote both wrote their plaintext in English, and memorized the 8 most frequent letters of English (to fill the top row of the checkerboard) through the mnemonic (and slightly menacing) phrase "a sin to err" (dropping the second "r").[2] The standard English straddling checkerboard has 28 character slots and in this cipher the extra two became "full stop" and "numbers shift". Numbers were sent by a numbers shift, followed by the actual plaintext digits in repeated pairs, followed by another shift. Then, similarly to the basic Nihilist, a digital additive was added in, which was called "closing". However a different additive was used each time, so finally a concealed "indicator group" had to be inserted to indicate what additive was used.

Unlike basic Nihilist, the additive was added by non-carrying addition (digit-wise addition modulo 10), thus producing a more uniform output which doesn't leak as much information. More importantly, the additive was generated not through a keyword, but by selecting lines at random from almanacs of industrial statistics. Such books were deemed dull enough to not arouse suspicion if an agent was searched (particularly as the agents' cover stories were as

116

businessmen), and to have such high entropy density as to provide a very secure additive. Of course the figures from such a book are not actually uniformly distributed (there is an excess of "0" and "1" (see Benford's Law), and sequential numbers are likely to be somewhat similar), but nevertheless they have much higher entropy density than passphrases and the like; at any rate, in practice they seem never to have been successfully cryptanalysed.

The weaker version generated the additive from the text of a novel or similar book (at least one *Rote Kapelle* member actually used *The Good Soldier Schweik*, which may not have been a good choice if one expected to be searched by Nazis!) This text was converted to a digital additive using a technique similar to a straddling checkerboard.

The ultimate development along these lines was the VIC cipher, used in the 1950s by Reino Häyhänen. By this time, most Soviet agents were instead using one-time pads. However, despite the theoretical perfection of the one-time pad, in practice they *were* broken, while VIC was not.

53.3 Internal mechanics

53.3.1 Straddling checkerboard

A straddling checkerboard is a device for converting an alphabetic plaintext into digits whilst simultaneously achieving fractionation (a simple form of information diffusion) and data compression relative to other schemes using digits. It also is known as a monôme-binôme cipher.

A straddling checkerboard is set up something like this:

The first row is populated with the ten digits, 0-9. They can be presented in order, as in the above table, or scrambled for additional security. The second row is typically set up with high-frequency letters (mnemonic ESTONIA-R), leaving two blank spots. It has no row label. The remaining rows are labeled with each digit that was not assigned a letter in the second row, and then filled out with the rest of the alphabet.

Much like the ordering of the digits in the top row, the alphabet can be presented in order (as it is here), or scrambled with a keyword or other technique. Since there are 30 slots in our grid, and we skipped two letters in the first row, there will be two spare cells in the other rows. We have filled these cells with a period '.', and a slash '/' to be used as a numeric escape character (indicating that a numeral follows). It doesn't matter where these spares go, so long as the sender and receiver use the same system.

To encipher, a letter in the second row is simply replaced by the number labeling its column. Letters in the third and fourth rows are replaced by a two-digit number representing their row and column numbers. Mapping one-digit numbers to common letters reduces the length of the ciphertext, while also concealing the identities of the two-digit numbers by reducing the frequency of their first digits. Here is an example:[3]

The resulting message, 3113212731223655, may be sent directly (if the table is scrambled), but is usually processed through a second cipher stage, such as transposition or substitution. As a simple example, we will add a secret key number (say, 0452) using modular (non-carrying) arithmetic:

Optionally, we could then use the same straddling checkerboard to convert the ciphertext back into letters:

Deciphering is simply the reverse of these processes. Although the size of groups can vary, deciphering is unambiguous because whenever the next element to be deciphered starts with a 2 or a 6, it is a pair; otherwise, it is a singleton.

53.3.2 Disrupted transposition

In a disrupted transposition, certain positions in a grid are blanked out, and not used when filling in the plaintext. This breaks up regular patterns and makes the cryptanalyst's job more difficult.

53.3.3 Fractionation

Transposition is particularly effective when employed with fractionation - that is, a preliminary stage that divides each plaintext symbol into several ciphertext symbols. For example, the plaintext alphabet could be written out in a grid, then every letter in the message replaced by its co-ordinates (see Polybius square). Another method of fractionation is to simply convert the message to Morse code, with a symbol for spaces as well as dots and dashes.

When such a fractionated message is transposed, the components of individual letters become widely separated in the message, thus achieving Claude E. Shannon's diffusion. Examples of ciphers that combine fractionation and transposition include the bifid cipher, the trifid cipher, the ADFGVX cipher and the VIC cipher.

Another choice would be to replace each letter with its binary representation, transpose that, and then convert the new binary string into the corresponding ASCII characters. Looping the scrambling process on the binary string multiple times before changing it into ASCII characters would likely make it harder to break. Many modern block ciphers use more complex forms of transposition related to this simple idea.

53.4   See also

- Topics in cryptography

53.5   References

[1] David Kahn. "Number One From Moscow". 1993.

[2] "The Rise Of Field Ciphers: straddling checkerboard ciphers" by Greg Goebel 2009

[3] http://asecuritysite.com/security/Coding/straddling?word=attackatdawn

53.6   External links

- FBI page on the hollow nickel case with images of the hollow nickel that contained the VIC encrypted message

- "The Cipher in a Hollow Nickel"

- The VIC Cipher

- Straddling Checkerboards Various different versions of checkerboards on Cipher Machines and Cryptology

- SECOM, a VIC variant with extended checkerboard

Chapter 54

Vigenère cipher

The Vigenère cipher is named for Blaise de Vigenère (pictured). Although Giovan Battista Bellaso had invented the cipher earlier, Vigenère developed a stronger autokey cipher.

The **Vigenère cipher** is a method of encrypting alphabetic text by using a series of different Caesar ciphers based on the letters of a keyword. It is a simple form of polyalphabetic substitution.[1][2]

The Vigenère (French pronunciation: [viʒnɛːʁ]) cipher has been reinvented many times. The method was originally described by Giovan Battista Bellaso in his 1553 book *La cifra del. Sig. Giovan Battista Bellaso*; however, the scheme was later misattributed to Blaise de Vigenère in the 19th century, and is now widely known as the "Vigenère cipher".

Though the cipher is easy to understand and implement,

A reproduction of the Confederacy's cipher disk on display in the US National Cryptologic Museum

for three centuries it resisted all attempts to break it; this earned it the description **le chiffre indéchiffrable** (French for 'the indecipherable cipher'). Many people have tried to implement encryption schemes that are essentially Vigenère ciphers.[3] Friedrich Kasiski was the first to publish a general method of deciphering a Vigenère cipher, in 1863.

54.1 History

The first well documented description of a polyalphabetic cipher was formulated by Leon Battista Alberti around 1467 and used a metal cipher disc to switch between cipher alphabets. Alberti's system only switched alphabets after several words, and switches were indicated by writing the letter of the corresponding alphabet in the ciphertext. Later, in 1508, Johannes Trithemius, in his work *Poligraphia*, invented the tabula recta, a critical component of the Vigenère cipher. The Trithemius cipher, however, only provided a progressive, rigid, and predictable system for switching between cipher alphabets.

What is now known as the Vigenère cipher was originally described by Giovan Battista Bellaso in his 1553 book *La cifra del. Sig. Giovan Battista Bellaso.* He built upon the tabula recta of Trithemius, but added a repeating "countersign" (a key) to switch cipher alphabets every letter. Whereas Alberti and Trithemius used a fixed pattern of substitutions, Bellaso's scheme meant the pattern of substitutions could be easily changed simply by selecting a new key. Keys were typically single words or short phrases, known to both parties in advance, or transmitted "out of band" along with the message. Bellaso's method thus required strong security for only the key. As it is relatively easy to secure a short key phrase, say by a previous private conversation, Bellaso's system was considerably more secure.

Blaise de Vigenère published his description of a similar but stronger autokey cipher before the court of Henry III of France, in 1586. Later, in the 19th century, the invention of Bellaso's cipher was misattributed to Vigenère. David Kahn in his book *The Codebreakers* lamented the misattribution by saying that history had "ignored this important contribution and instead named a regressive and elementary cipher for him [Vigenère] though he had nothing to do with it".[4]

The Vigenère cipher gained a reputation for being exceptionally strong. Noted author and mathematician Charles Lutwidge Dodgson (Lewis Carroll) called the Vigenère cipher unbreakable in his 1868 piece "The Alphabet Cipher" in a children's magazine. In 1917, *Scientific American* described the Vigenère cipher as "impossible of translation".[5] This reputation was not deserved. Charles Babbage is known to have broken a variant of the cipher as early as 1854; however, he didn't publish his work.[6] Kasiski entirely broke the cipher and published the technique in the 19th century. Even before this, though, some skilled cryptanalysts could occasionally break the cipher in the 16th century.[4]

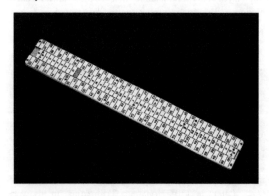

Cryptographic slide rule used as a calculation aid by the Swiss Army between 1914 and 1940.

The Vigenère cipher is simple enough to be a field cipher if it is used in conjunction with cipher disks.[7] The Confederate States of America, for example, used a brass cipher disk to implement the Vigenère cipher during the American Civil War. The Confederacy's messages were far from secret and the Union regularly cracked their messages. Throughout the war, the Confederate leadership primarily relied upon three key phrases, "Manchester Bluff", "Complete Victory" and, as the war came to a close, "Come Retribution".[8]

Gilbert Vernam tried to repair the broken cipher (creating the Vernam-Vigenère cipher in 1918), but, no matter what he did, the cipher was still vulnerable to cryptanalysis. Vernam's work, however, eventually led to the one-time pad, a provably unbreakable cipher.

54.2 Description

The Vigenère square or Vigenère table, also known as the tabula recta, can be used for encryption and decryption.

The Vigenère square or Vigenère table, also known as the tabula recta, *can be used for encryption and decryption.*

In a Caesar cipher, each letter of the alphabet is shifted along some number of places; for example, in a Caesar cipher of shift 3, A would become D, B would become E, Y would become B and so on. The Vigenère cipher consists of several Caesar ciphers in sequence with different shift values.

To encrypt, a table of alphabets can be used, termed a *tabula recta*, *Vigenère square*, or *Vigenère table*. It consists of the alphabet written out 26 times in different rows, each alphabet shifted cyclically to the left compared to the previous alphabet, corresponding to the 26 possible Caesar ciphers. At different points in the encryption process, the cipher uses a different alphabet from one of the rows. The alphabet used at each point depends on a repeating keyword.

For example, suppose that the plaintext to be encrypted is:

ATTACKATDAWN

The person sending the message chooses a keyword and repeats it until it matches the length of the plaintext, for example, the keyword "LEMON":

LEMONLEMONLE

Each row starts with a key letter. The remainder of the row holds the letters A to Z (in shifted order). Although there are 26 key rows shown, you will only use as many keys (different alphabets) as there are unique letters in the key string, here just 5 keys, {L, E, M, O, N}. For successive letters of the message, we are going to take successive letters of the key string, and encipher each message letter using its corresponding key row. Choose the next letter of the key, go along that row to find the column heading that matches the message character; the letter at the intersection of [key-row, msg-col] is the enciphered letter.

For example, the first letter of the plaintext, A, is paired with L, the first letter of the key. So use row L and column A of the Vigenère square, namely L. Similarly, for the second letter of the plaintext, the second letter of the key is used; the letter at row E and column T is X. The rest of the plaintext is enciphered in a similar fashion:

Decryption is performed by going to the row in the table corresponding to the key, finding the position of the ciphertext letter in this row, and then using the column's label as the plaintext. For example, in row L (from *L*EMON), the ciphertext L appears in column A, which is the first plaintext letter. Next we go to row E (from L*E*MON), locate the ciphertext X which is found in column T, thus T is the second plaintext letter.

54.3 Algebraic description

Vigenère can also be viewed algebraically. If the letters A–Z are taken to be the numbers 0–25 (i.e., $A \cong 0$, $B \cong 1$, etc.), and addition is performed modulo 26, then Vigenère encryption E using the key K can be written,

$$C_i = E_K(M_i) = (M_i + K_i) \mod 26$$

and decryption D using the key K ,

$$M_i = D_K(C_i) = (C_i - K_i) \mod 26$$

where $M = M_1 \dots M_n$ is the message, $C = C_1 \dots C_n$ is the ciphertext and $K = K_1 \dots K_n$ is the key obtained by repeating the keyword $\lceil n/m \rceil$ times, where m is the keyword length.

Thus using the previous example, to encrypt $A \cong 0$ with key letter $L \cong 11$ the calculation would result in $11 \cong L$.

$$11 = (0 + 11) \mod 26$$

Therefore, to decrypt $R \cong 17$ with key letter $E \cong 4$ the calculation would result in $13 \cong N$.

$$13 = (17 - 4) \mod 26$$

In general, let Σ be the alphabet of length ℓ . Denote by m the length of key. Then Vigenère encryption and decryption can be written as follows:

$$C_i = E_K(M_i) = (M_i + K_{(i \mod m)}) \mod \ell,$$

$$M_i = D_K(C_i) = (C_i - K_{(i \mod m)}) \mod \ell.$$

Note that M_i denotes the offset of the i-th character of the plaintext M in the alphabet Σ . For example, taking the 26 English characters as the alphabet $\Sigma = (A, B, C, \cdots, X, Y, Z)$, the offset of A is 0, and the offset of B is 1, etc. C_i and K_i are similar.

54.4 Cryptanalysis

The idea behind the Vigenère cipher, like all polyalphabetic ciphers, is to disguise plaintext letter frequencies, which interferes with a straightforward application of frequency analysis. For instance, if P is the most frequent letter in a ciphertext whose plaintext is in English, one might suspect that P corresponds to E, because E is the most frequently used letter in English. However, using the Vigenère cipher, E can be enciphered as different ciphertext letters at different points in the message, thus defeating simple frequency analysis.

The primary weakness of the Vigenère cipher is the repeating nature of its key. If a cryptanalyst correctly guesses the key's length, then the cipher text can be treated as interwoven Caesar ciphers, which individually are easily broken. The Kasiski examination and Friedman test can help determine the key length.

54.4.1 Kasiski examination

For more details on this topic, see Kasiski examination.

In 1863 Friedrich Kasiski was the first to publish a successful general attack on the Vigenère cipher. Earlier attacks relied on knowledge of the plaintext, or use of a recognizable word as a key. Kasiski's method had no such dependencies. Though Kasiski was the first to publish an account of the attack, it is clear that there were others who were aware of it. In 1854, Charles Babbage was goaded into breaking the Vigenère cipher when John Hall Brock Thwaites submitted a "new" cipher to the Journal of the Society of the Arts. When Babbage showed that Thwaites' cipher was essentially just another recreation of the Vigenère cipher, Thwaites challenged Babbage to break his cipher encoded twice, with keys of different length. Babbage succeeded in decrypting a sample, which turned out to be the poem "The Vision of Sin", by Alfred Tennyson, encrypted according to the keyword "Emily", the first name of Tennyson's wife. Babbage never explained the method he used. Studies of Babbage's notes reveal that he had used the method later published by Kasiski, and suggest that he had been using the method as early as 1846.[9]

The Kasiski examination, also called the Kasiski test, takes advantage of the fact that repeated words may, by chance, sometimes be encrypted using the same key letters, leading to repeated groups in the ciphertext. For example, Consider the following encryption using the keyword ABCD:

Key: ABCDABCDABCDABCDABCDABCDABCD
Plaintext: *CRYPTO*ISSHORTFOR*CRYPTO*GRAPHY
Ciphertext: *CSASTP*KVSIQUTGQU*CSASTP*IUAQJB

There is an easily seen repetition in the ciphertext, and the Kasiski test will be effective. Here the distance between the repetitions of CSASTP is 16. Assuming that the repeated segments represent the same plaintext segments, this implies that the key is 16, 8, 4, 2, or 1 characters long. (All factors of the distance are possible key lengths—a key of length one is just a simple Caesar cipher, where cryptanalysis is much easier.) Since key lengths 2 and 1 are unrealistically short, one only needs to try lengths 16, 8, or 4. Longer messages make the test more accurate because they usually contain more repeated ciphertext segments. The following ciphertext has two segments that are repeated:

Ciphertext: *VHVS*SP*QUCE*MRVBVBBB*VHVS*URQGIBDUGRNICJQUCERVUAXSSR

The distance between the repetitions of VHVS is 18. Assuming that the repeated segments represent the same plaintext segments, this implies that the key is 18, 9, 6, 3, 2, or 1 characters long. The distance between the repetitions of QUCE is 30 characters. This means that the key length could be 30, 15, 10, 6, 5, 3, 2, or 1 characters long. By taking the intersection of these sets one could safely conclude that the most likely key length is 6, since 3, 2, and 1 are unrealistically short.

54.4.2   Friedman test

The Friedman test (sometimes known as the kappa test) was invented during the 1920s by William F. Friedman. Friedman used the index of coincidence, which measures the unevenness of the cipher letter frequencies to break the cipher. By knowing the probability κ_p that any two randomly chosen source-language letters are the same (around 0.067 for monocase English) and the probability of a coincidence for a uniform random selection from the alphabet κ_r (1/26 = 0.0385 for English), the key length can be estimated as:

$$\frac{\kappa_p - \kappa_r}{\kappa_o - \kappa_r}$$

from the observed coincidence rate

$$\kappa_o = \frac{\sum_{i=1}^{c} n_i(n_i - 1)}{N(N-1)}$$

where c is the size of the alphabet (26 for English), N is the length of the text, and n_1 through nc are the observed ciphertext letter frequencies, as integers.

This is, however, only an approximation whose accuracy increases with the size of the text. It would in practice be necessary to try various key lengths close to the estimate.[10] A better approach for repeating-key ciphers is to copy the ciphertext into rows of a matrix having as many columns as an assumed key length, then compute the average index of coincidence with each column considered separately; when this is done for each possible key length, the highest average I.C. then corresponds to the most likely key length.[11] Such tests may be supplemented by information from the Kasiski examination.

54.4.3   Frequency analysis

Once the length of the key is known, the ciphertext can be rewritten into that many columns, with each column corresponding to a single letter of the key. Each column consists of plaintext that has been encrypted by a single Caesar cipher; the Caesar key (shift) is just the letter of the Vigenère key that was used for that column. Using methods similar to those used to break the Caesar cipher, the letters in the ciphertext can be discovered.

An improvement to the Kasiski examination, known as Kerckhoffs' method, matches each column's letter frequencies to shifted plaintext frequencies to discover the key letter (Caesar shift) for that column. Once every letter in the key is known, the cryptanalyst can simply decrypt the ciphertext and reveal the plaintext.[12] Kerckhoffs' method is not applicable when the Vigenère table has been scrambled, rather than using normal alphabetic sequences, although Kasiski examination and coincidence tests can still be used to determine key length in that case.

54.4.4 Key elimination

The Vigenère cipher with normal alphabets essentially uses modulo arithmetic, which is commutative. So if the key length is known (or guessed) then subtracting the cipher text from itself, offset by the key length, will produce the plain text encrypted with itself. If any "probable word" in the plain text is known or can be guessed, then its self-encryption can be recognized, allowing recovery of the key by subtracting the known plaintext from the cipher text. Key elimination is especially useful against short messages.

54.5 Variants

Confederate cipher wheel, captured at the surrender of Mobile, Alabama, in May 1865 – National Cryptologic Museum

The running key variant of the Vigenère cipher was also considered unbreakable at one time. This version uses as the key a block of text as long as the plaintext. Since the key is as long as the message the Friedman and Kasiski tests no longer work (the key is not repeated). In 1920, Friedman was the first to discover this variant's weaknesses. The problem with the running key Vigenère cipher is that the cryptanalyst has statistical information about the key (assuming that the block of text is in a known language) and that information will be reflected in the ciphertext.

If using a key which is truly random, is at least as long as the encrypted message, and is used only once, the Vigenère cipher is theoretically unbreakable. However, in this case it is the key, not the cipher, which provides cryptographic strength, and such systems are properly referred to collec-

tively as one-time pad systems, irrespective of which ciphers are employed.

Vigenère actually invented a stronger cipher: an autokey cipher. The name "Vigenère cipher" became associated with a simpler polyalphabetic cipher instead. In fact, the two ciphers were often confused, and both were sometimes called "*le chiffre indéchiffrable*". Babbage actually broke the much stronger autokey cipher, while Kasiski is generally credited with the first published solution to the fixed-key polyalphabetic ciphers.

A simple variant is to encrypt using the Vigenère decryption method, and decrypt using Vigenère encryption. This method is sometimes referred to as "Variant Beaufort". This is different from the Beaufort cipher, created by Francis Beaufort, which nonetheless is similar to Vigenère but uses a slightly modified enciphering mechanism and tableau. The Beaufort cipher is a reciprocal cipher.

Despite the Vigenère cipher's apparent strength it never became widely used throughout Europe. The Gronsfeld cipher is a variant created by Count Gronsfeld which is identical to the Vigenère cipher, except that it uses just 10 different cipher alphabets (corresponding to the digits 0 to 9). The Gronsfeld cipher is strengthened because its key is not a word, but it is weakened because it has just 10 cipher alphabets. Gronsfeld's cipher did become widely used throughout Germany and Europe, despite its weaknesses.

54.6 See also

- Roger Frontenac (Nostradamus quatrain decryptor, 1950)

54.7 References

54.7.1 Citations

[1] Bruen, Aiden A. & Forcinito, Mario A. (2011). *Cryptography, Information Theory, and Error-Correction: A Handbook for the 21st Century*. John Wiley & Sons. p. 21. ISBN 978-1-118-03138-4.

[2] Martin, Keith M. (2012). *Everyday Cryptography*. Oxford University Press. p. 142. ISBN 978-0-19-162588-6.

[3] Smith, Laurence D. (1943). "Substitution Ciphers". *Cryptography the Science of Secret Writing: The Science of Secret Writing*. Dover Publications. p. 81. ISBN 0-486-20247-X.

[4] David, Kahn (1999). "On the Origin of a Species". *The Codebreakers: The Story of Secret Writing*. Simon & Schuster. ISBN 0-684-83130-9.

[5] Knudsen, Lars R. (1998). "Block Ciphers—a survey". In Bart Preneel and Vincent Rijmen. *State of the Art in Applied Cryptography: Course on Computer Security and Industrial Cryptograph Leuven Belgium, June 1997 Revised Lectures.* Berlin ; London: Springer. p. 29. ISBN 3-540-65474-7.

[6] Singh, Simon (1999).   "Chapter 2:   Le Chiffre Indéchiffrable". *The Code Book.* Anchor Books, Random House. pp. 63–78. ISBN 0-385-49532-3.

[7] Codes, Ciphers, & Codebreaking (The Rise Of Field Ciphers)

[8] David, Kahn (1999). "Crises of the Union". *The Codebreakers: The Story of Secret Writing.* Simon & Schuster. pp. 217–221. ISBN 0-684-83130-9.

[9] Franksen, O. I. (1985) Mr. Babbage's Secret: The Tale of a Cipher—and APL. Prentice Hall.

[10] Henk C.A. van Tilborg, ed. (2005). *Encyclopedia of Cryptography and Security* (First ed.). Springer. p. 115. ISBN 0-387-23473-X.

[11] Mountjoy, Marjorie (1963).   "The Bar Statistics".   *NSA Technical Journal.* **VII** (2,4). Published in two parts.

[12] "Lab exercise: Vigenere, RSA, DES, and Authentication Protocols" (PDF). *CS 415: Computer and Network Security.* Retrieved 2006-11-10.

54.7.2   Sources

- Beutelspacher, Albrecht (1994). "Chapter 2". *Cryptology.* translation from German by J. Chris Fisher. Washington, DC: Mathematical Association of America. pp. 27–41. ISBN 0-883-85504-6.

- Singh, Simon (1999).   "Chapter 2: Le Chiffre Indéchiffrable". *The Code Book.* Anchor Book, Random House. ISBN 0-385-49532-3.

- Gaines, Helen Fouche (1939). "The Gronsfeld, Porta and Beaufort Ciphers". *Cryptanalysis a Study of Ciphers and Their Solutions.* Dover Publications. pp. 117–126. ISBN 0-486-20097-3.

- Mendelsohn, Charles J (1940). "Blaise De Vigenere and The 'Chiffre Carre'". *Proceedings of the American Philosophical Society.* **82** (2).

54.8   External links

Articles

- History of the cipher from Cryptologia

- Basic Cryptanalysis at H2G2

- Lecture Notes on Classical Cryptology including an explanation and derivation of the Friedman Test

- aolnews.com at the Wayback Machine (archived June 24, 2011)

Programming

- *Hacking Secret Ciphers with Python* Chapter 19, The Vigenère Cipher, Chapter 21, Hacking the Vigenère Cipher, with Python source code.

- Sharky's Online Vigenere Cipher – Encode and decode messages, using a known key, within a Web browser (JavaScript)

- PyGenere: an online tool for automatically deciphering Vigenère-encoded texts (6 languages supported)

- Vigenère Cipher encryption and decryption program (browser version, English only)

- Crypt::Vigenere – a CPAN module implementing the Vigenère cipher

- Breaking the indecipherable cipher: Perl code to decipher Vigenère text, with the source in the shape of Babbage's head

- Vigenère in BASH

- Java Vigenere applet with source code (GNU GPL)

- Vigenere Cipher in Java

- Vijner 974 Encryption Tool in C# (Vigenere Algorithm)

- Vigenère Cipher encryption tool – Browser

- Vigenère Cipher encryption tool – Google Chrome extension

Chapter 55

Wadsworth's cipher

Wadsworth's cipher was a cipher invented by Decius Wadsworth, a Colonel in the Ordnance Corps of the United States Army. In 1817, he developed a progressive cipher system based on a 1790 design by Thomas Jefferson, establishing a method that was continuously improved upon and used until the end of World War II.

Wadsworth's system involved a set of two disks, one inside the other, where the outer disk had the 26 letters of the alphabet and the numbers 2-8, and the inner disk had only the 26 letters. The disks were geared together at a ratio of 26:33. To encipher a message, the inner disk was turned until the desired letter was at the top position, with the number of turns required for the result transmitted as ciphertext. Due to the gearing, a ciphertext substitution for a character did not repeat until all 33 characters for the plaintext letter had been used. Wadsworth never got credit for his design because Charles Wheatstone invented an almost identical machine several years after Wadsworth, and got all the credit.

55.1   References

- "A Short History of Cryptography", Fred Cohen, 1995

- "Cryptography Primer", Jose Mari Reyes, 2001

- "Cryptography Timeline", Carl Ellison, December 11, 2004

- Codes, Richard A. Mollin, 2005

55.2 Text and image sources, contributors, and licenses

55.2.1 Text

- **Classical cipher** *Source:* https://en.wikipedia.org/wiki/Classical_cipher?oldid=740289295 *Contributors:* Inkling, Mcapdevila, Matt Crypto, Reallycoolguy, JemeL, Bender235, Davidgothberg, Wtmitchell, Gpvos, Drdefcom~enwiki, Jetekus, Vuong Ngan Ha, YurikBot, Cedar101, Peyna, Myrabella, SmackBot, Mmernex, Snori, Keycard, RekishiEJ, Chrumps, CBM, Nuwewsco, AlexAlex, DPdH, George A. M., KConWiki, NightFalcon90909, Jeffbadge, Dprust, Tiptoety, Crypter, Alexbot, Cenarium, 7, Addbot, Peridon, Tide rolls, Yobot, DataWraith, Alphapeeler, GuiderBob, Kimbo9324, FrescoBot, Ostevens, Nmaxcom, ClueBot NG, AlmaSA, BG19bot, Natuur12, HelpUsStopSpam and Anonymous: 18

- **A-1 (code)** *Source:* https://en.wikipedia.org/wiki/A-1_(code)?oldid=703067192 *Contributors:* Sadads, Hugo999, Nageh and Hazard-Bot

- **Acme Commodity and Phrase Code** *Source:* https://en.wikipedia.org/wiki/Acme_Commodity_and_Phrase_Code?oldid=713821764 *Contributors:* Sadads, Randy Kryn, Addbot, Nageh, RedBot, Jesse V. and Delusion23

- **ADFGVX cipher** *Source:* https://en.wikipedia.org/wiki/ADFGVX_cipher?oldid=742004833 *Contributors:* Imran, Iluvcapra, Ellywa, Muriel Gottrop~enwiki, Dcoetzee, Securiger, Mybot99999, Giftlite, Inkling, Matt Crypto, OldakQuill, Quistnix, ESkog, Davidgothberg, Jonsafari, Burn, Bookandcoffee, Miss Madeline, Apokrif, Eyreland, Pantagruel, Nneonneo, Lzz, DDOracle, Gaius Cornelius, SmackBot, Eskimbot, Sadads, Textor, FrankDynan, Nabokov, Smiteri, Shorelander, CommonsDelinker, Jevansen, Borat fan, VolkovBot, A4bot, Dprust, Jab416171, ClueBot, L'omo del batocio, Sv1xv, Alexbot, Avoided, Addbot, Sq7obj, Luckas-bot, Yobot, Ensei~enwiki, Żbiczek, AnomieBOT, Drilnoth, Erik9, Jesse V., Blacklunarsun, ClueBot NG, Helpful Pixie Bot, Pretzel29743, Fritz-X, Peterhurford, OS, Crjfluoxkp, InternetArchiveBot and Anonymous: 35

- **Affine cipher** *Source:* https://en.wikipedia.org/wiki/Affine_cipher?oldid=738526668 *Contributors:* Imran, Michael Hardy, Dcoetzee, Jeffq, Inkling, Matt Crypto, CryptoDerk, Two Bananas, TonyW, Perey, EmilJ, Davidgothberg, Burn, Feb30th1712, Jacklee, Cedar101, BiT, Gilliam, MatthewDaly, Cswhiz, Stotr~enwiki, JoeBot, Ntsimp, Thijs!bot, Tylop~enwiki, Pathan wannabe, MER-C, Hut 8.5, Wasell, Jkasprzak, Flyer22 Reborn, Smaug123, Mild Bill Hiccup, Starofale, Alexbot, PixelBot, Cenarium, Lak mee dee, Addbot, Luckas-bot, Yobot, Doglitbug, Capricorn42, Angelus1383, JimJam707, Sj31, FrescoBot, OldManInACoffeeCan, Jinsungy, ZéroBot, ClueBot NG, Kapanidze, Czg1989, BG19bot, Chmarkine, Mohammad.sajid.anwar, Red-eyed demon and Anonymous: 48

- **Alberti cipher** *Source:* https://en.wikipedia.org/wiki/Alberti_cipher?oldid=725573897 *Contributors:* Val42, Babbage, Eyreland, RussBot, HoratioVitero, Robert L, SmackBot, Jagged 85, Samanathon, Tenorcnj, Tom872, LibLord, Kaobear, Hut 8.5, Wasell, Waacstats, Uncle Dick, Brondahl, Jevansen, TreasuryTag, Blobinator11, Hqb, PipepBot, Antonio Giovanni Colombo, Addbot, Ronhjones, Gus Buonafalce, TheSuave, Yobot, Jim1138, Edgars2007, FrescoBot, Ronanletiec, ZéroBot, BG19bot, ChrisGualtieri, KasparBot and Anonymous: 13

- **The Alphabet Cipher** *Source:* https://en.wikipedia.org/wiki/The_Alphabet_Cipher?oldid=657419054 *Contributors:* Delirium, DavidWBrooks, Charles Matthews, Ww, Furrykef, Lunkwill, Inkling, Matt Crypto, N328KF, Brianhe, Rich Farmbrough, Bobo192, Tevildo, Sadads, Cydebot, Morrillonline, KConWiki, Lightbot, Erik9bot, ClueBot NG, Pishcal, Windjaguar56 and Anonymous: 6

- **Alphabetum Kaldeorum** *Source:* https://en.wikipedia.org/wiki/Alphabetum_Kaldeorum?oldid=544051270 *Contributors:* Imc, Inkling, DragonflySixtyseven, Stemonitis, Falconer, Gryffindor, FlaBot, MartinBot, Addbot, Erik9bot, WikitanvirBot and Anonymous: 2

- **Arnold Cipher** *Source:* https://en.wikipedia.org/wiki/Arnold_Cipher?oldid=408897240 *Contributors:* SimonP, Securiger, Inkling, Matt Crypto, Rklisowski, Geg, Gaius Cornelius, Wikidude775, Pb30, SmackBot, Bethpage89, Brother Officer, Jakedaniel, Ryan shell, Magicpiano, Erik9bot, Morgis and Anonymous: 9

- **Āryabhaṭa numeration** *Source:* https://en.wikipedia.org/wiki/%C4%80ryabha%E1%B9%ADa_numeration?oldid=742804784 *Contributors:* Arun, Jason Quinn, Chowbok, Icairns, Factitious, Dbachmann, MisterSheik, Kwamikagami, Swift, Paul Martin, Woohookitty, Shreevatsa, AndyKali, KSmrq, Tvarnoe~enwiki, SmackBot, Jagged 85, Srkris, MegA, Hyenaste, Vanisaac, CmdrObot, FilipeS, Thijs!bot, Headbomb, Tuncrypt, Krishnachandranvn, Zerokitsune, VolkovBot, Bigbenboa, John Garden, Niceguyedc, Wakari07, Addbot, LaaknorBot, Lightbot, Luckas-bot, Amirobot, Tom.Reding, Uanfala, EmausBot, AManWithNoPlan, Helpful Pixie Bot, Titodutta, Anooj Muljee, BattyBot, Subramanya sarma, Kephir, Kautilya3, Filpro, Fitindia and Anonymous: 15

- **Atbash** *Source:* https://en.wikipedia.org/wiki/Atbash?oldid=742795532 *Contributors:* Uriyan, Eclecticology, PierreAbbat, Shii, Imran, DopefishJustin, IZAK, Yaronf, Cimon Avaro, The Anomebot, Xanzzibar, VanishedUser kfljdfjsg33k, Inkling, Matt Crypto, Klemen Kocjancic, Volantwish, Euthydemos, Kbh3rd, Kwamikagami, Apollo2011, BrokenSegue, Davidgothberg, Offsky, Obradovic Goran, MPerel, Ross Burgess, Zsero, Jefromi, Grika, Julian Krause, Netan'el, Mga, Intgr, ThePlaz, LeCire~enwiki, YurikBot, Eraoul, Rufua, Bota47, Cedar101, Whaa?, Sue Anne, Alan smithee, A5b, SashatoBot, Louloufuentes, Nicodemas, Jumpwithjames, Thijs!bot, Seaphoto, JAnDbot, MER-C, Hut 8.5, Magioladitis, Newshunter~enwiki, Serguei S. Dukachev, Xnuala, TreasuryTag, TXiKiBoT, A4bot, Rei-bot, Philosp, Vituzzu, SchreiberBike, BOTarate, Ar2332, Jomital92, WikHead, Addbot, MrOllie, Agbad, Luckas-bot, Yobot, Ptbotgourou, Jeffz1, Jim1138, De 2.1, MauritsBot, J04n, Revipm, Loup émeraude, Nageh, MastiBot, ZéroBot, ClueBot NG, Kapanidze, BattyBot, FoCuSandLeArN, Isarra (HG), BorgiasRevenge, K scheik, Prinsgezinde, Barzamin, Jmcgnh, Somnum limax, Kuber yogi, AsfahGhazanfer, Vtecking12345, Mniles77, Anonymous 531, Blahkalomo, Arthur Goodhill and Anonymous: 63

- **Autokey cipher** *Source:* https://en.wikipedia.org/wiki/Autokey_cipher?oldid=712139782 *Contributors:* The Anome, Imran, Someone else, Bdesham, LenBudney, Delirium, 5ko, R3m0t, Jmabel, Ludraman, DavidCary, Inkling, Matt Crypto, TonyW, Davidgothberg, Gpvos, WriterHound, Frankd, Gilliam, TimBentley, Frap, Harryboyles, Jaksmata, Van helsing, Hut 8.5, Addbot, Gus Buonafalce, Jamesinc87, Yobot, Doctorhook, AnomieBOT, D'ohBot, Nmatvka, Skyerise, Gulbenk, Westley Turner, Cdated, Billatnapier, Pretzel29743, Yamaha5, R.javanmard and Anonymous: 18

- **Bacon's cipher** *Source:* https://en.wikipedia.org/wiki/Bacon{}s_cipher?oldid=736264807 *Contributors:* Llywrch, Haakon, Charles Matthews, Altenmann, Icairns, Rich Farmbrough, Antaeus Feldspar, BrokenSegue, Pearle, Licon, RJFJR, Notcarlos, Richard Arthur Norton (1958-), Xover, Shreevatsa, Eyreland, Hairy Dude, Briaboru, Doldrums, AndyJones, SmackBot, Herostratus, No Parking, Kcordina, The Man in Question, HJMG, Chris55, Cydebot, Thijs!bot, MER-C, Hut 8.5, Penubag, Vanish2, Wrad, Tdadamemd, TomCat4680, Edain Narsil, Brondahl, Ja

62, Jmrowland, Tom Reedy, Sfan00 IMG, ClueBot, Doloco, Johnuniq, MystBot, Addbot, Yobot, AnomieBOT, MagnusGuyra, Xqbot, Omni-paedista, Outback the koala, MondalorBot, Shakespearean Sherlock, Tommy2010, Beleary, ZéroBot, Josve05a, Erianna, Xanchester, Kapanidze, MichalisN, Dexbot, Matt.waa, Dragoonprogramming, Viva Caligula and Anonymous: 44

- **Beaufort cipher** *Source:* https://en.wikipedia.org/wiki/Beaufort_cipher?oldid=727558635 *Contributors:* The Anome, Matt Crypto, Jdege, SmackBot, Mmernex, Bobet, Frap, Zero sharp, Sable232, Isilanes, Spencer, Singularity, CommonsDelinker, VolkovBot, Haloangelboy, Macwinux, Bananabean, Pianosnake, Addbot, Luckas-bot, Yobot, MarioS, LilHelpa, Tom.Reding, Ronanletiec, Widr, Danielchatfield, Gian-mariot2, BrunetteBella, Rdavie3, Cmschaak, RoslinGenetics, Trepa Mayfield, Ajay poonia1992, Beifong3 and Anonymous: 5

- **Bifid cipher** *Source:* https://en.wikipedia.org/wiki/Bifid_cipher?oldid=706871161 *Contributors:* Imran, Robbot, Securiger, Inkling, Matt Crypto, Mouser, TonyW, Davidgothberg, Gpvos, SmackBot, Mmernex, Brammers, Bluebot, Frap, SashatoBot, Ilias.vanpeer, Ntsimp, Ty-lop~enwiki, AntiVandalBot, MER-C, Hut 8.5, OKBot, Addbot, Lightbot, Yobot, Jeffz1, AnomieBOT, Kapanidze, Harmon758 and Anonymous: 12

- **Book cipher** *Source:* https://en.wikipedia.org/wiki/Book_cipher?oldid=735212996 *Contributors:* Imran, Frecklefoot, Michael Hardy, Paddu, Silverfish, Ww, Phr, Securiger, Rfc1394, DavidCary, Inkling, BigHaz, Matt Crypto, TonyW, Robophilosopher, Mikkel, Stbalbach, Davidgoth-berg, Inky, Paul Magnussen, SmackBot, Mmernex, Hmains, Colonies Chris, Trekphiler, Tamfang, BrentRockwood, Crouchbk, TenPoundHam-mer, AndrewHowse, Xaiver0510, Olaf, Smfrick, GrahamHardy, TreasuryTag, Andreas Kaganov, WereSpielChequers, The Thing That Should Not Be, PixelBot, Arjayay, Austinburk, XLinkBot, Mbrsart, Addbot, Lightbot, Luckas-bot, FlavusBelisarius, DataWraith, Winterwater, Fres-coBot, SuperFlo, Gijargan, Mjbmrbot, Helpsome, ClueBot NG, ThaddeusSholto, Altaïr, BattyBot, Amisom, Lord Kryten, Dexbot, F3ndot, Libertarian12111971, AnnaComnemna and Anonymous: 46

- **Thomas Brierley** *Source:* https://en.wikipedia.org/wiki/Thomas_Brierley?oldid=740432093 *Contributors:* Morwen, Jackiespeel, Klemen Koc-jancic, Dave.Dunford, Doc glasgow, Bgwhite, Welsh, Wknight94, Open2universe, SmackBot, Chris the speller, Blueboar, Candorwien, SMas-ters, Dl2000, Cydebot, A876, Alaibot, PKT, Nick Number, DShamen, Jmorrison230582, Boleyn, Yobot, Raven1977, LilHelpa, DefaultsortBot, RjwilmsiBot, AvicAWB, ChrisGualtieri, Hmainsbot1, Spirit of Eagle, Periglio, Acalycine, Nuclear pulse, Stormmeteo, Cracker2013, Ashbyku-mar, Mildchild, KasparBot and Anonymous: 2

- **Caesar cipher** *Source:* https://en.wikipedia.org/wiki/Caesar_cipher?oldid=739045363 *Contributors:* Damian Yerrick, Bryan Derksen, Arvindn, Fubar Obfusco, Kurt Jansson, Panairjdde~enwiki, Imran, Hephaestos, Michael Hardy, Wwwwolf, Wapcaplet, Theresa knott, Marumari, Cimon Avaro, Timwi, Dcoetzee, Ww, Dysprosia, The Anomebot, Didactylos, Furrykef, Taxman, Leus, Topbanana, Carbuncle, Fito, Naddy, Bkell, Hadal, GreatWhiteNortherner, Cedars, Lunkwill, Inkling, Lupin, No Guru, Anville, DO'Neil, Avsa, Matt Crypto, Just Another Dan, Bobblewik, CryptoDerk, Kuralyov, Mike Rosoft, Mormegil, Discospinster, Rich Farmbrough, Mat cross, Quistnix, Tsujigiri~enwiki, Closeapple, Brian0918, Lankiveil, EmilJ, BrokenSegue, Davidgothberg, Offsky, Minghong, Crust, SPUI, Captmjc, 119, Pforret, Craigy144, Ashley Pomeroy, Demi, Ciaran H, Zsero, Chronophasiac, Yuckfoo, Rshin, Randy Johnston, Wayward, Marskell, Rjwilmsi, Oblivious, FlaBot, Ian Pitchford, Mfeadler, RobertG, Gurch, Intgr, Valentinian, Chobot, DVdm, JesseGarrett, Bgwhite, Kokyong, YurikBot, Phantomsteve, Aminto, Wiki alf, BOT-Superzerocool, Nikkimaria, JLaTondre, KNHaw, KnightRider~enwiki, SmackBot, Mmernex, Mdd4696, BiT, Bluebot, A. B., Ealster2004, Bart v M, Paulschou, BillFlis, Noah Salzman, JoGusto, Neddyseagoon, KlaudiuMihaila, Doc Daneeka, RekishiEJ, Tawkerbot2, One19, Ntsimp, Mat-tisse, Thijs!bot, Biruitorul, Headbomb, RichardVeryard, Tylop~enwiki, Centrepull, JAnDbot, Hut 8.5, Magioladitis, Robby, Soulbot, Nyttend, KConWiki, 28421u2232nfenfcenc, Ravihansa3000, MartinBot, Glrx, Yonaa, CommonsDelinker, FANSTARbot, DrKay, Trusilver, Maurice Carbonaro, Hut 6.5, Jc4p, Jevansen, Treisijs, Sgeureka, Anton Rakitskiy, VolkovBot, WOSlinker, Philip Trueman, A4bot, Pookey gb, KjellG, Castlebianca, Arkwatem, BotMultichill, Yintan, Boromil, ClueBot, The Thing That Should Not Be, CrazyGlu, Paulcmnt, PixelBot, Estirabot, Lartoven, Aitias, Joedaddy09, XLinkBot, XalD, Kwjbot, Vanished user ijenqwkjnvi3ij4htnasjh239j092nf, PenComputingPerson, Mojska, Ad-dbot, JoeMoron2000, BabelStone, MrOllie, MrVanBot, AndersBot, LinkFA-Bot, Luckas-bot, Yobot, Ptbotgourou, Amirobot, Jeffz1, Citation bot, Xqbot, Capricorn42, Angelus1383, GrouchoBot, AlSweigart, Revipm, VS6507, Citation bot 1, RedBot, Serols, TobeBot, Trappist the monk, RjwilmsiBot, Kastchei, Marco Guzman, Jr, Wikipelli, Evanh2008, Ὁ οἶστρος, Mentibot, ClueBot NG, Essterling, Wcherowi, Joefromrandb, Widr, Kapanidze, Prbindia, Theblogger01, Crh23, Geilamir, Rmad 89, BattyBot, David.moreno72, Dexbot, Jaculator, Grubby7, E19293001, Sam Sailor, JaconaFrere, Monkbot, Filedelinkerbot, Santhoshsivarajan, ToonLucas22, Ejs1985, 3 of Diamonds, Joseph Bagnall, The Quixotic Potato, Qwesad, PlutoniumPhilosopher, Harvi004 and Anonymous: 203

- **Chaocipher** *Source:* https://en.wikipedia.org/wiki/Chaocipher?oldid=620445459 *Contributors:* The Anome, Babbage, Davidgothberg, Miss Madeline, Eyreland, Shae, Snottily, SmackBot, Mmernex, Autarch, OrphanBot, Moshe Rubin, Alaibot, Dalliance, Gavia immer, Tgeairn, Tid-Miste, Addbot, Yobot, Nageh, TjBot, Belman Brisk, ChuispastonBot, Laertes2, Mullins1949 and Anonymous: 8

- **Copiale cipher** *Source:* https://en.wikipedia.org/wiki/Copiale_cipher?oldid=743348754 *Contributors:* Frecklefoot, Nealmcb, Rursus, Nunh-huh, Beland, Pol098, Edison, Bgwhite, Banaticus, Arthur Rubin, Elonka, Skintigh, Riggwelter, Blueboar, Loadmaster, Glrx, Gnebulon, Rumping, WurmWoode, MystBot, Addbot, Yobot, Антон Черный, AnomieBOT, JackieBot, Cameron Scott, FrescoBot, Nageh, Bmclaughlin9, EmausBot, John of Reading, ZéroBot, 2blackdogs, Card Zero, CasualVisitor, Regulov, BG19bot, ClanCularius, Svenstein, ChrisGualtieri, Weirvile, Corinne, YiFeiBot and Anonymous: 10

- **DRYAD** *Source:* https://en.wikipedia.org/wiki/DRYAD?oldid=546754201 *Contributors:* Inkling, Matt Crypto, ArnoldReinhold, Closeapple, Cmdrjameson, Paullaw, Fche, JdforresterBot, Sacxpert, SmackBot, Bluebot, Saejinn, Cydebot, SoxBot, Yobot, Cerabot~enwiki and Anonymous: 4

- **Dvorak encoding** *Source:* https://en.wikipedia.org/wiki/Dvorak_encoding?oldid=743868537 *Contributors:* Charles Matthews, Rursus, Matt Crypto, Beland, Shreddy, TMott, SmackBot, Elonka, Nerd42, Legoguy, Doc Daneeka, AnAj, MER-C, Osndok, Ronald S. Davis, Addbot, Favonian, Yobot, Fraggle81, Citation bot, Omnipaedista, TuHan-Bot, EdoBot, Mjbmrbot, Yourmomblah, Cyberbot II, Eyesnore, Hannasnow, SalmonCat, GreenC bot and Anonymous: 22

- **Four-square cipher** *Source:* https://en.wikipedia.org/wiki/Four-square_cipher?oldid=742697830 *Contributors:* AxelBoldt, Lowellian, Matt Crypto, Mouser, Davidgothberg, Burn, Skotte, Scope creep, Mmernex, Can't sleep, clown will eat me, Tylop~enwiki, Dinoceras, Addbot, Yobot, Frosted14, Bamyers99, KLBot2, Pretzel29743, Jordiherrera, Bobjin and Anonymous: 11

- **Great Cipher** *Source:* https://en.wikipedia.org/wiki/Great_Cipher?oldid=742693216 *Contributors:* Danny, Mintguy, Charles Matthews, Ww, Birkett, Securiger, Inkling, Matt Crypto, Livajo, Captain Blood~enwiki, Eyreland, YurikBot, SmackBot, GôTô, Thumperward, Lazulilasher,

KConWiki, Philg88, TreasuryTag, Perebourne, Addbot, Lightbot, Luckas-bot, Yobot, Rofflebuster, RjwilmsiBot, GoingBatty, Helpful Pixie Bot, SkateTier and Anonymous: 9

- **Grille (cryptography)** *Source:* https://en.wikipedia.org/wiki/Grille_(cryptography)?oldid=738284840 *Contributors:* Ww, AnonMoos, Sverdrup, Pabouk, Matt Crypto, ArnoldReinhold, QVanillaQ, NormanEinstein, Ligulem, SmackBot, Mmernex, Hmains, AndrewHowse, RenamedUser2, Scottiscool, SimonDeDanser, Stevebkk, Smatprt, Gavia immer, KConWiki, ClovisPt, EagleFan, Lucasbfrbot, Texnic, Tom Reedy, Auntof6, Addbot, Yobot, FrescoBot, OgreBot, I dream of horses, RedBot, Beleary, BattyBot, Cyberbot II, 32RB17, GreenC bot and Anonymous: 13

- **Hill cipher** *Source:* https://en.wikipedia.org/wiki/Hill_cipher?oldid=738263445 *Contributors:* Securiger, Elysdir, DavidCary, Matt Crypto, Colinb, Davidgothberg, Snowolf, Brookie, Eyreland, YurikBot, Laurentius, Syth, Closedmouth, FRR~enwiki, SmackBot, Gaff, Iignotus, Colonies Chris, Otus, Marc-André Aßbrock, Dognosh, Seaphoto, MER-C, Anaxial, Abeer.ag, Jon Fawkes, OKBot, Kmassey, Alexbot, Spock of Vulcan, XLinkBot, Utdiscant, Addbot, Freakmighty, Lightbot, Yobot, AnomieBOT, Materialscientist, Telementor, OgreBot, I dream of horses, Vectornaut, Cipher726, EmausBot, Sailor20, Wikipelli, ZéroBot, ClueBot NG, KLBot2, Thekillerpenguin, Jithji3, Kn330wn, Jbeyerl, Abizabber, Jitesh sunhala, Season4, Adam Van Prooyen and Anonymous: 62

- **Keyword cipher** *Source:* https://en.wikipedia.org/wiki/Keyword_cipher?oldid=744636509 *Contributors:* ArnoldReinhold, Sin-man, Mmernex, McGeddon, Ioannes Pragensis, Bigdavejob, Darklilac, Schmloof, Smaug123, Yobot, GermanJoe, ClueBot NG, TigertailZLC, Netromdk and Anonymous: 5

- **M-94** *Source:* https://en.wikipedia.org/wiki/M-94?oldid=588313252 *Contributors:* Wapcaplet, Alan Liefting, Inkling, Matt Crypto, ArnoldReinhold, Davidgothberg, Boblord, Segv11, Imzadi1979, Hmains, Robbie Cook, Parmandil, ImageRemovalBot, Addbot, Lightbot, Yobot, Aditya, Slappydrewit, 777sms and Anonymous: 4

- **Mirror writing** *Source:* https://en.wikipedia.org/wiki/Mirror_writing?oldid=735030326 *Contributors:* Patrick, Zanimum, Ellywa, Julesd, Ineuw, Fuzheado, Donreed, ZimZalaBim, Mirv, Texture, Meelar, Diberri, MikeCapone, Michael Devore, Matt Crypto, Beland, JoJan, Tsemii, Sonett72, Shagmaestro, Cacycle, ArnoldReinhold, Warpflyght, Janderk, Bcjordan, Haham hanuka, Alansohn, Velella, Woohookitty, Scriberius, Zealander, Ratzer, Mandarax, Rjwilmsi, X1987x, YurikBot, AjaxSmack, Pb30, BorgQueen, Hollerama, Oneirist, Lviatour, SmackBot, Rentier, Mscuthbert, Eskimbot, Gilliam, Hmains, Anonymous coward, Durova, Bluebot, OrangeDog, Sadads, Patriarch, Da Vynci, CARAVAGGISTI, Armend, MilitaryTarget, Geekening, Beetstra, Moj0, Ginkgo100, Sinaloa, Apathetic duck, JohnCD, Anil1956, Cydebot, Arrowned, Sobreira, Missvain, Asmeurer, ThomasO1989, Ssier1am, JMyrleFuller, Lunakeet, MartinBot, Rrawpower, ElenaZam, Rob ten Berge, Tulpan, Sporti, Vipinhari, Anna Lincoln, WazzaMan, Jlhw, Dpbalazs~enwiki, RaseaC, AlleborgoBot, Smilesfozwood, Ossicle, ClueBot, Keraunoscopia, DumZiBoT, XLinkBot, Addbot, DOI bot, Tcncv, CanadianLinuxUser, LaaknorBot, The-sand-monkey, Debresser, OlEnglish, He A, Luckasbot, AnomieBOT, Materialscientist, ArthurBot, RibotBOT, Bigweeboy, Citation bot 1, ANDROBETA, Miracle Pen, EmausBot, Heracles31, Dcirovic, Donner60, Prakayas, Sonicyouth86, ClueBot NG, Helpful Pixie Bot, Lehetm, Titodutta, HueSatLum, Hasler101, Aaronbb97, Callousiamnot, I am One of Many, HEMANT GUPTA1985, Blackbombchu, Iamcreative1000, JustBerry, FDMS4, Believeittoo, Leonardo the Florentine, Khandakarnnan and Anonymous: 101

- **Mlecchita vikalpa** *Source:* https://en.wikipedia.org/wiki/Mlecchita_vikalpa?oldid=732543438 *Contributors:* Dawnseeker2000, Krishnachandranvn, Arjayay, LilHelpa and Anonymous: 1

- **Nihilist cipher** *Source:* https://en.wikipedia.org/wiki/Nihilist_cipher?oldid=654604697 *Contributors:* Jimfbleak, Val42, Matt Crypto, Makomk, Davidgothberg, JIP, Kolbasz, Quuxplusone, Mmernex, Hmains, Zickzack, Dvunkannon, Jevansen, Railfence, Richard-of-Earth, MystBot, Addbot, Lightbot, Yobot, Randombabbleblah, Jesse V., Peterhurford, LukasMatt and Anonymous: 9

- **Null cipher** *Source:* https://en.wikipedia.org/wiki/Null_cipher?oldid=725793836 *Contributors:* The Anome, Danny, TakuyaMurata, The Anomebot, Furrykef, Pakaran, Saforrest, Matt Crypto, Longhair, Eyreland, Sepand, SmackBot, Mmernex, Indeterminate, Nuwewsco, CharlotteWebb, Player 03, Dthomsen8, TutterMouse, FrescoBot, DexDor and Anonymous: 9

- **Pig Latin** *Source:* https://en.wikipedia.org/wiki/Pig_Latin?oldid=744301752 *Contributors:* Chuck Smith, Mav, The Anome, Stevertigo, Ubiquity, Infrogmation, Fuzzie, Lousyd, Liftarn, Ixfd64, Tregoweth, Jpatokal, UserGoogol, Kimiko, Charles Matthews, Timwi, Nohat, Denni, HappyDog, Furrykef, Populus, Fibonacci, Topbanana, Pakaran, Noldoaran, AlainV, Gandalf61, Merovingian, Matty j, Wayland, Smjg, Graeme Bartlett, WiseWoman, ZeroJanvier, Jackol, Chowbok, Alexf, J. 'mach' wust, R. fiend, Eregli bob, DragonflySixtyseven, Ary29, Bepp, Burschik, Everlong, Haruo, Random contributor, Discospinster, Rich Farmbrough, Factitious, ArnoldReinhold, Android79, MBisanz, El C, Bletch, Shanes, Art LaPella, Bobo192, Aetherfukz, Smalljim, Ejrrjs, Neg, Man vyi, Alphax, Rje, Jonsafari, Jonathunder, Zellin, Alansohn, Pinar, Mo0, Keenan Pepper, Queson, Ricky81682, Messerschmitts, PRH, Hu, Dmismir, KJK::Hyperion, Wtmitchell, RainbowOfLight, Mikeo, Pookleblinky, Dave.Dunford, Scott Gall, IJzeren Jan, Jess Cully, Kazvorpal, Feezo, Thryduulf, LOL, Pol098, JeremyA, Tylerni7, Damicatz, Xiong Chiamiov, Ravpapa, Atatncnu~enwiki, Mandarax, Tslocum, Qwertyus, Jetekus, Reisio, Coneslayer, TurtleTurtle, Chipuni, Kinu, Harro5, The wub, Volfy, MLRoach, Platypus222, Yamamoto Ichiro, St. Chris, Fantom~enwiki, Scottinglis, TheDJ, Intgr, TeaDrinker, Chobot, Korg, Bgwhite, KX675, Bobdablob, IBlender, Mercury McKinnon, YurikBot, Hairy Dude, RussBot, Red Slash, Icarus3, MoriyaMug, Rubber cat, Gaius Cornelius, CambridgeBayWeather, Daveswagon, Finbarr Saunders, NawlinWiki, Wiki alf, Danactro, Aeusoes1, RattleMan, Grafen, Oberst, Ankologist, Kortoso, Alhen, Bmju, Daniel C, Tanet, Zzuuzz, Nebuchadnezzar o'neill, BenBildstein, Closedmouth, Fang Aili, SMcCandlish, SigmaEpsilon, Tropylium, Darrel francis, Rcharman, EgyptianSushi, Cmglee, Sardanaphalus, SmackBot, Dweller, EvilCouch, Monkeyblue, Benjaminb, Reedy, Martin.Budden, FlashSheridan, Wehwalt, DCDuring, Proficient, Maplebed, Rbreen, Gary Kirk, Strabismus, Big Adamsky, Ifnord, Jon Phillips, Gjs238, Kintetsubuffalo, Imzadi1979, HeartofaDog, HalfShadow, SmartGuy Old, Yamaguchi先生, Gilliam, Ghosts&empties, Betacommand, Jushi, ERcheck, JorgePeixoto, Chris the speller, Dogbreathcanada, Thumperward, Caissa's DeathAngel, Miquonranger03, Jerome Charles Potts, Jxm, Colonies Chris, Gracenotes, Yanksox, Emurphy42, Royboycrashfan, Kemperb, Can't sleep, clown will eat me, Amber388, Ultra-Loser, TKD, Wombler, Metalmallow, Khukri, Nakon, Teehee123, B jonas, Aelffin, DoubleAW, Mini-Geek, Derek R Bullamore, Arantor, RyGuy17, Kukini, Andrew Dalby, Lambiam, Michael J, RickO5, Andymc, Haring123, Whitesoxfanatic, Ocatecir, Dingobaby, A. Parrot, Waggers, SandyGeorgia, Splintor, Jvlm.123, Peyre, DabMachine, Fredil Yupigo, Eeyore tim, Jaksmata, Fsotrain09, Dp462090, Buddy13, Kori126, Tawkerbot2, DJGB, JForget, Thedemonhog, Marbles, L'œuf, AlbertSM, BeenAroundAWhile, Machchunk, Joelholdsworth, Pyrotek7x7, Lordmaster913, George cowie, HalJor, Cydebot, Cahk, 7on, Boaz Benzvi, Cschulen, Clayoquot, Corpx, Islander, PuckUdroc, Chirp Cricket, JodyB, Zalgo, Cutekangaroo, UberScienceNerd, Thijs!bot, Epbr123, Barticus88, Kenifh, N5iln, Andyjsmith, 24fan24, JustAGal, PJtP, Citizensmith, Arrozal, Stui, AntiVandalBot, The Obento Musubi, Majorly, Wainson, Widefox, Mrmoocow, Jj137, Byornski, Res2216firestar,

Tohru Honda13, Endlessdan, Salubrious, Acroterion, Smeddlesboy, Bongwarrior, VoABot II, Voodoodriver, Sardinas, Drahreg01, Phunting, YA1YB4FIGKYlTQ0FB8AR, Avicennais, KConWiki, Soleado, Catgut, Allstarecho, JMyrleFuller, DerHexer, Wdflake, Esanchez7587, StopItTidyUp, Patstuart, Flami72, NatGertler, B. Wolterding, Ztobor, Crabhain, Hdt83, MartinBot, Hugo Dufort, Juansidious, Jarhed, Chrishy man, J.delanoy, Pharaoh of the Wizards, Thomasolson, Sp3000, Eliz81, Xam123456, Aboutmovies, Hut 6.5, NewEnglandYankee, Nwbeeson, BostonRed, ACBest, Vanished user 39948282, SixteenBitJorge, Mydogtrouble, Pdcook, Useight, Netjunkie66, Sapphiregurl08, CardinalDan, Fainites, Khjkhjkhgjgj m, Craitman17, Graphite Elbow, ABF, Jeff G., Indubitably, Jmrowland, Paugus, Leadmanfly, Philip Trueman, Fran Rogers, Admantine5, MarkKeegan, Oshwah, Anselmocisneros~enwiki, Captain Wikify, Bobthehobo60, Pauloppelt, WikiReaderer, Lradrama, Jackfork, Super Smartypants, Emi emu, Dvmedis, Dirkbb, Some Guy421, Trobinson41, Ghostofandy, Brianga, Monty845, Zx-man, FlyingLeopard2014, RedRabbit1983, Snip3rNife, SPQRobin, Timmytop16, Jauerback, Caltas, Sg647112c, Toddst1, Flyer22 Reborn, Exert, Socal gal at heart, Nk.sheridan, Ianrosenberg1, Nro92, IdreamofJeanie, Svick, Wookydl, StaticGull, Johnson487682, Rotovia, Upphed, Denisarona, RoIn22, LarRan, Kellyx3, KBYU, ClueBot, LAX, Ghakim, The Thing That Should Not Be, TinyMark, Page1pourvous, Drmies, Artyom, Michael.Urban, Niceguyedc, Blanchardb, Rapidchoper, Xxcarriexx, Auntof6, Jeffrey shin, Jusdafax, John Nevard, KC109, Bde1982, Hannahjmlee, M.O.X, Razorflame, La Pianista, 9Nak, Aitias, Luke Farrelly-Spain, Playasolmar, Antti29, Piratemurray, Qwaerdtyuiytresrtgyt, Spitfire, Luke inc, Rror, Little Mountain 5, Mitch Ames, NellieBly, Agameofchess, Subversive.sound, Otaknam, Addbot, Fyrael, DougsTech, Ronhjones, TutterMouse, One cookie, Fieldday-sunday, Raziel Anarki, Kman543210, Dcole4321, Glane23, Latiligence, Tassedethe, Ehrenkater, MWestera, Whatsyourname, Tide rolls, OlEnglish, Jarble, Legobot, Luckas-bot, Yobot, Cobolsaurus, Fraggle81, Sean662005, Drunken Shinobi, THEN WHO WAS PHONE?, KamikazeBot, AnomieBOT, Marauder40, Rjanag, Cedargang, Mark1295, Fahadsadah, Kentoutcourt, 580freak, Cinciguy, Xqbot, Sionus, Capricorn42, Alliemhanson, Mononomic, Vanroc, InsérerNombreHere, GrouchoBot, Chicken pot pie rocks!, Kirroha, Geodilly24, Wikidity, MathsPoetry, Gordonrox24, Shadowjams, E0steven, FrescoBot, Whore123435, D'ohBot, Footyfanatic3000, DrilBot, Pinethicket, I dream of horses, Arianehd, Sophiethenerdfighter, PrincessofLlyr, A8UDI, Zyoi, Barras, Ticklewickleukulele, Jordgette, Zakawer, GregKaye, ProjectSHiNKiROU, Vrenator, Despondentblue, Amkilpatrick, Diannaa, Suffusion of Yellow, Tbhotch, Rock drum, Andrea105, Onel5969, Mean as custard, MohrGould, IIT AGORA, ArlaxleJayTemisAray, DRAGON BOOSTER, Beyond My Ken, GoldenSandslash15, Deagle AP, EmausBot, WTM, Immunize, Nø, GoingBatty, NotAnonymous0, Winner 42, Wikipelli, Dcirovic, Recesstime, Daonguyen95, Ephilios, Yammabro, Anir1uph, Lapidar, Aeonx, Tolly4bolly, Erianna, L Kensington, Champion, MonoAV, Donner60, David Rolek, Intellec7, AnddoX, Helpsome, ClueBot NG, AlbertBickford, Gareth Griffith-Jones, Loginnigol, Jayeshrchinchole, Ert304, Asukite, Widr, Theonesean, MerlIwBot, 0zero9nine, Alexbee2, BG19bot, Hearthk98, Chess, Kaltenmeyer, Northamerica1000, Trumpkinius, Danieljr1992, AdventurousSquirrel, VegetaSaiyan, CitationCleanerBot, Heilongjiang2011, JZCL, InTheRevolution2, Achowat, Argleyetty, EricEnfermero, BattyBot, Zhaofeng Li, DeerMtn, Element Knight 375, Codeh, Packer1028, Znailxxor, Kevinzhang27, Cwobeel, Belac1, Mogism, Makecat-bot, Cerabot~enwiki, Matt723star, Nicolas ANCEAU, MisterShiney, Raven011, Hillbillyholiday, Popabar, Epicgenius, Theo's Little Bot, Jamesmcmahon0, Tentinator, Jdaudier, Clr324, Popa Bar Abba, Morrasl, Ugog Nizdast, Luxure, Timothymiko, Danerdreal, Inforceptable, Admiral Caius, Malcolm Mcquane, Rabdill, Furn54321, Bilorv, Melcous, Mollyella, Batfan1966, Prof. Mc, Atxfilm, Paradise77, DaNiEl13DJ, SSF12, Stew2710, Konitakat57, Nescophe, Haaaaaaaaaapy, DevilishDB, Devin0314, Forever acrobate, Wikibenboy123, Liance, Wolfmanbrad, Ckmarvelous, Mgnny12816, Sundayclose, Journicool, Bennyboy 321, Gamingforfun365, DopeWaffle, Maquelaa, MB298, LumStone, Kevon kevono, Efs1ee, EmberFire135, Big guy 99, G-reynolds92, Marianna251, Marvellous Spider-Man, AndThemsTheFactsFolks, Deez nuts in yo mouth, DatingMona and Anonymous: 839

- **Pigpen cipher** *Source:* https://en.wikipedia.org/wiki/Pigpen_cipher?oldid=732639317 *Contributors:* Cimon Avaro, Mrklingon, AnonMoos, Donreed, DavidCary, Matt Crypto, Peter Ellis, SarekOfVulcan, Bumm13, WegianWarrior, Causa sui, Sortior, Smalljim, Davidgothberg, Hashar-Bot~enwiki, Alansohn, V2Blast, Lokicarbis, The JPS, Sburke, Eyreland, Cacimar, Zef, Atratus, YurikBot, Rsrikanth05, Anomie, Ptcamn, Lexicon, Stijn Calle, MSJapan, Thnidu, Nikkimaria, JDspeeder1, SmackBot, Elonka, Grye, Hmains, Skizzik, Zephyrad, Lmblackjack21, Vanisaac, Apathetic duck, Synergy, Chrislk02, James086, AntiVandalBot, MER-C, Hut 8.5, DerHexer, R'n'B, Dubhe.sk, KylieTastic, VolkovBot, Deconstructhis, SieBot, Yintan, Keilana, Ultimatedevr, Mr. Granger, PipepBot, XLinkBot, Addbot, Grayfell, Numbo3-bot, Lightbot, The Bushranger, MileyDavidA, Yobot, Jim1138, CCCElian, Materialscientist, Xqbot, Omnipaedista, Mhageman, FrescoBot, FFraenz, Neophytesage, Waltbucher, Calmer Waters, Sumone10154, Mugishaernestisaac, JakeTununda, EmausBot, WikitanvirBot, Griffinxyz, Dcirovic, K6ka, بدر الإسلام, ClueBot NG, Essterling, MelbourneStar, ThaddeusSholto, Archtktn, Helpful Pixie Bot, Addihockey10 (automated), TheGeneralUser, Vikinggyrli, Klilidiplomus, Fylbecatulous, Fiddlersmouth, AllenZh, Sakuya Hiyama, MrLinkinPark333, Liz, Adeptzare3, Yoshi0110sana, KH-1, Rider ranger47, Yo 'tsup, Emily4644 and Anonymous: 101

- **Playfair cipher** *Source:* https://en.wikipedia.org/wiki/Playfair_cipher?oldid=738058721 *Contributors:* Arvindn, Ellmist, Imran, RTC, Stib, Ww, AnonMoos, Proteus, Johnleemk, Slawojarek, Sander123, Lowellian, VanishedUser kfljdfjsg33k, JamesMLane, Inkling, Tom harrison, Gamaliel, Matt Crypto, Vanished user 1234567890, SimonArlott, Mouser, TonyW, Quistnix, Syp, PhilHibbs, CDN99, Davidgothberg, Wrs1864, Mailer diablo, Burn, Kurivaim, Oleg Alexandrov, Pugwash, Angr, Eyreland, Pfalstad, Gerbrant, Cmsg, FlaBot, YurikBot, Wavelength, Borgx, Skotte, Grafen, Fitzsimons, Moe Epsilon, SmackBot, Verne Equinox, Snori, Michel SALES, MatthewDaly, Cybercobra, Daqu, Clean Copy, DMacks, Mr. Vernon, Allamericanbear, Zepheus, Keycard, Alex Selby, Ed Crossword, Viennese Waltz, Nabokov, Nthep, Hut 8.5, Bongwarrior, Ahecht, Kiore, Yonaa, J.delanoy, Yonidebot, NewEnglandYankee, KylieTastic, Hugo999, Deor, VolkovBot, TreasuryTag, Aaron Rotenberg, Michaeldsuarez, Radagast3, Cwkmail, Jenflex, MarkMLl, Ari14850, Broboman, El bot de la dieta, XLinkBot, SilvonenBot, Addbot, LatitudeBot, Lightbot, Zorrobot, Wiso, Yobot, Vini 17bot5, Davidtheterp, AnomieBOT, ArthurBot, Lulzwutnow, FrescoBot, Pinethicket, DBrianWilson, At.shakil, Abesolom, Ripchip Bot, John of Reading, ZéroBot, ChuispastonBot, Xanchester, ClueBot NG, Wcherowi, Helpful Pixie Bot, Prbindia, BG19bot, Crosthwaitgin, Abhradeep05Ghosh, Wikitom24, Packer1028, Wallmajik2, Maniesansdelire, Ugog Nizdast, Xxelite beast swagUK420 QSxX, Dilidor, Swagggr and Anonymous: 89

- **Poem code** *Source:* https://en.wikipedia.org/wiki/Poem_code?oldid=671151779 *Contributors:* Ap, Ww, Securiger, Inkling, Folks at 137, Matt Crypto, Lvl, TonyW, Rich Farmbrough, That Guy, From That Show!, SmackBot, Hmains, Chris the speller, OrangeDog, Bezapt, Cydebot, Dawkeye, Tylop~enwiki, TreasuryTag, Download, Legobot and Anonymous: 7

- **Polyalphabetic cipher** *Source:* https://en.wikipedia.org/wiki/Polyalphabetic_cipher?oldid=710844370 *Contributors:* Imran, Bdesham, LenBudney, Delirium, Cema, Ww, The Anomebot, Val42, Theta682, Securiger, Inkling, BigBen212, Matt Crypto, TonyW, Murtasa, Eric Shalov, BrokenSegue, Davidgothberg, Yuckfoo, IHendry, Nightscream, Yrithinnd, Dialectric, Ninly, SmackBot, Mmernex, Jagged 85, Hmains, Jprg1966, Samanathon, Wen D House, Synergy, Tylop~enwiki, Hut 8.5, Allstarecho, Binba, STSS, Hqb, TedColes, Jackfork, Soler97, ClueBot, Addbot, Gus Buonafalce, MrOllie, Yobot, Ciphers, Revipm, Thehelpfulbot, DrilBot, ClueBot NG, Krautw68, Cdated, BattyBot, Skr15081997, Horseless Headman, BethNaught, VexorAbVikipædia, HelpUsStopSpam, Anycards and Anonymous: 26

- **Polybius square** *Source:* https://en.wikipedia.org/wiki/Polybius_square?oldid=740396094 *Contributors:* Matusz, Iluvcapra, Jpatokal, Julesd, Cema, Val42, Securiger, Giftlite, Inkling, Matt Crypto, Ukexpat, Bill Thayer, Davidgothberg, HasharBot~enwiki, DV8 2XL, Scratchy, DePiep, YurikBot, Wavelength, Neilbeach, Deucalionite, Mysid, NorsemanII, SmackBot, Mmernex, Elonka, Adrigon, Myrtone86, Cydebot, Alaibot, Tylop~enwiki, MER-C, Hut 8.5, Ariel., LordAnubisBOT, VolkovBot, TXiKiBoT, CultureDrone, ClueBot, Catalographer, WikHead, Addbot, SamatBot, Luckas-bot, Yobot, Ptbotgourou, McKaot, DrilBot, Jesse V., Igor Yalovecky, WikitanvirBot, Mjbmrbot, ClueBot NG, Kapanidze, AvocatoBot, Comatmebro, Danielchatfield, JPaestpreornJeolhlna, Glovacki and Anonymous: 29

- **Rail fence cipher** *Source:* https://en.wikipedia.org/wiki/Rail_fence_cipher?oldid=677888457 *Contributors:* David4286, Rl, Rich Farmbrough, Xezbeth, Davidgothberg, Offsky, Jdege, Eyreland, SmackBot, Elonka, GiantSnowman, Alaibot, MER-C, Kevinsam, KylieTastic, Oshwah, Blueyeru, Alexbot, Railfence, El bot de la dieta, Addbot, Yobot, Vicenarian, ZéroBot, ClueBot NG, Derick1259, Helpful Pixie Bot, Rmehtany, અક્ષય માકડિયા, Schladow, Ugog Nizdast, Marc renault and Anonymous: 22

- **Rasterschlüssel 44** *Source:* https://en.wikipedia.org/wiki/Rasterschl%C3%BCssel_44?oldid=738394676 *Contributors:* Drdefcom~enwiki, Eyreland, Scope creep, DéRahier, LanternLight, Daytona2, DH85868993, Yobot, Mullins1949, Wncude and Anonymous: 1

- **Reihenschieber** *Source:* https://en.wikipedia.org/wiki/Reihenschieber?oldid=727569210 *Contributors:* Fifelfoo, Matt Crypto, Austin Hair, One-dimensional Tangent, Davidgothberg, Eyreland, Rjwilmsi, DrHok, DantheCowMan, KjellG, Addbot, Lightbot, Yobot, Tom.Reding, ZéroBot and Anonymous: 3

- **Reservehandverfahren** *Source:* https://en.wikipedia.org/wiki/Reservehandverfahren?oldid=699818379 *Contributors:* Omegatron, Folks at 137, Matt Crypto, ArnoldReinhold, Davidgothberg, Bellhalla, Rjwilmsi, Gaius Cornelius, Tadpole256, Colonies Chris, LanternLight, Olaf Davis, Cydebot, Thadius856, Dodo19~enwiki, Nick2491, JoDonHo, Oeropium, Magus732, Yobot, Nageh, Rmehtany and Anonymous: 3

- **ROT13** *Source:* https://en.wikipedia.org/wiki/ROT13?oldid=742419100 *Contributors:* The Cunctator, Vicki Rosenzweig, Bryan Derksen, The Anome, Karl E. V. Palmen, Eijkhout, Arvindn, Fubar Obfusco, Ben-Zin~enwiki, Nknight, Stevertigo, Bdesham, Infrogmation, Michael Hardy, DopefishJustin, Isomorphic, Norm, SGBailey, Pcb21, Haakon, J'raxis, Nikai, Cimon Avaro, Hashar, Timwi, Dcoetzee, JeffTL, Ww, Fuzheado, The Anomebot, Jogloran, Itai, VeryVerily, Bevo, AnonMoos, Finlay McWalter, UninvitedCompany, Denelson83, Phil Boswell, Donarreiskoffer, Gentgeen, Nufy8, Fredrik, Psychonaut, Mattflaschen, Ludraman, David Gerard, Decrypt3, DocWatson42, Lunkwill, Mshonle~enwiki, N12345n, Robin Patterson, Luis Dantas, Inkling, Lupin, JimD, Xinoph, Matt Crypto, Jrdioko, Geoffspear, Joshuamcgee, Quadell, MisfitToys, Sebbe, Codeman38, TreyHarris, Deewiant, Austin Hair, TonyW, Ropers, Ultrarob, Karl Dickman, Grm wnr, Chmod007, Leonid Korchenko, Thorwald, Mariko~enwiki, Rich Farmbrough, Avriette, FiP, Flynns32547, Izogi, Ponder, SocratesJedi, Bender235, Kbh3rd, Foolip, Sgeo, Chewie, Syp, CanisRufus, Sietse Snel, JRM, Apollo2011, John Vandenberg, BrokenSegue, SpeedyGonsales, Matt McIrvin, Photonique, Davidgothberg, Alansohn, Rxc, M7, Sl, JoaoRicardo, Sligocki, Yuckfoo, Werty8472, Mikenolte, Ceyockey, Stvangel, Ods15, Radiant!, Ashmoo, Graham87, Marskell, Sinar~enwiki, Rjwilmsi, MordredKLB, Oblivious, Brighterorange, Fred Bradstadt, Fish and karate, Andrew Rodland, FlaBot, Weihao.chiu~enwiki, Intgr, Chobot, RobotE, Gaius Cornelius, CambridgeBayWeather, Pseudomonas, Stassats, DouglasHeld, Randolf Richardson, Scs, Tony1, Ospalh, Cedar101, Kriscotta, SMcCandlish, Peyna, ArielGold, SmackBot, F, Mangoe, CyclePat, Eskimbot, BiT, Xaosflux, Maetrics, Oli Filth, MalafayaBot, Bazonka, Emurphy42, Tsca.bot, Olddocks, Aumakua, Djcapelis, Arantor, SU182, Attys, John, Minna Sora no Shita, Needlenose, PseudoSudo, Ckatz, Hvn0413, Kyoko, Hyenaste, SandyGeorgia, Ginkgo100, White Ash, Tawkerbot2, Tungazzio, Mapsax, Mattyrottn, DannyKitty, Gunny01, TheTito, Edlin2, Kozuch, Thijs!bot, Alex Forencich, PeteX, AntiVandalBot, Luna Santin, Hut 8.5, JGarbett, MasterA113, Sethiroth66, Magioladitis, Kennercat, JMyrleFuller, BunsenH, Keith D, MattMattMattLoLoLoLuh, Peewack, Glrx, DrKay, Hut 6.5, Omes, Jevansen, Treisijs, Ajfweb, Pete Kleinberg, VolkovBot, TXiKiBoT, Yugsdrawkcabeht, Shaka Kaan, JhsBot, PaladinWhite, Random seed, Rublev, Agvulpine, SieBot, Brian787, X-Fi6, MinorContributor, Canislupusarctos, Lightmouse, SallyForth123, Badger Drink, Trivialist, Leonard^Bloom, The Dot Matrix, XLinkBot, HexaChord, Addbot, Coaliton, Victor-435, SpBot, LinkFA-Bot, Tide rolls, Yobot, Denispir, Wargo, Jeffz1, AnomieBOT, IRP, Frankenpuppy, Cldream, Capricorn42, The Interior, Alan.A.Mick, Einheitlix, FFraenz, Qwertysledge, AstaBOTh15, I dream of horses, Aoidh, Acather96, RA0808, The Blade of the Northern Lights, H3llBot, Fb46, Stephanemoore, George Makepeace, Petrb, ClueBot NG, BarrelProof, Bstan10, Widr, Kapanidze, BG19bot, Kouhi, GrammarFascist, HTML2011, Dexbot, Harrycol123, Isarra (HG), Mahan, C5st4wr6ch, Maniesansdelire, Govindarajan Devarajan, Epicgenius, AMartinez1986, Chris troutman, Myconix, DavidLeighEllis, One Of Seven Billion, Vandergay, Monkbot, Mhmd fm, Kethrus, Yo 'tsup, User000name, RichardCareaga, SSTflyer and Anonymous: 171

- **Running key cipher** *Source:* https://en.wikipedia.org/wiki/Running_key_cipher?oldid=740288517 *Contributors:* Dcoetzee, Securiger, Hemanshu, Hadal, DocWatson42, DavidCary, Inkling, Everyking, Matt Crypto, TonyW, Davidgothberg, MattGiuca, Mandarax, Capi, Cedar101, Mmernex, RomanSpa, Jimbobl, Yobot, Eugene-elgato, 32RB17, StephenBishop3rd, LukasMatt and Anonymous: 11

- **Scytale** *Source:* https://en.wikipedia.org/wiki/Scytale?oldid=701790548 *Contributors:* Bryan Derksen, PierreAbbat, Glenn, Rl, Geirem, Ww, Lfh, The Anomebot, Zero0000, Rhys~enwiki, Securiger, Sverdrup, Jleedev, Matt Crypto, Antandrus, Jackiespeel, Trevor MacInnis, Kwamikagami, Ypacaraí, BrokenSegue, Davidgothberg, Mrzaius, Jwinius, Eyreland, Deltabeignet, Rjwilmsi, Nihiltres, Quuxplusone, Manscher, Gaius Cornelius, Segv11, Redmess, Bluebot, MalafayaBot, Oatmeal batman, W1tgf, WeggeBot, Thijs!bot, Barticus88, Deflective, Idioma-bot, Leonard^Bloom, Jcreek201, Railfence, Catalographer, DumZiBoT, Gazzadel, Addbot, AkhtaBot, West.andrew.g, Luckas-bot, Yobot, GrouchoBot, Telofy, Citation bot 1, Cramyourspam, Kgrad, ZéroBot, ClueBot NG, Electriccatfish2, Proxyma, Elize louw, 32RB17, Per82 and Anonymous: 36

- **Substitution cipher** *Source:* https://en.wikipedia.org/wiki/Substitution_cipher?oldid=741062470 *Contributors:* Damian Yerrick, Matusz, Imran, Michael Hardy, Lquilter, Charles Matthews, Ww, ZeWrestler, Phil Boswell, Astronautics~enwiki, R3m0t, Securiger, Sverdrup, Inkling, Nunh-huh, KuniShiro~enwiki, Matt Crypto, Beland, Austin Hair, Kelson, Kevin Rector, Chmod007, CALR, Rich Farmbrough, Roybb95~enwiki, Quistnix, BrokenSegue, Davidgothberg, RussBlau, Haham hanuka, CyberSkull, Andrewpmk, Alexg~enwiki, Brentdax, Cbdorsett, Waldir, Gimboid13, Sinar~enwiki, Tangotango, Gwernol, RussBot, Gustavb, -OOPSIE-, Deville, Thnidu, Luk, SmackBot, Mmernex, Sydius, BiT, Hmains, Bluebot, William Allen Simpson, OrphanBot, KaiserbBot, LeoNomis, Ohconfucius, Stelio, Renmiri, דניאל צבי, Japoniano, Grgarza, Ntsimp, Arruah, Nuwewsco, Jepler, Tylop~enwiki, Dajagr, Prolog, Kraelis, JAnDbot, Omeganian, MER-C, Hypnometal, Midnightdreary, Hut 8.5, CountingPine, B9 hummingbird hovering, D2B, R'n'B, Nono64, DH85868993, IPSOS, TedColes, Dprust, Neonsignal, Arkwatem, Ellusion, OKBot, Anchor Link Bot, Mild Bill Hiccup, Niceguyedc, Excirial, Socrates2008, Razorflame, SchreiberBike, Ratna0, Paulmnguyen, Richard-of-Earth, Addbot, Grayfell, Morriswa, MrOllie, Morning277, Ehrenkater, Lightbot, MaBoehm, Zorrobot, Qwertymith, Luckas-bot, Yobot, OrgasGirl, TaBOT-zerem, Ciphers, Materialscientist, MauritsBot, Xqbot, TinucherianBot II, Semioptimist, GrouchoBot,

Revipm, FrescoBot, Dr.sliderule, LaukkuTheGreit, Jschnur, ChartaxS, Jesse V., DARTH SIDIOUS 2, Alph Bot, Lauri.pirttiaho, EmausBot, John of Reading, Orphan Wiki, Quondum, ClueBot NG, Maklen, Ososolax, Mouse20080706, Prbindia, BG19bot, AvocatoBot, Samswimmer, Skunk44, Sfarney, ChrisGualtieri, Kupiakos, Dexbot, Alysq, Harshul.mittal.se, Tshubham, HelpUsStopSpam and Anonymous: 110

- **Tabula recta** *Source:* https://en.wikipedia.org/wiki/Tabula_recta?oldid=740288133 *Contributors:* Tarquin, LapoLuchini, Bdesham, Michael Hardy, LenBudney, Cema, Itai, Matt Crypto, دبعل, ArnoldReinhold, Davidgothberg, Eyreland, Allen Moore, Dake~enwiki, Cedar101, Smack-Bot, Mmernex, BiT, MalafayaBot, Wvmarle, Synergy, Christian75, PKT, Thijs!bot, Doranchak, VolkovBot, Osho-Jabbe, Addbot, Lightbot, Yobot, AnomieBOT, Joostik, FrescoBot, Ronanletiec, Justincheng12345, Cdated, Especially Lime, JustAMuggle and Anonymous: 9

- **Tap code** *Source:* https://en.wikipedia.org/wiki/Tap_code?oldid=739263941 *Contributors:* David4286, Furrykef, AnonMoos, Securiger, David-Cary, WiseWoman, Wwoods, Mjuarez, Discospinster, Davidgothberg, Offsky, Eyreland, Davidrust, DePiep, Angusmclellan, Orville Eastland, Bgwhite, Wasted Time R, RussBot, NawlinWiki, Sandstein, Light current, Katieh5584, Bluebot, Thumperward, O keyes, Twas Now, Krator, Tawkerbot4, Alaibot, Magioladitis, Parsecboy, NewEnglandYankee, Jevansen, Jarry1250, Slysplace, Josepy, Collin Stocks, AHMartin, Flyer22 Reborn, Ailuro Dragon, ClueBot, Alchaemist, Yobot, AnomieBOT, Materialscientist, LilHelpa, Srich32977, Slightsmile, Wikipelli, ClueBot NG, Helpful Pixie Bot, Epicgenius, JPaestpreornJeolhlna, Monkbot, Katyandreakatya, Dominico Fantini200128 and Anonymous: 49

- **Templar cipher** *Source:* https://en.wikipedia.org/wiki/Templar_cipher?oldid=740426899 *Contributors:* AnonMoos, Rich Farmbrough, Dbachmann, SmackBot, Baronnet, Addbot, Yobot, AnomieBOT, McSush, Xqbot, Alvin Seville, Gattacca, MrLinkinPark333, Justin15w and Anonymous: 5

- **Transposition cipher** *Source:* https://en.wikipedia.org/wiki/Transposition_cipher?oldid=735897954 *Contributors:* PierreAbbat, Imran, Michael Hardy, Dominus, Eric119, Ellywa, Darkwind, Nikai, Charles Matthews, Dysprosia, Frazzydee, Securiger, Auric, Inkling, Matt Crypto, Discospinster, Xezbeth, Davidgothberg, Alexg~enwiki, Jdege, Feezo, Firsfron, Eyreland, Gimboid13, Jb-adder, Imnotminkus, YurikBot, Wavelength, SmackBot, Mmernex, Eskimbot, Cyclopaedic, Minna Sora no Shita, Hu12, Ericka Dawn, Aherunar, Grgarza, Ntsimp, Tylop~enwiki, Dawnseeker2000, Dvunkannon, Hut 8.5, Magioladitis, Logan, Hac13, OKBot, Anchor Link Bot, Denisarona, Arakunem, Addbot, Profplan, Issyl0, Luckas-bot, Yobot, Ptbotgourou, Amirobot, Doctorhook, AnomieBOT, Materialscientist, Xqbot, DSisyphBot, Almabot, Basvb, GrouchoBot, Louperibot, Full-date unlinking bot, Majanko, ZéroBot, Quondum, ChuispastonBot, ClueBot NG, Wcherowi, MelbourneStar, Gilderien, Widr, MusikAnimal, Smart00boy, Wjcw, Ekips39, Epicgenius, KodoTheDon264, Dough34, Param Mudgal, Articleediter3.1415926535, Davidgeller123, J4kepearce, M.R.40it, Yoshi0110sana, PLNech, Ryan Pohlman and Anonymous: 80

- **Trifid cipher** *Source:* https://en.wikipedia.org/wiki/Trifid_cipher?oldid=740236375 *Contributors:* The Anome, AnonMoos, Securiger, Mouser, Davidgothberg, Offsky, Gpvos, Eyreland, Mikedelsol, YurikBot, RobotE, Cedar101, SmackBot, RDBury, Mmernex, Lingbeek, Addbot, Lightbot, Yobot, Fraggle81, Jeffz1, Matthiaspaul, GeorgeGibson and Anonymous: 3

- **Two-square cipher** *Source:* https://en.wikipedia.org/wiki/Two-square_cipher?oldid=737979896 *Contributors:* Mouser, Sietse Snel, Davidgothberg, Eyreland, Rjwilmsi, Skotte, Scope creep, Mmernex, CmdrObot, Ntsimp, Mahousu, Agentgonzo, Josepy, Yobot, Mmeijeri, BG19bot and Anonymous: 5

- **VIC cipher** *Source:* https://en.wikipedia.org/wiki/VIC_cipher?oldid=740237095 *Contributors:* Imran, Michael Hardy, Dominus, Ww, AnonMoos, Securiger, DavidCary, Inkling, DO'Neil, Matt Crypto, DÅ‚ugosz, Eric Shalov, Eritain, Drdefcom~enwiki, Eyreland, Ground Zero, Cedar101, SmackBot, Addisonbr, Tec15, MER-C, UDoWs, Magioladitis, R'n'B, TreasuryTag, Richard-of-Earth, Addbot, Lightbot, Yobot, Materialscientist, MauritsBot, Frietjes, SubTenebra, BG19bot, Dark Silver Crow, GodofDarkness01 and Anonymous: 21

- **Vigenère cipher** *Source:* https://en.wikipedia.org/wiki/Vigen%C3%A8re_cipher?oldid=738180817 *Contributors:* The Anome, Maury Markowitz, LapoLuchini, Imran, Mintguy, Youandme, Bdesham, Michael Hardy, LenBudney, 5ko, Julesd, AugPi, Nikai, Charles Matthews, Ww, Zoicon5, Birkett, Itai, AnonMoos, Johnleemk, Catskul, Chealer, R3m0t, Lowellian, Decrypt3, Giftlite, Lunkwill, Inkling, Matt Crypto, Andycjp, Phe, Two Bananas, Aerion, Thorwald, Mormegil, Rama, Bender235, El C, Kwamikagami, EmilJ, JRM, BrokenSegue, Davidgothberg, Petdance, Binabik80, Yuckfoo, Jdege, Bsadowski1, Kell, Feezo, The Wordsmith, Jacj, Mathbot, Nihiltres, Korg, RadioFan, Square87~enwiki, Thnidu, That Guy, From That Show!, SmackBot, Glvgfz, Hmains, Bluebot, Alan smithee, Jack324, Kimero, Giancarlo Rossi, JorisvS, Michael miceli, IronGargoyle, Dante Shamest, TwistOfCain, JoeBot, Jaksmata, Aleph 1, Eric, Xumx, Endareth, Lokal Profil, Synergy, Doug Weller, JLD, Tylop~enwiki, GiM, JAnDbot, Deflective, MER-C, Jheiv, Hut 8.5, DAGwyn, KConWiki, Slartibartfast1992, Gerrardperrett, David Eppstein, J.delanoy, Mike.lifeguard, Thegreenj, Notreallydavid, BMBTHC, Ocsic, Dubhe.sk, Joshua Issac, Koinseb, TraceyR, TXiKiBoT, Answr42, TedColes, Kmhkmh, KjellG, Sue Rangell, Arkwatem, Svick, Pvdl, Behrat, Tuntable, Antonio Giovanni Colombo, Muhandes, Toastking13, Versus22, WikHead, Addbot, Tent405, Lightbot, Legobot, Luckas-bot, Yobot, TaBOT-zerem, Julia W, Avilena, AnomieBOT, Shadyabhi, Citation bot, Capricorn42, Angelus1383, AlSweigart, RibotBOT, FrescoBot, Jc3s5h, JMS Old Al, Izecksohn, Citation bot 1, Pinethicket, Nmatavka, Lotje, EmausBot, Dewritech, Shajinjohns, Cal-linux, Isdhbcfj, Westley Turner, Ὁ οἶστρος, ClueBot NG, Wcherowi, Cdated, Mesoderm, Widr, Helpful Pixie Bot, Sanketsaurav, Sunnypavan, Jmcontra, Cyberbot II, PedroStadler, Dexbot, Jbeyerl, Nicojonesgodel, 1doknowyouNever, Soham, Altonlee68, Wikistormer, InternetArchiveBot, Anareth, GreenC bot, Shiyu Ji and Anonymous: 149

- **Wadsworth's cipher** *Source:* https://en.wikipedia.org/wiki/Wadsworth'{}s_cipher?oldid=522060222 *Contributors:* Davidgothberg, Mangojuice, NawlinWiki, BusterD, Spondoolicks, Elonka, Bluebot, Rattle1337, JoeBot, Malleus Fatuorum, R'n'B, Anticipation of a New Lover's Arrival, The, Yobot, Lashman69 and Clockadile

55.2.2 Images

- **File:A-pigpen-message.svg** *Source:* https://upload.wikimedia.org/wikipedia/commons/b/ba/A-pigpen-message.svg *License:* Public domain *Contributors:* Transferred from en.wikipedia to Commons. *Original artist:* Of the SVG version, Roland Geider (Ogre), the original uploader was Matt Crypto at en.wikipedia

- **File:Acap.svg** *Source:* https://upload.wikimedia.org/wikipedia/commons/5/52/Acap.svg *License:* Public domain *Contributors:* Own work *Original artist:* F l a n k e r

- **File:Alphabet_templier.svg** *Source:* https://upload.wikimedia.org/wikipedia/commons/a/a0/Alphabet_templier.svg *License:* Public domain *Contributors:*

- **File:Exodus_4_-_reference_to_spiritual_possession_putting_words_in_mouths.jpg** *Source:* https://upload.wikimedia.org/wikipedia/ commons/9/9e/Exodus_4_-_reference_to_spiritual_possession_putting_words_in_mouths.jpg *License:* Public domain *Contributors:* Own work *Original artist:* Accuruss

- **File:Fleissner.png** *Source:* https://upload.wikimedia.org/wikipedia/commons/9/96/Fleissner.png *License:* CC BY-SA 2.0 *Contributors:* en.wikipedia.org *Original artist:* Stephen Colbourn

- **File:Folder_Hexagonal_Icon.svg** *Source:* https://upload.wikimedia.org/wikipedia/en/4/48/Folder_Hexagonal_Icon.svg *License:* Cc-by-sa-3.0 *Contributors:* ? *Original artist:* ?

- **File:Free-to-read_lock_75.svg** *Source:* https://upload.wikimedia.org/wikipedia/commons/8/80/Free-to-read_lock_75.svg *License:* CC0 *Contributors:* Adapted from 9px|Open_Access_logo_PLoS_white_green.svg *Original artist:* This version:Trappist_the_monk (talk) (Uploads)

- **File:Gaius_Julius_Caesar_(100-44_BC).JPG** *Source:* https://upload.wikimedia.org/wikipedia/commons/2/26/Gaius_Julius_Caesar_ %28100-44_BC%29.JPG *License:* Public domain *Contributors:* H. F. Helmolt (ed.): *History of the World.* New York, 1902 (University of Texas Library Portrait Gallery) *Original artist:* ?

- **File:Great_Cipher.png** *Source:* https://upload.wikimedia.org/wikipedia/commons/8/89/Great_Cipher.png *License:* Public domain *Contributors:* Scanned from the journal Cryptologia, January 2005, volume XXIX, number 1, p. 47. Image from Paris, Service historique ...... Archives Serie A. *Original artist:* Unknown<a href='//www.wikidata.org/wiki/Q4233718' title='wikidata:Q4233718'><img alt='wikidata:Q4233718' src='https://upload.wikimedia.org/wikipedia/commons/thumb/f/ff/Wikidata-logo.svg/20px-Wikidata-logo.svg.png' width='20' height='11' srcset='https://upload.wikimedia.org/wikipedia/commons/thumb/f/ff/Wikidata-logo.svg/30px-Wikidata-logo.svg.png 1.5x, https://upload.wikimedia.org/wikipedia/commons/thumb/f/ff/Wikidata-logo.svg/40px-Wikidata-logo.svg.png 2x' data-file-width='1050' data-file-height='590' /></a>

- **File:GrigliaRotante.png** *Source:* https://upload.wikimedia.org/wikipedia/commons/6/66/GrigliaRotante.png *License:* CC BY-SA 2.0 *Contributors:* Transferred from it.wikipedia
Original artist: Stevebkk. Original uploader was Leo72 at it.wikipedia

- **File:Hill'{}s_message_protector.png** *Source:* https://upload.wikimedia.org/wikipedia/commons/9/9a/Hill%27s_message_protector.png *License:* Public domain *Contributors:* A cropped, cleaned up version of figure 4 from Hill's "Message Protector" patent, US patent 1,845,947 of 1929. Sourced from http://www.und.nodak.edu/org/crypto/crypto/.hill4.html where it was scanned in by the American Cryptogram Association. Securiger 08:24, 22 Nov 2004 (UTC) *Original artist:* American Cryptogram Association

- **File:KTV1400D.jpg** *Source:* https://upload.wikimedia.org/wikipedia/commons/0/05/KTV1400D.jpg *License:* Public domain *Contributors:* ? *Original artist:* ?

- **File:Lyon_Playfair.jpg** *Source:* https://upload.wikimedia.org/wikipedia/commons/9/96/Lyon_Playfair.jpg *License:* Public domain *Contributors:* National Portrait Gallery: NPG x133395 *Original artist:* Lock & Whitfield

- **File:Merge-arrows.svg** *Source:* https://upload.wikimedia.org/wikipedia/commons/5/52/Merge-arrows.svg *License:* Public domain *Contributors:* ? *Original artist:* ?

- **File:Mirror_writing2.jpg** *Source:* https://upload.wikimedia.org/wikipedia/commons/3/32/Mirror_writing2.jpg *License:* Public domain *Contributors:* Library of Congress[1] *Original artist:* Mahmoud Ibrahim

- **File:Numeral_Systems_of_the_World.svg** *Source:* https://upload.wikimedia.org/wikipedia/commons/c/c0/Numeral_Systems_of_the_ World.svg *License:* CC BY-SA 4.0 *Contributors:* Own work *Original artist:* Psihedelisto

- **File:People_icon.svg** *Source:* https://upload.wikimedia.org/wikipedia/commons/3/37/People_icon.svg *License:* CC0 *Contributors:* OpenClipart *Original artist:* OpenClipart

- **File:Pigpen_cipher_key.svg** *Source:* https://upload.wikimedia.org/wikipedia/commons/3/36/Pigpen_cipher_key.svg *License:* Public domain *Contributors:* Own work *Original artist:* Anomie

- **File:Playfair_Cipher_01_HI_to_BM.png** *Source:* https://upload.wikimedia.org/wikipedia/commons/4/40/Playfair_Cipher_01_HI_to_BM. png *License:* CC0 *Contributors:* Own work *Original artist:* Davidtheterp

- **File:Playfair_Cipher_02_DE_to_OD.png** *Source:* https://upload.wikimedia.org/wikipedia/commons/4/44/Playfair_Cipher_02_DE_to_OD. png *License:* CC0 *Contributors:* Own work *Original artist:* Davidtheterp

- **File:Playfair_Cipher_03_TH_to_ZB.png** *Source:* https://upload.wikimedia.org/wikipedia/commons/1/1b/Playfair_Cipher_03_TH_to_ZB. png *License:* CC0 *Contributors:* Own work *Original artist:* Davidtheterp

- **File:Playfair_Cipher_04_EG_to_XD.png** *Source:* https://upload.wikimedia.org/wikipedia/commons/f/fb/Playfair_Cipher_04_EG_to_XD. png *License:* CC0 *Contributors:* Own work *Original artist:* Davidtheterp

- **File:Playfair_Cipher_05_OL_to_NA.png** *Source:* https://upload.wikimedia.org/wikipedia/commons/7/79/Playfair_Cipher_05_OL_to_NA. png *License:* CC0 *Contributors:* Own work *Original artist:* Davidtheterp

- **File:Playfair_Cipher_10_EX_to_XD.png** *Source:* https://upload.wikimedia.org/wikipedia/commons/2/29/Playfair_Cipher_10_EX_to_XD. png *License:* CC0 *Contributors:* Own work *Original artist:* Davidtheterp

- **File:Playfair_Cipher_building_grid_omitted_letters.png** *Source:* https://upload.wikimedia.org/wikipedia/commons/e/ef/Playfair_ Cipher_building_grid_omitted_letters.png *License:* CC0 *Contributors:* Own work *Original artist:* Davidtheterp

- **File:Portal-puzzle.svg** *Source:* https://upload.wikimedia.org/wikipedia/en/f/fd/Portal-puzzle.svg *License:* Public domain *Contributors:* ? *Original artist:* ?

- **File:Question_book-new.svg** *Source:* https://upload.wikimedia.org/wikipedia/en/9/99/Question_book-new.svg *License:* Cc-by-sa-3.0 *Contributors:* ? *Original artist:* ?

55.2.3 Content license

www.ingramcontent.com/pod-product-compliance
Lightning Source LLC
LaVergne TN
LVHW060123070326
832902LV00019B/3102